VOLUME 491   MAY 1987

THE ANNALS

of The American Academy *of* Political
and Social Science

RICHARD D. LAMBERT, *Editor*
ALAN W. HESTON, *Associate Editor*

THE FULBRIGHT EXPERIENCE
AND ACADEMIC EXCHANGES

Special Editor of this Volume

NATHAN GLAZER

Graduate School of Education
Harvard University
Cambridge
Massachusetts

⑤ SAGEPUBLICATIONS *NEWBURY PARK BEVERLY HILLS LONDON NEW DELHI*

THE ANNALS

© 1987 *by* The American Academy *of* Political *and* Social Science

ERICA GINSBURG, *Assistant Editor*

Editorial Office: 3937 Chestnut Street, Philadelphia, Pennsylvania 19104.

For information about membership* (individuals only) and subscriptions (institutions), address:

SAGE PUBLICATIONS, INC.

2111 West Hillcrest Drive   275 South Beverly Drive
Newbury Park, CA 91320   Beverly Hills, CA 90212

From India and South Asia,   *From the UK, Europe, the Middle*
write to: *East and Africa, write to:*

SAGE PUBLICATIONS INDIA Pvt. Ltd.   SAGE PUBLICATIONS LTD
P.O. Box 4215   28 Banner Street
New Delhi 110 048   London EC1Y 8QE
INDIA   ENGLAND

SAGE Production Editor: JACQUELINE SYROP

* Please note that members of The Academy receive THE ANNALS with their membership.

Library of Congress Catalog Card Number 86-063024
International Standard Serial Number ISSN 0002-7162
International Standard Book Number ISBN 0-8039-3007-0 (Vol. 491, 1987 paper)
International Standard Book Number ISBN 0-8039-3006-2 (Vol. 491, 1987 cloth)
Manufactured in the United States of America. First printing, May 1987.

The articles appearing in THE ANNALS are indexed in *Book Review Index; Public Affairs Information Service Bulletin; Social Sciences Index; Monthly Periodical Index; Current Contents; Behavioral, Social Management Sciences;* and *Combined Retrospective Index Sets.* They are also abstracted and indexed in *ABC Pol Sci, Historical Abstracts, Human Resources Abstracts, Social Sciences Citation Index, United States Political Science Documents, Social Work Research & Abstracts, Peace Research Reviews, Sage Urban Studies Abstracts, International Political Science Abstracts, America: History and Life,* and/or *Family Resources Database.*

Information about membership rates, institutional subscriptions, and back issue prices may be found on the facing page.

Advertising. Current rates and specifications may be obtained by writing to THE ANNALS Advertising and Promotion Manager at the Newbury Park office (address above).

Claims. Claims for undelivered copies must be made no later than three months following month of publication. The publisher will supply missing copies when losses have been sustained in transit and when the reserve stock will permit.

Change of Address. Six weeks' advance notice must be given when notifying of change of address to insure proper identification. Please specify name of journal. Send change of address to: THE ANNALS, c/o Sage Publications, Inc., 2111 West Hillcrest Drive, Newbury Park, CA 91320.

Origin and Purpose. The Academy was organized December 14, 1889, to promote the progress of political and social science, especially through publications and meetings. The Academy does not take sides in controverted questions, but seeks to gather and present reliable information to assist the public in forming an intelligent and accurate judgment.

Meetings. The Academy holds an annual meeting in the spring extending over two days.

Publications. THE ANNALS is the bimonthly publication of The Academy. Each issue contains articles on some prominent social or political problem, written at the invitation of the editors. Also, monographs are published from time to time, numbers of which are distributed to pertinent professional organizations. These volumes constitute important reference works on the topics with which they deal, and they are extensively cited by authorities throughout the United States and abroad. The papers presented at the meetings of The Academy are included in THE ANNALS.

Membership. Each member of The Academy receives THE ANNALS and may attend the meetings of The Academy. Membership is open only to individuals. Annual dues: $26.00 for the regular paperbound edition (clothbound, $40.00). Add $9.00 per year for membership outside the U.S.A. Members may also purchase single issues of THE ANNALS for $6.95 each (clothbound, $10.00).

Subscriptions. THE ANNALS (ISSN 0002-7162) is published six times annually—in January, March, May, July, September, and November. Institutions may subscribe to THE ANNALS at the annual rate: $52.00 (clothbound, $68.00). Add $9.00 per year for subscriptions outside the U.S.A. Institutional rates for single issues: $10.00 each (clothbound, $15.00).

Second class postage paid at Philadelphia, Pennsylvania, and at additional mailing offices.

Single issues of THE ANNALS may be obtained by individuals who are not members of The Academy for $7.95 each (clothbound, $15.00). Single issues of THE ANNALS have proven to be excellent supplementary texts for classroom use. Direct inquiries regarding adoptions to THE ANNALS c/o Sage Publications (address below).

All correspondence concerning membership in The Academy, dues renewals, inquiries about membership status, and/or purchase of single issues of THE ANNALS should be sent to THE ANNALS c/o Sage Publications, Inc., 2111 West Hillcrest Drive, Newbury Park, CA 91320. *Please note that orders under $20 must be prepaid.* Sage affiliates in London and India will assist institutional subscribers abroad with regard to orders, claims, and inquiries for both subscriptions and single issues.

THE ANNALS

of The American Academy *of* Political
and Social Science

RICHARD D. LAMBERT, *Editor*
ALAN W. HESTON, *Associate Editor*

———————— **FORTHCOMING** ————————

UNEMPLOYMENT: A GLOBAL CHALLENGE
Special Editors: Bertram Gross and Alfred Pfaller
Volume 492   July 1987

THE INFORMAL ECONOMY
Special Editors: Louis A. Ferman, Stuart Henry, and Michele Hoyman
Volume 493   September 1987

A NEIGHBORHOOD, FAMILY, AND EMPLOYMENT POLICY
TO PREVENT CRIME
Special Editor: Lynn A. Curtis
Volume 494   November 1987

See page 3 for information on Academy membership and
purchase of single volumes of **The Annals.**

CONTENTS

BOOK DEPARTMENT CONTENTS

PREFACE

Since a very modest beginning 40 years ago, some 156,000 men and women have participated in the international educational exchange program outlined in the Fulbright Act of 1946. Many of these men and women now occupy positions of importance and influence in their respective societies.

These people have acquired a capacity for empathy: they bring to their communities an understanding of other countries, their customs, religions, and history and are thereby capable of sound judgment in making decisions affecting the relationship of their respective countries with other countries with different traditions and cultures. In this era of strife and violence, people who are capable of understanding and of mitigating the passions that arise from the conflict of ideological convictions are essential if the community of nations is to find a way to adjust to the reality of the age of nuclear weapons.

I do not think it is pretentious to believe that the exchange of students, that intercultural education, is much more important to the survival of our country and of other countries than is a redundancy of hydrogen bombs or the Strategic Defense Initiative. Conflicts between nations result from deliberate decisions made by the leaders of nations, and those decisions are influenced and determined by the experience and judgment of the leaders and their advisers. Therefore our security and the peace of the world are dependent upon the character and intellect of the leaders rather than upon the weapons of destruction now accumulated in enormous and costly stockpiles.

The direct result of the exchange program is significant, but we should not overlook the fact that after the American program demonstrated the validity of the concept, other countries have themselves initiated their own government-supported exchanges, so there has been a considerable proliferation of similar schemes. This is gratifying, but, in truth, all together the numbers pale into insignificance compared to the enormous expenditures of money and talent on military armaments. It is a critical question whether the truce we now enjoy under the auspices of deterrence based upon the parity of military power will last long enough for the effect of intercultural exchange and other joint ventures to rise to the level of leadership in the United States and the Soviet Union, as it has already done in some smaller countries.

The fundamental challenge in this nuclear high-tech era is one of psychology and education in the field of human relations. It is not the kind of problem that is likely to be resolved by expertise, even the sophisticated expertise of our most gifted military thinkers, who delight in exotic weapons and strategic doctrines that threaten the solvency of the richest nations as well as their physical survival. The attributes upon which we must draw are the human attributes of compassion and common sense, of intellect and creative imagination, and of empathy and understanding between cultures.

The cultivation of these attributes is the highest calling of all true educators, a calling to which the American Academy of Political and Social Science has made a very significant contribution.

J. WILLIAM FULBRIGHT

ANNALS, *AAPSS,* **491,** May 1987

The Making of the Fulbright Program

By RALPH H. VOGEL

ABSTRACT: The nature and character of the Fulbright program were shaped by the 1946 legislation that gave it life, by the circumstance of its foreign currency financing generated by surplus property sales, by those in the State Department and in a few private organizations, and by members of the first Board of Foreign Scholarships, who transformed the Fulbright Act into the worldwide educational exchange program we know today. Early decisions by the Board were the building blocks on which the program has grown and flourished. The first bilaterial Fulbright programs depended on the negotiation of executive agreements with participating governments and the establishing of binational commissions abroad. The latter played a key role in the initial acceptance of the exchange program, in its planning and administration, and in eventual joint financing by many participating governments. Today the Fulbright program looks to the future with confidence as it proudly claims over 156,000 alumni in the United States and abroad.

Ralph H. Vogel is a graduate of Harvard College. He earned a law degree at George Washington University and is a member of the District of Columbia bar. His association with educational and cultural exchange activities began in 1950 as a foreign affairs officer in the Department of State. In 1965 he was named staff director, Board of Foreign Scholarships, the position he now holds. He has participated in numerous educational exchange conferences in the United States and abroad and has frequently chronicled the activities of the Board and the Fulbright program.

NOTE: The views expressed are those of the author and not those of the Board of Foreign Scholarships or the United States Information Agency.

THERE was scarcely a hint as the Fulbright program began that it would one day be considered by many the flagship of international exchange programs, that at 40 it could lay claim to over 156,000 alumni, with 4500 new exchanges each year in 120 participating countries, or that it would be the catalyst for countless other public and private exchanges. A don at Oxford once described the Fulbright program as "the biggest, most significant movement of scholars across the face of the earth since the fall of Constantinople in 1453."[1]

A profile of the program today shows that:

—over 1000 American scholars—faculty and professionals—annually hold Fulbright lectureships or research awards in colleges and universities in more than 100 countries;

—visiting scholars from abroad—almost 1200 each year—receive similar Fulbright research or teaching awards at universities and colleges across the United States;

—student exchanges, embracing the largest single category of Fulbright awards, include 550 grants annually to Americans for a year of graduate study abroad, more than 1300 new grants to foreign students for graduate studies in the United States, and about 650 foreign-student renewal grants to continue studies begun under a Fulbright award;

—almost 350 American elementary and secondary school teachers receive Fulbright awards yearly to teach in schools abroad or participate in seminars, including over 200 on direct exchange with their host-country counterparts; about 250 teachers from overseas teach in the United States annually on Fulbright awards;

—the Humphrey Fellowship Program, initiated in 1978 in memory of the late Senator and Vice-President Hubert H. Humphrey, awards 150 grants to professionals in public service from developing countries for a year's study and internship in the United States; and

—about 30 American universities each year are selected for university affiliation grants, seed money toward establishing a long-term linkage with a counterpart university in another country.

THE FULBRIGHT ACT

In September 1945, J. William Fulbright, then a freshman senator from Arkansas, introduced legislation to amend the Surplus Property Act of 1944. The amendment allowed the use of foreign credits accruing to the United States from the sale of idle surplus war property overseas for the financing of educational exchange—a disarmingly simple idea.

He had in mind two significant precedents in American history supporting the idea that educational exchange could affect the attitudes of the participants toward foreign nations: the Boxer Indemnity Fund and the Belgian-American Educational Foundation. He recalled also the wrangle over war debts after World War I, as well as his own experience as a Rhodes scholar in the 1920s.[2]

Senator Fulbright, adroitly choosing not to invite attention to the larger purposes of the legislation, emphasized

1. Eric Sevareid, CBS commentary, 18 May 1976.

2. J. William Fulbright, Remarks at the fortieth anniversary observance of the Fulbright program, The Hague, The Netherlands, Apr. 1986.

instead its modest scope and cost so as not to invite opposition. The bill passed the Congress and was signed by President Harry Truman on 1 August 1946, with scarce public notice. Years later Arnold Toynbee said, "Along with the Marshall Plan, the Fulbright Program is one of the really generous and imaginative things that have been done in the world since World War II."[3]

Several distinctive features helped gain the Fulbright program early acceptance from its diverse constituency. Those features have also given it stability and continuity while allowing it to evolve in response to vast political, economic, and social change here and abroad during the past four decades.

Giving shape and meaning to the new program, first of all, was the creative legislation itself. Second were those in the State Department and a few private organizations called upon to develop a mechanism for transforming the Fulbright Act into a reality. Finally, there were those individuals appointed to the first Board of Foreign Scholarships and their successors. Mandated by the Congress to supervise the program and select its participants, the Board established guidelines and standards of excellence that have stood the test of time. The result was an academic exchange program recognized throughout the world for quality and merit selection, peer review, open competition, public-private cooperation, and binational administration, leading later to joint financing.

3. Board of Foreign Scholarships, *A Quarter Century* (Washington, DC: Department of State, 1971). See also Francis A. Young, "Educational Exchanges and the National Interest," *American Council of Learned Societies Newsletter*, 20(2) (1969).

NEGOTIATING FULBRIGHT AGREEMENTS

A key feature of the legislation gave the secretary of state authority to enter into executive agreements with foreign governments. Educational exchanges under these agreements, financed with credits or currencies resulting from surplus property sales, were to be administered by foundations or by other means. Since the foreign currencies were readily expendable overseas, it was natural that such foundations, governed by binational boards, should be situated in the participating countries.

There were many anxious for the exchanges to begin, but a number of preliminary steps were necessary. A serious problem was the lack of dollars, since the Fulbright Act allowed only for utilizing nonconvertible foreign currencies. Dollars had to be found to pay costs incurred in the United States. American universities responded by offering fellowships, assistantships, and visiting lectureships to selected foreign applicants, with Fulbright funds providing the international travel. The Carnegie Corporation and the Rockefeller Foundation agreed to defray the costs of selecting American grantees for the first six months so that the first Fulbright exchanges could get under way. Thus was initiated the symbiotic relationship between private American institutions and the U.S. government that has been a basic characteristic of the Fulbright program to the present day.

It was a year after the new legislation before a concrete program developed that satisfied Secretary Dean Acheson's injunction "to take the fullest advantage of the opportunity offered by the Fulbright Act to improve common understanding among the peoples of the world."[4] In that time some funds had been identified, claimed, and set aside, negotiation of agreements with other countries had begun, and ways and means of financing and conducting the program had been devised.

In November 1947 the first executive agreement was concluded with China; shortly afterward, Derk Bodde, a well-known sinologist from the University of Pennsylvania, became the first American scholar to receive a Fulbright award. Within six months, agreements had also been signed with Burma, the Philippines, and Greece. These and the Fulbright agreements that followed achieved several objectives. The agreements identified the financial basis for the exchange program, established a binational board in each host country with specific shared program responsibilities, and empowered that board to employ a staff, disburse funds, maintain offices, draw up annual program plans and selection criteria, and recommend to the Board of Foreign scholarships candidates for awards, as well as receive nominations of Americans from the Board of Foreign Scholarships.

Early in 1948 the Congress was to approve the United States Information and Educational Exchange Act, thus solving the dollar problem. The State Department could then seek appropriations to pay contractual costs and some dollar expenses of foreign grantees, as well as to carry out academic exchanges in countries with minimal surplus property sales.

The Congress later authorized the use for educational exchanges of other foreign currencies owed the United States, most notably in a 1954 provision dealing

4. Board of Foreign Scholarships, *Quarter Century*, p. 9.

with surplus agricultural commodity sales abroad. This enabled exchanges to continue in some countries where surplus property proceeds were exhausted. It also allowed extending exchanges in the mid 1950s to additional countries, including eight in Latin America, where there had been no binational agreements. By the 1970s, U.S. government support for the program was almost entirely in dollar funds since few foreign currencies were held by the government.

In negotiating and financing educational exchange agreements and in countless other tasks, the Fulbright program is greatly indebted to the Department of State, and since 1978 to the United States Information Agency. They have carried responsibility for the management of the Fulbright program from the beginning; without them the program could not have been sustained.

BINATIONAL COMMISSIONS

In its landmark statement setting forth the goals for educational exchange in the 1970s, the Board made special reference to the binational character of the program:

The uniqueness of the exchange program is enhanced by the strong strain of *binationalism* that infuses it. Citizens of both countries share in its planning and administration, and bring talent and breadth to this responsibility. They protect its quality. They insulate it against partisan pressures. They keep it flexible and responsive to new ideas. They enlist many talents in support of its activities. They move a program that is governmental in origin outside the routine processes and controls of government; this condition makes participation in it more attractive to some, and makes it less likely to be affected in passing periods of political strain.[5]

5. Board of Foreign Scholarships, *A State-*

Over the history of the program, 51 binational Fulbright agreements have been negotiated with as many countries. The agreement with Morocco, signed in February 1982, is the most recent. Today commissions operate Fulbright exchanges in 42 of these countries. Commissions in the nine other countries have become inactive for various reasons, although some Fulbright exchanges administered by the American embassy have continued with most of these countries. Fulbright exchanges also take place in an additional 75 countries where no binational commissions exist; these are operated abroad by officers of the United States Information Agency posted at American embassies.

As binational commissions were established in each participating country, they became the focal point for all Fulbright exchanges with that country. The commission acts as the bridge to the universities that accept American Fulbright lecturers, research scholars, and students in priority fields specified by the commission. It also nominates the visiting Fulbright scholars and students coming to the United States. More recently commissions have counseled and advised substantial numbers of foreign students wishing to study in the United States under other auspices.

Commissions have attracted capable and dedicated staffs, some of whom have served the program for many years. A number of commissions have been headed by talented directors who have become the permanent Fulbright presence in their respective countries.

The board of the commission, appointed, respectively, by the American ambassador and the minister of foreign affairs or the minister of education, has been important in establishing the binational character of the program and in its ready acceptance by the host country, countering the charge by some of cultural imperialism. Commission members have later lent their personal support to the cost-sharing of Fulbright exchanges by many host governments. Beyond program acceptance, the most significant long-term result of the binational approach has undoubtedly been the willingness of many governments to join with the United States in financing the Fulbright program. Today 27 countries contribute over $12 million annually in direct support of binational commission programs.

THE BOARD OF FOREIGN SCHOLARSHIPS

In the original drafts of the 1946 legislation, Senator Fulbright made no provision for a Board of Foreign Scholarships. Before final passage, however, two points impressed him: domestic politics might influence the selection of American participants; and short-term foreign policy goals might come to determine the character of the program.

Later, appearing before the House Committee on Expenditures in Executive Departments, he was ready with an amendment providing for a ten-member presidentially appointed Board of Foreign Scholarships "for the purpose of selecting students and educational institutions qualified to participate in this program and to supervise the exchange program authorized."[6]

---

ment on *Educational Exchanges in the Seventies* (Washington, DC: Department of State, 1971).

6. The Fulbright Act, signed into law on 1 Aug. 1946 (Pub. L. No. 79-584), superseded by the Mutual Educational and Cultural Exchange Act of 1961 (Pub. L. No. 87-256).

Years later, on the program's twentieth anniversary, Board chairman Oscar Handlin stated that the Board existed as "the product of an intention to keep the program free of either political or bureaucratic interference."[7] In 1983, when the Senate Foreign Relations Committee adopted a legislative charter for the exchange programs carried out by the United States Information Agency's Bureau of Educational and Cultural Affairs, its report stated, "The Committee expects that the Board of Foreign Scholarships, which is essential to the administration of the academic programs of the . . . Bureau, shall be a completely nonpartisan institution."[8]

It became the duty of the first appointed Board of Foreign Scholarships, meeting initially in October 1947, to make prompt decisions on a number of issues of historic significance to the future direction of the new program. There were few if any precedents.

Since this Board chartered the basic course for the future direction of the new Fulbright program, its membership deserves special attention. Elected chairman was Francis Spaulding, the dynamic commissioner of education of the state of New York. Other members were Sarah Blanding and Charles Johnson, presidents, respectively, of Vassar and Fisk; Martin R.P. McGuire, dean of the Graduate School of Arts and Sciences at Catholic University in Washington, D.C.; and Laurence Duggan, long-term director of the Institute of International Education. Included also were three noted scholars—E. O. Lawrence of the University of California, Nobel Prize winner in physics; Walter

Johnson, historian from the University of Chicago; and Helen C. White, English professor and writer from the University of Wisconsin. Two other members representing constituencies specified in the legislation were General Omar Bradley, administrator of veteran affairs; and John W. Studebaker, U.S. commissioner of education.

SELECTING FULBRIGHTS

The Board's most urgent task was to set up the criteria by which preliminary and final selections might be made and to devise ways and means of using such criteria effectively with the thousands of persons, American and foreign, soon applying for grants. The Board pledged that

in all aspects of the program the highest standards will be developed and maintained . . . the individuals to benefit will be of the highest caliber, persons who demonstrate scholastic and professional ability and whose personalities and characters will contribute to the furtherance of the objectives of the program.[9]

The emphasis on excellence was not narrowly construed. The Fulbright Act was to be "interpreted broadly to include persons of all kinds of educational activities, for example, librarians, museum personnel, and agricultural extension consultants."[10] At its second meeting in December 1947, the Board elaborated on this list to specify "artists, musicians . . . writers, journalists, and similar profes-

7. Board of Foreign Scholarships, *Quarter Century*, p. 26.

8. USIA Authorization Act, Fiscal years 1984-85 (Tit. 2, Pub. L. No. 98-164).

9. Board of Foreign Scholarships, *Quarter Century*, pp. 27-28. These and other decisions setting forth Board policy are included in the summary minutes of Board meetings. These decisions are described in more detail in Walter Johnson and Francis J. Colligan, *The Fulbright Program: A History* (Chicago: University of Chicago Press, 1965).

10. Board of Foreign Scholarships, *Quarter Century*, p. 28.

sional people . . . as well as such fields as adult education, labor and workers' education."[11] One of the first grantees to Burma was a retired agricultural extension agent, Otto K. Hunerwardel, who with his wife, Helen, was sent on a Fulbright to the Shan States of Burma to teach and demonstrate improved methods of agriculture.[12]

The Board also specified that all persons receiving grants "must be acceptable to the host country and to the institution in connection with which they propose to pursue their projects." This precaution was necessary "so that we would not seem to be imposing individuals on any one country"; and "consideration should be given to whether a candidate is temperamentally suited" to promote international understanding as well.[13]

In most of these decisions, the emphasis was on the individual student and scholar, selected on a merit basis after an open national competition. As the Board announced publicly, "Awards will not be made to projects or institutions, as such." One of the latter submitted a single project for microfilming records that could have used up all the funds available in these early years. Even though conceivably it might have been possible to justify such an award as consonant with the letter of the Fulbright Act, the Board was confident it did not accord with its spirit.

With this emphasis on the individual in competition, the Board accepted a responsibility it knew it could not fulfill without considerable outside help. Thus there was the necessity for turning to cooperating agencies, which would channel information to the prospective American applicant, receive and analyze his or her papers, and bring in qualified experts to evaluate credentials and make recommendations to the Board.

The Institute of International Education, with over 25 years' experience in student exchanges, agreed to perform these screening functions for U.S. student grants. The U.S. Office of Education would serve for grants to U.S. teachers and administrators in elementary and secondary education, and the Conference Board of Associated Research Councils was asked by the Board of Foreign Scholarships and the State Department to establish a screening mechanism for U.S. senior scholars applying for lecturing or research assignments abroad.

These organizations and others coming later became essential elements in linking the Fulbright program to the educational community in the United States and abroad. They have drawn on the voluntary services of thousands of American scholars and other professionals, who sit on screening committees to judge the qualifications of applicants and give nominations of Fulbright candidates to the Board of Foreign Scholarships. The cooperating organizations have also sought university admissions, including private scholarships, fellowships, and other support, for many of the 100,000 Fulbrighters from abroad over the life span of the program.

Expenses for Fulbright program administration by the cooperating organizations, as well as salaries and expenses of government administrators, are now included in the U.S. president's annual appropriation request to the Congress for the operations of the United States Information Agency.

11. Ibid.

12. Johnson and Colligan, *Fulbright Program,* p. 181.

13. Board of Foreign Scholarships, *Quarter Century,* p. 29.

The role and contributions of these organizations have been vital to the success of the program; they are not ones that can be readily duplicated. Not surprisingly, there have been times when that significance has not been fully understood and appreciated.

ADVISE OR SUPERVISE?

The Board's second mandate under the authorizing legislation was "to supervise the program." Before the members of the first Board met, there had been some in the State Department disposed to interpret "supervise" as "advise." They reasoned that since there was no apparent precedent for vesting supervisory responsibility in a part-time board, however distinguished, Congress must have really intended only a limited, ceremonial function.

But the wording of the legislation was undeniable; and the Board at its first meeting clearly accepted the authority it had been given.

The Board assumes the responsibility for policies and general directives to govern the program and determine the qualifications of individuals and participating institutions. The Board's responsibility includes such functions as (a) the determination of the types of programs and projects which are to be carried out under the Act, (b) the final selection of all grantees, both foreign and American, (c) review of reports of program operations, (d) statements of policy regarding the objectives and directions of the Fulbright program.[14]

This statement has served the Board well through the years. In 1972 a new statement of objectives took into account the broader authority bestowed on the Board by the Fulbright-Hays Act. This

14. Ibid., p. 32.

act had increased Board membership to 12 and gave the Board authority for the selection and supervision of academic exchange programs with all countries where the United States engages in such exchanges, not merely those with binational commissions, as under the earlier Fulbright Act.

In elaborating on its supervisory role in the 1972 statement, the Board could not resist the opportunity to lament its lack of a "statutory role in the budget process" and the necessity to "accommodate the exercise of its responsibilities to financial ceilings and allocations of funds determined by others."[15] Nonetheless, the Board's policy guidelines, which have evolved over the lifetime of the program, together with its selection role, have been the most important single factors influencing the character of the Fulbright program worldwide.

PROGRAM GROWTH

As the number of executive agreements increased steadily—from the 7 reported to Congress by Secretary Dean Acheson for 1948 to the 39 active in 1961—grants to American and foreign participants kept pace, with 84 awards the first year and over 4800 in the latter.

In 1965 new Fulbright exchanges climbed to 6000, the largest one-year total achieved until then, not yet to be surpassed. Five years later exchanges had dropped to half that number, reflecting the sharp governmentwide budget cuts necessitated by the rising costs of the Vietnam war and the political fallout

15. "Statement of Objectives," Minutes, Eighty-fifth meeting of the Board of Foreign Scholarships, 5-6 Dec. 1968. See also *Policy Statements, Board of Foreign Scholarships,* rev. ed. (Washington, DC: Bureau of Educational and Cultural Affairs, United States Information Agency, 1986).

over the bitter antiwar sentiment on many university campuses.

More recently, the number of new exchanges rose from 3500 in 1980 to about 5000 in 1986, no small achievement considering the devastating effects of inflation here and abroad on travel and living costs. Maintaining and expanding these numbers were possible largely because of an action taken by the U.S. Congress, prompted in part by a proposed major reduction in funding in the fall of 1981 that severely threatened the program. Under the so-called Percy-Pell amendment to the authorizing bill for Fulbright and other basic exchange activities of the United States Information Agency, the Congress in 1982 mandated a doubling of exchange-of-persons programs between fiscal years 1982 and 1986. Funding for these exchanges had declined by 40 percent since 1965, when the budget was $27 million; the congressional action sought to reverse that trend. The Congress voted $42 million for Fulbright exchanges in 1982, $58 million in 1984, and about $81 million for 1986. This rate of growth will undoubtedly be slowed by congressional budgetary restrictions in place for 1987 and beyond.

A second significant long-term source of funding has been the cost-sharing contributions to binational Fulbright commissions by participating governments with which the United States has exchange agreements. The 1961 Fulbright-Hays Act encouraged such joint financing, and the State Department vigorously pursued the amending of existing agreements to this end. Germany, which had initially signed an exchange agreement a decade earlier, was the first to sign a new cost-sharing agreement in 1962. It agreed to finance 80 percent of the program, or $800,000, annually for

the ensuing 5 years to make up in part for earlier years when the United States funded the entire program. Germany has since continued the practice of contributing the larger share of the now much larger annual budget.

In 1966 foreign governments in 10 countries contributed $1.6 million directly to the support of binational commission exchanges. By 1985, 27 governments were giving $12.2 million annually. While largely a joint financial investment, cost sharing also represents a more lasting commitment to the concept and principle of binationalism in the conduct of long-term educational and cultural exchanges. Beyond direct financial support to the binational commissions, many of the 120 participating countries provide some indirect support such as free or subsidized university housing and other partial costs of Fulbright grantees.

How much has the U.S. government invested in the Fulbright program since it began? One estimate is $997.7 million, averaging less than $25 million per year. There are many who believe that on any scale of government expenditures this is surely a modest investment in the cause of promoting better mutual understanding between the peoples of the world.

CONTINUITY AND CHANGE

We have seen a glimpse of the institutions that have given style and substance to the Fulbright program. They have also given it continuity. One measure of its success is that the program has not only survived to age 40 but has remained true to its initial goals. In that time it has enjoyed the enormous goodwill and support of many thousands throughout the world, who continue to give it strength and vitality.

With continuity also comes change, and the program has kept pace with the changing political and social environment in which it must operate. New countries, developing countries, spell fresh challenges. Limited budgets dictate hard choices and the setting of exchange priorities. Fewer exchange candidates call for innovative programs and new initiatives.

The first Board of Foreign Scholarships pioneered educational exchanges on a global scale. Shared binational planning and administering of scholarly exchanges were introduced for the first time. The introduction of American studies at universities abroad was fostered under the Fulbright program.

Successive Boards in the 1950s presided over the program's expansion to several Third World countries and introduced the first binational commissions to Latin America. Boards in 1959 and 1961 met personally with President Eisenhower and President Kennedy to report on the Fulbright program.

With the passage of the Fulbright-Hays Act, the Boards of the sixties took on new responsibilities as Fulbright exchanges were extended to some seventy additional countries including many newly emerged in Africa.

The Board that ushered in the decade of the seventies was especially creative. It produced a blueprint for future Fulbright exchanges, advocating a sharper program focus for such activities. The Board also urged increased exchanges in nonacademic professions, experimental grants to scholarly teams and institutions, and increased counseling services to nonsponsored foreign students.

This Board of the seventies also launched a program for distinguished Fulbright scholars, attracting some of the best minds in America and abroad.

Finally, it sponsored the publication of an unofficial history of the program on its twenty-fifth anniversary.

More recent Boards have carried their share of program responsibilities in extending the legacy of their predecessors to ensure the continued flourishing of the Fulbright program.

TOMORROW'S AGENDA

Several issues deserve the attention of Fulbright program administrators as we look to the future:

1. Alternative sources of funding for the Fulbright program should be explored and expanded. Some commissions now administer Fulbright-type exchanges financed by foreign banks, local Fulbright alumni groups, and other sponsors. Since there are limits to U.S. and foreign government funding, these and other public-private funding efforts should be encouraged. Other types of funding should also be explored. These include joint Fulbright awards with private industry, state and local governments and institutions, and other groups. Finally, the advantages of establishing a national or international endowment for Fulbright and other exchanges should be explored and encouraged.

2. Effective binational participation in the conduct of the Fulbright program should be expanded. Binational participation in the conduct and administration of academic exchanges abroad is an important element in the success of the Fulbright program. Steps should be taken to strengthen and expand the binational commission network to additional countries where program levels and other favorable factors are present. Simple, effective alternatives such as binational Fulbright advisory committees should

be explored in other instances to make clearly visible the binational character of the program.

3. Active national and local Fulbright alumni organizations here and abroad should be supported. Fulbright alumni are one of the program's great untapped resources. The Fulbright Alumni Association in the United States and similar groups elsewhere should be encouraged to share program experiences; advise present, former, or potential grantees; and offer local hospitality to visiting Fulbrighters. They could assist in grantee recruitment, advise on program issues, and aid in keeping the public informed about the program. Finally, some alumni groups have raised financial support to provide additional Fulbright awards in specific countries.

4. American colleges should be enlisted to offer incentives for faculty participation in the Fulbright program. Many American faculty accept Fulbright awards at a financial sacrifice and with some adverse effects on professional careers. An appeal should be made in the national interest to American colleges and universities to offer career incentives—or eliminate disincentives—for faculty members who accept Fulbright lectureships abroad.

Fulbright Internationalism

By RANDALL BENNETT WOODS

ABSTRACT: In 1946 Senator J. William Fulbright introduced and guided through Congress legislation establishing an international exchange program in education. The Fulbright program, which has produced the largest migration of students and scholars in modern history, was the result first of the senator's personal experience. His goal was to make available to thousands the enlightening experience of foreign study and travel he had enjoyed as a Rhodes scholar. The exchange legislation was also an integral part of the internationalist movement that swept America in the mid-1940s. Finally, Fulbright's brainchild was a result of his disillusionment with America's diplomatic leadership and his determination to raise up an educated, sophisticated elite capable of guiding the nation and the world.

Randall Bennett Woods is the John A. Cooper Professor of Diplomacy in the Fulbright Institute of International Relations at the University of Arkansas. He earned his Ph.D. at the University of Texas in 1972 and has taught diplomatic history at Arkansas since 1971. Woods is the author of two books and numerous articles on various aspects of American history. He is currently president of the Arkansas Endowment for the Humanities.

NOTE: This article is the product of research for a projected biography of J. William Fulbright.

A T the outset of his public career, J. William Fulbright had an extraordinary vision: an American-sponsored international exchange program that would educate thousands of scholars and students from every part of the globe. Such a program, he believed, would do much to help rid the world of the twin evils of parochialism and nationalism. Fulbright began his tenure in the Senate near the close of World War II, when much of Europe and Asia lay in ruins. Two new superpowers, Russia and the United States, faced each other across a devastated world. One already possessed atomic weapons and the other, it was commonly agreed, would shortly develop a nuclear-strike capability. Like many of his generation, Bill Fulbright believed that humanity had been given a second chance and that the heritage and largess of the United States imposed upon it a special responsibility to lead the world into a new era. He did not argue that it was America's destiny to force its culture on others. Rather, its mission was to make the world safe for diversity.

Fulbright recognized that in a democracy an enlightened foreign policy depends upon an educated electorate. He saw clearly that xenophobia breeds intolerance and aggression. The ability of the United States, the most powerful nation in the world in 1946, to protect its democratic institutions and to facilitate the establishment of a peaceful and stable world in the atomic age depended in large part on the nation's ability to learn about and appreciate foreign cultures. To this end he founded the program that was to bear his name.

In this sense the Fulbright exchange program was an integral part of the internationalist movement that swept America during and after World War II.[1] Fulbright was a primary actor and a major intellectual contributor to that movement. His speeches traced isolationism and nationalism to a common source and claimed that in the modern world, with its technologically advanced communications and armament systems, national sovereignty was impossible. Only if the international community accepted collective security and economic interdependency could the endless cycle of aggression and war be broken. An international exchange program was a prime method, Fulbright believed, of weaning the peoples of the world away from the sacred cow of national sovereignty.

At the same time, however, the genesis of the exchange program grew out of Fulbright's disillusionment with the selfsame internationalism or, rather, with America's commitment to it. He was alarmed by the intense opposition in Congress to the Bretton Woods legislation and to the British loan of 1946, an opposition spearheaded, he believed, by isolationists and economic nationalists. He was concerned about the Truman administration's increasingly obvious intent to get tough with the Soviet Union in 1945-46. Its unwillingness to internationalize atomic energy also disturbed him. When the State Department and White House agreed to a U.N. Charter that seemed to preserve rather than diminish national sovereignty, he began to wonder if America's leaders really understood what Woodrow Wilson had been talking about. Perhaps his countrymen, particularly those in power, did not comprehend the obligations and requirements that a "parliament of man"

1. See Robert A. Divine, *Second Chance: The Triumph of Internationalism in America during World War II* (New York: Atheneum, 1967).

would entail. But the event that seemed to have been most disillusioning to him, one that caused him to despair of America's diplomatic leadership, was the seating of Argentina in April 1945 as a permanent member of the United Nations over the violent objections of the Russians. This power play, he believed, was the work of Edward Stettinius, the inexperienced secretary of state whom Truman had inherited from Roosevelt, and members of the State Department old guard wedded to the outdated strategies of power politics and spheres of interest.

THE UNITED STATES AND INTERNATIONAL EXCHANGE

The idea of international exchange as a means of sharing knowledge and breaking down barriers was certainly not original with Fulbright; the concept is as old as organized society itself.[2] The development of Western civilization, and to a certain extent Eastern, is in large part a study in the exchange of ideas and technology between cultures. Fulbright is perhaps remarkable for seeing international exchange as a prerequisite for the proper functioning of any kind of world government.

Nor was the Fulbright exchange program the first formal mechanism for the interchange of students and scholars in the United States. Between the two world wars 5564 students studied in the United States and abroad under the auspices of the Institute of International Education.[3]

In addition, there emerged during the early years of the twentieth century two bilateral programs of note. In 1908 the United States remitted $16 million of an indemnity it had forced China to pay following the Boxer Rebellion. The money was to be channeled into an educational fund to enable Chinese students to come to America. China set up Tsing Hua College at Peking, where, until World War II intervened, approximately 400 students annually prepared for admission to an American university.[4] Herbert Hoover, a life-long advocate of international education, was responsible for setting up America's second country-to-country exchange. In 1920, with the liquidation of the Belgian Relief Commission, he established the Belgian-American Educational Foundation. That agency, using left-over relief funds, exchanged 762 Belgians and Americans during its 25 years of existence.[5] By the outbreak of World War II, one-quarter of the faculty at Belgian universities, one prime minister, and six cabinet members had studied in America. In 1923, as secretary of commerce, Hoover tried to divert $100 million in war debts to educational exchange, and subsequently as president he attempted to found a Latin American program. Both efforts failed.

Throughout the interwar period the U.S. government assumed a posture of indifference toward scholarly exchange. In the inter-American understanding signed at the Buenos Aires Conference in 1936, Washington did bind itself to trade two professors and two graduate students each year with the other Ameri-

---

2. See Henry J. Kellermann, *Cultural Relations as an Instrument of U.S. Foreign Policy* (Washington, DC: Department of State, Bureau of Educational and Cultural Affairs, 1978).

3. I. L. Kandel, *U.S. Activities in International Cultural Relations* (Washington, DC: American Council on Education Studies, 1945), p. 40.

4. Richard L. Strout, "Changing Cannons to Cultural Currency," *Christian Science Monitor*, 2 Mar. 1946.

5. William Starr Meyers, *The Foreign Policy of Herbert Hoover, 1929-1933* (New York: Charles Scribner's Sons, 1940), pp. 1-4.

can republics, but Congress was never called upon to provide funding. The prospects for international exchange brightened when in 1938 the State Department established a Cultural Affairs Division. During World War II the division ran a small-scale operation that included China, Africa, and the Middle East, but its activities were devoted mostly to persuading American universities to start their own programs.[6] In an effort to combat Axis propaganda, the Roosevelt administration persuaded Congress in 1943 to establish the Office of Coordinator of Inter-American Affairs. Under Nelson Rockefeller, this agency sponsored travel in and scholarship on the Americas, but its programs were sporadic and unfocused.[7]

THE FULBRIGHT PROGRAM BECOMES LAW

In September 1945 Senator J. William Fulbright introduced an amendment to the Surplus Property Act of 1944 that would use proceeds from the sale of U.S. surplus property overseas to fund an educational exchange program. In the process of defeating the Axis, the U.S. military and its civilian appendages had built more than $6.5 billion in manufacturing industries in various countries and had stockpiled $2.8 billion in goods, including everything from machine tools and rolling stock to raw cotton and jeeps.[8] Although various domestic groups

sought either to distribute these products free or to allow them to be bought at cut rate, Congress resisted. The cost of re-importation would be immense and the dumping of large quantities of stocks on the domestic market would cripple the private sector in its efforts to convert from a wartime to a peacetime footing.[9]

Fulbright's short, thirty-line bill authorized the use of proceeds from the sale of surplus property overseas for educational exchange in the areas of science, culture, and education. The junior senator from Arkansas believed that the juxtaposition of surplus property, a shortage of dollars abroad with which to purchase that property, and widespread sympathy in the United States for a more active role in world affairs was sufficient to overcome a tight-fisted Congress and the historic indifference of official Washington to international educational exchange. As Harry Jeffrey points out, the impetus for the program came almost solely from Fulbright. In 1945 there was no organized pressure from educators and certainly not from the Truman administration to launch such a program.[10]

In November 1945 Fulbright abandoned his first proposal in favor of a second, broader bill that made more explicit his ideas on international education. It also reflected extensive consultation with the State Department. Under this second measure, which was finally adopted, the State Department was to

6. Harry P. Jeffrey, "Senator Fulbright and the Passage of the Fulbright Exchange Program" (Paper presented to special symposium commemorating the fortieth anniversary of the Fulbright exchange program, Fayetteville, AR, 28-30 Sept. 1986), pp. 5-6.

7. *Federal Records of World War II*, vol. 1, *Civilian Agencies* (Washington, DC: Government Printing Office, 1950), pp. 226-27.

8. U.S., Congress, Committee on Expenditures in the Executive Departments, *Surplus Property Disposal: Hearings*, 79th Cong., 1st sess., 1946, pp. 1-40.

9. Robert Donovan, *Conflict and Crisis: The Presidency of Harry S. Truman, 1945-1948* (New York: W. W. Norton, 1977), p. 109. See also Fred Vinson to Harry Truman, 7/19/45, Box 4, Naval Aide File, Papers of Harry S. Truman, Truman Library, Independence, MO.

10. Jeffrey, "Senator Fulbright," p. 1.

be the sole disposal agency for surplus property located outside the United States and its possessions. The Division of Cultural Affairs could accept dollars, foreign currency, or promissory notes, and it could enter into agreements with foreign governments to use the proceeds from these transactions to finance educational activities for Americans in other countries, study by foreign nationals in overseas U.S. institutions, and transportation of visitors from abroad to study in America.[11] As finally amended, the legislation established a nonpartisan Board of Foreign Scholarships to administer the project and limited the amount that could be spent in any one country to $1 million. After obtaining Harry Truman's offhanded endorsement of the bill, the Arkansan quietly secured the support of the Democratic and Republican leadership of both houses of Congress. As a result his pet scheme passed without opposition. On 1 August 1946 President Truman signed the bill into law and the Fulbright scholarship program came into being.[12]

THE PROGRAM AS A PROJECTION OF PERSONAL EXPERIENCE

J. William Fulbright sponsored his historic bill in part because he wanted to institutionalize the experience that had converted him from a narrow-gauged resident of the American heartland into a citizen of the world. The fourth of six children, he was born on a farm near Sumner, Missouri, on 9 April 1905. When he was a year old the family moved to another farm, near Fayetteville, Arkansas, a college community situated in the foothills of the Ozarks. The future

senator's father was a hard-working, prosperous farmer who invested successfully in a lumber yard, a bottling plant, and the local newspaper. His mother, Roberta, a tough-minded woman who assumed the editorship of the *Northwest Arkansas Times*, instilled in her son an appreciation for education and a sense of public duty. Fulbright enrolled at the University of Arkansas, where he was involved in athletics and campus politics and majored in liberal arts. However, when his father died suddenly, the young student left school briefly during his junior year. With the family's affairs in order, he was able to return and graduate. Just as he was about to assume management of the Fulbright business network, one of his professors suggested that he apply for a Rhodes Scholarship. Following an interview in Little Rock, the young Arkansan learned, to his surprise, that he was to be the Rhodes scholar from his state for that year.[13]

When he sailed for England, Fulbright had never journeyed east of the Mississippi River, visited a large metropolitan area, or seen the ocean. His time at Oxford with vacations spent in Europe profoundly impressed the man whose travel hitherto had been largely limited to football trips to Oklahoma and Texas. He met students from every continent and began to understand something of the world's vast array of political and religious beliefs. After a full diet of tutorials, rugby, lacrosse, and the Oxford Union, the Arkansas traveler graduated from Pembroke College with a concentration in modern history.

At the time Fulbright finished at Oxford in 1928 the family business was going so well that he decided that he

---

11. U.S., Congress, Senate, *Congressional Record*, 79th Cong., 2d sess., 1946, 92, pt. 12:A4766.
12. Jeffrey, "Senator Fulbright," pp. 9-12.

13. "Egghead from the Ozarks," *Saturday Evening Post*, 2 May 1959.

could afford to spend some time on the Continent before returning. His stay lengthened into more than a year. The freshly minted Rhodes scholar gravitated to Vienna, the cultural and political crossroads of interwar Europe, and there he fell in with a veteran American correspondent for the *Philadelphia Public Ledger*, M. W. Fodor. He and Mike Fodor, who was to correspond with Fulbright regularly for the next thirty years, explored the highways and byways of central and southeastern Europe. Through Fodor he met many of the top political figures of the era. In 1929 Fulbright returned home, his education complete. The Rhodes Scholarship and his sojourn with Fodor impressed forever upon him the value of foreign travel and international education.[14]

FULBRIGHT INTERNATIONALISM

The Fulbright exchange program was more than just an extension of the man's personal history; it was also a product of the internationalist resurgence of the mid-1940s and an integral part of Fulbright's own special brand of internationalism. During World War II Americans self-consciously studied the lessons of the immediate past. Munich had clearly demonstrated that appeasement only fed aggression. Woodrow Wilson had been right; the only alternative to war and depression was a world organization with the will and power to maintain collective security. In the fall of 1943 America's best-known neo-internationalist, Secretary of State Cordell Hull, journeyed to the Moscow Foreign Minister's Conference and there secured Russia's and Great Britain's agreement to participate in a revised League of Nations. That same year Senator Tom Connally of Texas and freshman Congressman J. William Fulbright pushed through the House and Senate a resolution pledging U.S. support for a postwar collective security organization. The Roosevelt administration, impressed by the outpouring of public support for the Moscow Declaration and the Fulbright-Connally Resolution, boarded the bandwagon. With Washington leading the way, representatives of the Grand Alliance gathered at Dumbarton Oaks in late 1944 to sketch the outline of a global organization. That framework was subsequently fleshed out at the United Nations Conference on International Organization (UNCIO) held in San Francisco in April and May 1945. Later that same year the U.S. Senate unanimously approved the Charter of the United Nations.[15]

As his coauthorship of the Fulbright-Connally Resolution indicated, Fulbright as a congressman and as a senator was a leading figure in the internationalist movement. In part his commitment to Wilsonian principles was an offshoot of his years at Oxford. The most important acquaintance he made at Pembroke College was his young tutor, Ronald Buchanan McCallum, whose guidance and instruction were crucial in shaping the young American's intellect and worldview. From that first autumn after-

14. Ibid. See also "Well Adjusted Realist from Arkansas Takes Senate Seat of Hattie Caraway," 14 Feb. 1945, Series 78, Box 31, Folder 4, Papers of J. William Fulbright, Special Collections, Mullins Library, University of Arkansas, Fayetteville (hereafter cited as Fulbright Papers); Haynes Johnson and Bernard M. Gwertzman, *Fulbright: The Dissenter* (New York: Curtis Books, 1966), pp. 17-64.

15. Gaddis Smith, *American Diplomacy during the Second World War, 1941-1945* (New York: John Wiley, 1966), pp. 71-74, 147-48, and 156.

noon when they met and cycled together to view the tomb of William Lenthall of Long Parliament fame, the two men maintained a close personal and intellectual relationship until McCallum's death in 1973.

A Liberal, McCallum was an ardent admirer of Woodrow Wilson, revering both the man and his vision. In 1944 the Oxford don published *Public Opinion and the Lost Peace*, in which he challenged the long-standing view of John Maynard Keynes that the peace structure worked out at the Versailles Conference was predestined to fail. The concept of the League was sound; the organization had not worked because political figures on both sides of the Atlantic had never been willing to make a true commitment to the principles that underlay it and had attempted to use it for their own selfish, political purposes. Eventually, due to ignorance, ambivalence, selfishness, and especially a lack of leadership, Anglo-American public opinion became intensely disillusioned with the Versailles peace settlement. McCallum concluded his book with an appeal to Americans and Britons to rediscover and rededicate themselves to the principles of Wilsonian internationalism. He not only urged the two powers to bring to fruition plans for an International Monetary Fund and International Bank for Reconstruction and Development, but also called for an elimination of barriers to trade. McCallum warned against a revival of political isolationism in the United States, and he appealed for postwar cooperation with Russia. Above all, if the modern world were to survive, there would have to be "some abnegation of formal state sovereignty."[16]

16. George Herbert Gunn, "The Continuing Friendship of James William Fulbright and Ronald

Meanwhile, in the United States, J. William Fulbright, the practicing politician, began to develop and promulgate his own version of Wilsonian internationalism. In speeches inside and outside Congress and in debates on the floor of the House and Senate, the outline of his vision began to emerge. Like Wilson, Fulbright believed that it was imperative that American leaders develop a set of principles to guide their foreign policy and that they fashion bipartisan support for these principles.[17] Also like Wilson— and Theodore Roosevelt before him— Fulbright sensed that the time was ripe for a new foreign policy. Perhaps if he could define and articulate the direction America should take, he could simultaneously advance his own interests and those of his country.

Underlying Fulbright's internationalism was the assumption that there existed a body of ideas and a constellation of economic and political institutions that together defined Western civilization, that the United States shared in these ideals and institutions, and that therefore it had an obligation to defend them. If it were true, he told the Senate, that Americans, Britons, Scandinavians, and Italians had in common "the love of family, the regard for contractual obligation, the abhorrence of torture and persecution, the distrust of tyrannical and oppressive government . . . then we should acknowledge them in order that a definite policy based upon sound considerations be firmly adopted."[18] The United States had not been willing in the

Buchanan McCallum," *South Atlantic Quarterly*, 83(4):417-19 (Autumn 1984).

17. J. William Fulbright (hereafter JWF) to Edward J. Meeman, 19 Mar. 1945, BCN24, Folder 29, Fulbright Papers.

18. U.S., Congress, Senate, *Congressional Record*, 79th Cong., 1st sess., 1945, 91, pt. 3:2898.

past to acknowledge its debt to this common culture, much less its obligation to defend it. Fulbright, like most internationalists, was reacting to a particular interpretation of the immediate past. He, like Harry Truman, Dean Acheson, and so many others of his generation, accepted what Gaddis Smith has called a great cycle theory of history.[19] According to this view the story of the twentieth century was largely a recurring pattern of American isolation, European aggression, and American intervention. It was up to his generation, Fulbright believed, to break that cycle. The lesson of Munich was that appeasement strengthened the forces of totalitarianism and encouraged aggression. The United States, he said, must fight World War II for more than just the selfish reason of self-preservation. When the war ended isolationists would sing their siren song once again, but the American people must turn a deaf ear. It was the nation's duty "to wage a creative war for a creative peace."[20]

Time and again the former Rhodes scholar tried to demonstrate that isolationism was merely a facet of old-fashioned nationalism. Those of his contemporaries who posed as defenders of national sovereignty were in fact advocating a return to the policies of the interwar period, when the United States refused to acknowledge that its fate was tied up with those of other democracies. National sovereignty was in fact a trick, an illusion, especially in the world of airplanes, submarines, and atomic weapons. "If it means anything today," he told his Senate colleagues, "sovereignty as applied to a state surely means that a state is sufficiently independent econom-

ically, politically, and physically to defend itself and provide for the security and happiness of its own people." In this turbulent world, he asked, "can it be seriously contended that the vast majority of existing states are sovereign powers?"[21] After equating isolationism with obsessive nationalism, he observed that both led to a laissez-faire attitude toward international affairs. Abnegation, in turn, made possible oppression and poverty—the twin seeds of war.

With the end of the struggle against the Axis, the United States and the world stood at a crossroads. The path selected would determine the shape of the future—tyranny or freedom, peace or annihilation. "We must," he told the George Washington School of Law in 1943, "make this choice now while the minds and hearts of men are concerned with universal and fundamental problems, while danger and sacrifice give us humility and understanding."[22] At first, Fulbright's view of America's mission in the world took on the same messianic and parochial characteristics of Wilson's missionary diplomacy. In his early speeches, Fulbright argued that America must help other nations develop their own version of democracy. Implicit in this view was the assumption that given the freedom to choose, all people would opt for a society characterized by democracy, individual liberty, and free enterprise.[23] By late 1945, however, the senator had developed a sense of cultural relativity. He observed to the Senate that capitalism was not "divine and inviolable [sic]," something handed down by the Almighty from above. It had

19. Gaddis Smith, *Dean Acheson* (New York: Cooper Square, 1972).

20. U.S., Congress, House, *Congressional Record*, 78th Cong., 1st sess., 1943, 8, pt. 9:A477.

21. U.S., Congress, Senate, *Congressional Record*, 79th Cong., 1st sess., 1945, 91, pt. 3:2899.

22. U.S., Congress, House, *Congressional Record*, 78th Cong., 1st sess., 1943, 8, pt. 9:A477.

23. Ibid.

worked for America because a particular set of circumstances and material conditions prevailed at a particular time in history. The peoples of the earth should be free to develop their own economic and political traditions.[24]

But the principle of self-determination would not in and of itself preserve the world from the deadly cycle of aggression and war. Something more was needed. To an extent Fulbright believed that the inability of the United States to develop a coherent, consistent foreign policy that would enable it to lead the world into a new era of peace and prosperity stemmed from flaws in the American federal system. Like Wilson, Fulbright was something of an anglophile and was a great admirer of the parliamentary system. At one point he proposed the creation of an executive-legislative cabinet that would consult on a regular basis and develop in camera a rational, consistent foreign policy.[25] But Fulbright quickly decided that, constitutional problems aside, the idea lacked merit, and he began instead to focus on the international sphere and specifically on a new experiment in world government. In one remarkable address to the Foreign Policy Association in New York, Fulbright declared that the progress and welfare of modern humanity depended on the simultaneous and synchronized advance of technology and statecraft. While technology had produced machines that could fly above the earth and cruise beneath the sea, and weapons that could destroy whole cities in the blinking of an eye, there had been no new developments in political theory and practice since the American and French revolutions. Just as the trend in

economics had been toward larger and more complex units, the trend in government had been toward larger and more complex structures. A social evolutionist, Fulbright proclaimed this was all for the good.[26]

What the freshman senator had in mind was an authentic international federation run on democratic principles. In a speech to the American Bar Association, Fulbright laid his cards on the table: "The history of government over the centuries, which is largely the chronicle of man's efforts to achieve freedom by the control of arbitrary force, indicate [sic] that only by the collective action of a dominant group can security be obtained." The hope of the world was the establishment of a global organization with a collective security mandate and a police-keeping force sufficient to enforce that mandate. The United States must participate and contribute to such a force. Participation required—indeed, necessitated—surrender of a portion of the national sovereignty.[27] Once the U.N. Charter was ratified, it should have been clearly understood that the president through his delegate would have the authority to commit American troops to military action authorized by the Security Council. Fulbright urged his countrymen to cooperate while the times were propitious—before would-be aggressors had the opportunity to develop the means of aggression. Was it not better to cooperate with the superpowers of the future, Russia and China, while they were still relatively weak? "It seems clear to me," he told an Arkansas audience in 1944, "that either we cooperate with

24. U.S., Congress, Senate, Congressional Record, 79th Cong., 1st sess., 1945, 91, pt. 3:2899.
25. Ibid., pt. 11:A1586.

26. U.S., Congress, House, Congressional Record, 78th Cong., 1st sess., 1945, 89, 11:A4652-54.
27. U.S., Congress, Senate, Congressional Record, 79th Cong., 1st sess., 1945, 91, pt. 13: A4652-53.

Russia and the other nations in a system to preserve peace or we must look forward to a time when, in a chaotic world of warring nations we may have to compete for survival with an industrialized Russia of 250,000,000 or a China of 450,000,000."[28] To those of his conservative constituents who complained that the proposed United Nations was so much globaloney Fulbright argued that international cooperation was essential if the free enterprise system were to be preserved. Without a collective security organization, America would be forced to fight one costly war after another, or at least be prepared to do so. This would require huge defense budgets and regimentation of the economy. In such an environment bureaucracy and red tape would choke the private sector to death.[29]

J. William Fulbright was an economic as well as a political internationalist; that is, he, along with his friend Will Clayton, was a thoroughgoing multilateralist. Clayton, the Houston cotton broker Franklin Roosevelt appointed assistant secretary of state for economic affairs in 1944, was to be the chief architect of the Marshall Plan. These intellectual heirs of Adam Smith looked forward to the creation of an economically interdependent world free of tariffs, preference, quotas, and exchange controls. They insisted that competition for the wealth of the world among national economies protected by high tariff walls restricted trade, wasted resources, and bred war; competition between individuals and corporations based on price, product quality, and market demand bred efficiency, promoted economic expansion, and raised living standards. The

world had not begun to realize its productive potential. As long as nations tried to protect infant industries and inefficient agricultural operations with artificial, uneconomic trade barriers, the world would continue to be made up of relatively inefficient national economies or clusters of such economies.[30] The multilateralists looked forward to the creation of a world market in which the citizens of each region concentrated on producing that commodity which they could produce most cheaply and efficiently. This specialization coupled with the elimination of trade barriers would mean the manufacture and distribution of the greatest number of goods at the cheapest possible price.[31]

To this end Fulbright helped lead the fight in the Senate in 1945 for approval of the Bretton Woods Agreement, which established the World Bank and the International Monetary Fund. Then in 1946 the Arkansas legislator played a crucial role in persuading other cotton-state senators to vote for the British loan. That transaction forced Great Britain, in return for a $3.75 billion credit, to undertake the early and free conversion of sterling into other currencies.[32]

INTERNATIONAL EXCHANGE AND AMERICA'S DIPLOMATIC LEADERSHIP

Certainly the Fulbright exchange program was an integral part of Fulbright

28. U.S., Congress, House, *Congressional Record*, 78th Cong., 2d sess., 1944, 90, pt. 8:A412.

29. Ibid.

30. See, for example, Winant Memorandum, n.d., *Foreign Relations of the United States, 1945* (Washington, DC: Government Printing Office, 1960), 6:22-24; U.S., Congress, Senate, Committee on Banking and Currency, *Anglo-American Financial Agreement: Hearings*, 79th Cong., 2d sess., 1946.

31. Committee on Banking and Currency, *Anglo-American Financial Agreement.*

32. Warren F. Kimball, ed., *Churchill and Roosevelt: The Complete Correspondence*, vol. 2, *Alliance Forged* (Princeton, NJ: Princeton University Press, 1984), p. 709.

internationalism. Xenophobia and cultural barriers were major obstacles to the creation of an integrated, interdependent, and peaceful world. But what lent a sense of urgency to the senator's campaign to establish an international exchange program was his growing conviction in 1945-46 that the United States was not willing to surrender any part of its sovereignty for the good of the global village and that the political and diplomatic elite in America was incapable of leading the world into a new era of collective security and economic interdependency.

In reality neither Franklin Roosevelt nor Harry Truman was committed to internationalism as either Woodrow Wilson or J. William Fulbright defined it. FDR was a devotee of realpolitik.[33] His pet scheme for ensuring peace and prosperity in the postwar world had been the Four Policemen concept, in which the United States, Russia, China, and Great Britain kept the peace in their respective spheres of interest. Roosevelt, always the astute politician, had become a convert to internationalism in name only.[34] Some have argued that the United Nations was the Four Policemen in internationalist clothing. Did not the great powers have the right of absolute veto; did not Article 52 permit regional alliances; and did not the Charter exempt from U.N. action matters deemed purely internal?

Harry Truman was a hardheaded politician from Missouri who found internationalism appealing in theory but believed that the major questions of the day would continue to be resolved by direct negotiation between superpowers.

Moreover, first Roosevelt and then Truman took a spheres-of-interest approach to European politics. FDR had been willing to concede Eastern Europe to the Soviets in 1944, but an ironic combination of residual isolationism and internationalism in the United States kept him from doing so. Very early in his administration, Harry Truman began to perceive the Soviet Union as the principal threat to European stability. Nonetheless, he vacillated between a policy of conciliation and one of resistance throughout 1945. By early 1946, however, the president, responding to the breakdown of the Moscow Foreign Minister's Conference in December 1945 and to George Kennan's Long Telegram and Stalin's two-camp speech of February 1946, decided that Russia was an expansionist power bent on world domination, a threat as dangerous to Western civilization as Nazi Germany. Britain and America gave notice of their intention to stand up to the Soviets in Churchill's iron-curtain speech in March, and then that same month Washington proved its resolve by forcing Moscow to back down over Iran.[35]

As early as the summer of 1945 J. William Fulbright began to express doubts about America's commitment to internationalism. He wondered aloud to the Senate why there was unanimous support for ratification of the U.N. Charter while only weeks before economic nationalists and neo-isolationists had fought tooth and nail against the Bretton Woods Agreement and the British loan. Could it be, he asked, that they believed that the Charter did not impinge on the nation's sovereignty and that

---

33. Ibid., p. 767.
34. Memo on joint U.S.-U.K. relations in connection with approach to third countries, 10 Nov. 1944, Clayton-Thorp Papers, Truman Library.

35. See Michael S. Sherry, *Preparing for the Next War: American Plans for Postwar Defense, 1941-1945* (New Haven, CT: Yale University Press, 1976), pp. 43-44.

despite its membership in the United Nations, the United States still retained absolute freedom of action? Contemplating the results of the Yalta Conference, Fulbright detected a return to the old pattern of power politics and spheres-of-influence diplomacy that had led the world into one war after another.[36] He tended to blame "the devotees of protocol and the status quo in the Department of State" rather than Stalin or Churchill for the breakdown of wartime cooperation.[37] Why, the Arkansas legislator inquired, was the White House not willing to trust the United Nations?

Fulbright also deplored the refusal of the United States to offer a convincing strategy to the Soviets for the internationalization of atomic energy. He had at first enthusiastically supported the Acheson-Lilienthal Plan, which called for the creation of an international agency that would take possession of all the world's known uranium and thorium deposits.[38] Instead, the United States offered Russia a scheme devised by Bernard Baruch, a plan that would preserve U.S. control of these deposits.[39] The Arkansas senator also decried the reappearance of Pacific imperialism in American foreign policy. At the same time that Washington attacked Russia for claiming territory in Manchuria and southeastern Europe, and Britain and France for attempting to hold on to parts of their empires, it demanded the right to annex such strategically important islands as Okinawa and Tarawa.[40]

But the incident that disturbed Fulbright perhaps more than any other was the seating of Argentina at the UNCIO over the strenuous objections of the Russians. As delegates from around the world assembled in San Francisco in May 1945 to breathe life into the United Nations, American diplomats provoked a storm of controversy at home and abroad by sponsoring Argentina for full membership. In doing so, Washington supported a country that for two years after the U.S. entry into the war had maintained diplomatic ties with the Axis powers, served as a base for German espionage in the Western Hemisphere, and submitted to the rule of two autocratic, militaristic governments. With the backing of the other twenty American republics, the United States out-

36. See James F. Schnabel, "The History of the Joint Chiefs of Staff and National Policy," vol. 1: "1945-1947" (Manuscripts, Division of Modern Military Records, National Archives, Washington, DC, 1979), pp. 14-15.

37. See Wesley T. Wooley, Jr., "The Quest for Permanent Peace—American Supranationalism, 1945-1947," *Historian*, 35(1):18-27.

38. Roosevelt agreed to the generous sums of $3.5 billion for munitions and $3.0 billion for nonmunitions. He also agreed to drop restrictions imposed in 1941 on British exports, restrictions that forbade the United Kingdom to export certain items as long as it was receiving lend-lease. When Roosevelt returned to Washington from the second Quebec Conference, he encountered a storm of protest from the secretary of state and others over the concessions he made to Churchill. Hull was furious that the Chief had given away so much without securing an ironclad commitment to liberalized trade policies. Others warned that Congress would not tolerate such generosity, especially in view of the fact that British exports could now compete freely with American merchandise. As a result, the administration pared down the amount of aid Britain was to receive to $2.7 billion for munitions and $2.0 billion for nonmunitions, and placed British exports back in harness. Richard P. Hedlund, "Congress and the British Loan of 1946" (Ph.D. diss., University of Kentucky, 1978), pp. 11-12.

39. See Larry G. Gerber, "The Baruch Plan and the Origins of the Cold War," *Diplomatic History*, 6(1):69-95 (Winter 1982).

40. JWF to S.Sgt. Robert Hobson, 6 Nov. 1945, BCN24, Folder 27, Fulbright Papers; see also U.S., Congress, Senate, *Congressional Record*, 79th Cong., 2d sess., 1946, 92, pt. 3:3508.

voted the Soviet Union in an acrimonious showdown over the Argentine issue. Walter Lippmann led a national chorus of disapproval. Prevailing opinion held that in their first internationalist test U.S. diplomats had engineered a political power play rather than forging a consensus.[41]

Fulbright, along with much of the rest of the nation, was incensed. "I have been very upset about the turn our delegation took at San Francisco," he confided to an acquaintance. "I do not approve in the least of our backing of Argentina at this time . . . I am fearful that in the long run it will cause us much trouble in dealing with Russia."[42] He believed in an active, powerful executive with the ability and will to conduct foreign policy, limiting the legislative branch to consultation and the articulation of broad principles.[43] But to function properly the system required an enlightened, sophisticated leadership. Apparently, America lacked such leadership. Fulbright was particularly appalled at Stettinius, a handsome General Motors executive with little intellectual ability and with even less academic attainment and diplomatic experience. Roosevelt and Harry Hopkins had brought Stettinius into the State Department in late 1944 to be their front man while they conducted foreign policy themselves.[44] First-term Senator Fulbright, who was deeply disappointed at not having been invited to the UNCIO, complained to a constituent:

Frankly, I have not been very pleased with the way our Secretary of State is handling the San Francisco Conference. . . . I attribute this [the Argentine imbroglio] largely to his own inexperience and lack of knowledge. After all, it is fantastic that our country should be represented in these important and complicated matters by a man with less than a year's experience in office.[45]

But Stettinius was symptomatic of a larger problem, Fulbright believed. At this crucial juncture in the history of the world, with the god of internationalism standing in the doorway beckoning with a loud voice, and with humanity suspended over the pit of nationalism and war, America was being led by a combination of empty-headed bureaucrats and relics of the ancien régime who knew only power politics backed by arms and treaties. Fulbright had always claimed that in a democracy, the cream rises to the top; a meritocracy would inevitably emerge to lead the nation.[46] But he was beginning to have his doubts. "The greatest weakness of this country is getting brains into our public service," he wrote in May 1945. "I am sure we will continue to make mistakes until we devise some means to attract able men into the government at an early age in

41. Randall B. Woods, "Conflict or Community? The United States and Argentina's Admission to the United Nations," *Pacific Historical Review*, 56(3):361-86 (Aug. 1977).

42. JWF to E. A. Matthews, 4 May 1945, BCN24, Folder 31, Fulbright Papers. See also U.S., Congress, Senate, *Congressional Record*, 79th Cong., 2d sess., 1946, 92, pt. 3:3508.

43. Memo on the authority of the U.S. delegate to the Security Council, 1945, BCN24, Folder 36, Fulbright Papers.

44. *New York Times*, 29 Mar. 1944; Joseph Newman, "Latin American Republics Eager to Renew Argentine Ties," *New York Herald Tribune*, 15 Mar. 1944; *Foreign Relations of the United States, 1944* (Washington, DC: Government Printing Office), 6:14-15.

45. JWF to Charles A. Stick, 22 May 1945, BCN24, Folder 49, Fulbright Papers.

46. U.S., Congress, House, *Congressional Record*, 78th Cong., 1st sess., 1943, 89, pt. 10:A2398; U.S., Congress, Senate, *Congressional Record*, 79th Cong., 1st sess., 1945, 91, pt. 10:A187.

order that they may grow up and know what it is all about."[47]

It was at this juncture that the idea of an international exchange program to train an educated and enlightened elite began to take shape in his mind. On 24 May an Arkansas acquaintance of Fulbright's stationed in San Francisco wrote, bemoaning the tendency of the American delegation to the UNCIO to "operate like the backstage of a country convention." The friend, Lieutenant Commander Bernal Seamster, accused the Americans of "playing up to the conflict between the capitalistic and communisitic system on all sides" and blamed this tendency on "the lack of understanding and knowledge of the conditions other than in their own circle." The solution to the problem, he concluded, "might well be for the federal government to sponsor a major exchange of students from this country to other countries, and from other nations to our own colleges, universities, and trade schools." Seamster suggested a minimum of 100,000 students a year.[48] Fulbright's friend had articulated an idea that had been formulating in his own mind, and he responded enthusiastically. "Your views are in complete agreement wth my own," he replied. "Your sugges-

tion about the exchange of students is a very appropriate one."[49]

CONCLUSION

The Fulbright exchange program was undeniably a reflection, a projection, of J. William Fulbright's personal experience. What he proposed in 1946 was the institutionalization of his own overseas odyssey. It would do for thousands of young people what it had done for him—remove cultural blinders and instill tolerance and a sense of public service. The program was also a natural corollary of Fulbright internationalism. It was the cultural equivalent of collective security and multilateralism. But it was also a specific response to a specific set of circumstances and perceived shortcomings. Events of 1945-46 convinced the junior senator from Arkansas that the United States and particularly its leadership either did not understand or did not accept internationalism. If nationalism and isolationism were not to reappear as the dominant strains in American foreign policy, the United States would have to raise up an educated, enlightened elite with extensive firsthand knowledge of at least one other culture. The Fulbright exchange program was designed to bring just such an elite into existence.

47. JWF to E. A. Matthews, 4 May 1945, BCN24, Folder 31, Fulbright Papers.
48. Lt. Comdr. Bernal Seamster to JWF, 24 May 1945, BCN24, Folder 32, Fulbright Papers.

49. JWF to Seamster, 26 May 1945, BCN24, Folder 32, Fulbright Papers.

ANNALS, *AAPSS*, **491**, May 1987

Legislative Origins of
the Fulbright Program

By HARRY P. JEFFREY

ABSTRACT: This article briefly summarizes the scope of the Fulbright scholarship program. A biographical sketch of J. William Fulbright indicates how his experiences before he ran for public office and his activities and concerns as a representative and senator shaped the origin of the exchange program. In some depth the article examines the strategy Fulbright employed to produce a politically palatable bill and his tactics of quietly pushing the proposal through to enactment. More than most pieces of congressional legislation, the Fulbright exchange program is the product of the efforts of one man, Senator Fulbright.

Harry P. Jeffrey received a Ph. D. from Columbia University and is associate professor of history at California State University, Fullerton. An oral historian, he directed oral history projects on Robert Taft, Richard Nixon, and the United States Cost of Living Council. He is the author of The Republican Party as a Minority Party in Wartime, 1943-1944 *and presented papers about the Fulbright scholarship program at the American Historical Association and the University of Arkansas.*

THE Fulbright scholarship program is the largest and most important project of international educational exchange in the history of the world. Indeed, Ronald B. McCallum, J. William Fulbright's Oxford tutor, maintained that his former pupil had been "responsible for the largest and most significant movement of scholars across the earth since the fall of Constantinople in 1453." However, the law setting up this educational activity slipped through Congress with little notice or debate. Perhaps more than any other major piece of congressional legislation in post-World War II American history, the Fulbright exchange program is the product of one man, former Senator Fulbright.[1]

THE FULBRIGHT PROGRAM TODAY

Since the Fulbright Act became law in 1946, some 54,000 American professors, researchers, teachers, and students have gone abroad, and approximately 101,000 foreign scholars have come to the United States via the program. Today, over 1000 American scholars and professionals travel to other countries yearly, and an equal number of foreign professors, researchers, and specialists visit the United States under Fulbright auspices. In addition, large numbers of American students have studied in other countries, and many foreign nationals have gone to college in the United States or in American universities abroad through the program. Over 500 American students currently study overseas while 1500 foreign students pursue academic training in America. More than 200 schoolteachers, American and foreign, now work abroad each year as Fulbrighters.

Some 117 nations presently participate in the Fulbright program. At this time, individuals receive Fulbright awards in approximately fifty academic disciplines ranging from American studies and agriculture to social work and zoology. Moreover, grants are made for cross-disciplinary areas such as Japanese-American trade relations, North Atlantic Treaty Organization research fellowships, Islamic civilization, and the production of small animals in tropical regions.[2]

FULBRIGHT'S EARLY YEARS

James William Fulbright, the father of the Fulbright scholarship program, was born in Missouri in 1905. While still a baby, Bill Fulbright, who never used his first name, moved with his family to the Ozark Mountain town of Fayetteville, Arkansas, close to the Kansas and Oklahoma borders. There he grew up, secure in a prosperous and respected family, attending public school and the University of Arkansas in Fayetteville, where he was a solid *B* student, campus leader, and star football halfback. Because of the death of his father, Bill Fulbright dropped out of the university for a semester to help his mother manage the multiple family businesses, so at 18 he became the youngest railroad vice-

1. John Richardson, Jr., "Preparing for a Human Community," in *A Process of Global Enlightenment*, ed. Robert Armbruster (Washington, DC: Board of Foreign Scholarships, 1976), p. 32; Tristam Coffin, *Senator Fulbright: Portrait of a Public Philosopher* (New York: E.P. Dutton, 1966), p. 87; Don Oberdorfer, "Common Noun Spelled f-u-l-b-r-i-g-h-t," *New York Times*, 4 Apr. 1965.

2. "Fulbright Program: Fact Sheet" (Letter, United States Information Agency, 1986); "Fulbright Scholar Program: Faculty Grants, 1987-1988" (Pamphlet, Council for International Exchange of Scholars, 1986).

president in the country. At age 20 he won a Rhodes Scholarship.

Until sailing for England, Fulbright had never taken a drink, been to a big city, journeyed east of the Mississippi River, or seen the ocean. Staying abroad four years, Fulbright earned two Oxford degrees and traveled throughout Britain and much of the European continent, sometimes in the company of sophisticated journalists. Returning to the United States, he spent a little time in Fayetteville, then left for Washington, D.C., where he married a Philadelphia Main Line woman, Betty Williams, and graduated second in his law school class. He worked in the Justice Department during the early New Deal on the Schecter sick-chicken case and taught law at his alma mater, George Washington University Law School.

Leaving Washington in 1936, he came back to Fayetteville, where he taught at the University of Arkansas Law School, again became involved in the family businesses, and lived as a gentleman farmer in a three-story so-called log cabin, Rabbit Foot's Lodge. When the university president unexpectedly died, the local boy who had made good was the dark-horse choice who became the new college president—at 34 the youngest in the nation.[3]

Politics had a good deal to do with Fulbright's becoming president of the University of Arkansas, and politics had everything to do with his being fired from that position. Roberta Fulbright, Bill's mother, was perhaps the leading citizen of Fayetteville and thus of northwest Arkansas. Using her position as a newspaper owner and columnist, she

had launched a successful crusade to oust a corrupt courthouse ring from office in her hometown. Mindful of her political influence and Bill Fulbright's accomplishments, and his own lack of political strength in that part of the state, Governor Carl Bailey tapped young Bill for the university presidency. But Bailey lost a reelection bid to Homer Adkins, a Bible-belt fundamentalist whom Roberta Fulbright characterized in a column as a mere "handshaker." A self-styled common man, Adkins had no use for the establishment Fulbright clan. After packing the university board of trustees with his own people, Adkins arranged for the firing of Bill Fulbright, without cause, after less than two years in office.[4]

FULBRIGHT'S EARLY POLITICAL CAREER

Much to Adkins's regret, politics then became Bill Fulbright's profession. Repeatedly, Fulbright had urged involvement in politics and public affairs to his students and through his speeches. When an open seat became available for the U.S. House of Representatives in the Fayetteville area, a former pupil reminded his old professor of his own injunction. Fulbright did run, beating an Adkins-backed candidate in the Democratic primary. In overwhelmingly Democratic Arkansas, that meant victory in the November general election.[5] Although only 38 years old when

3. Coffin, *Senator Fulbright*, pp. 35-50; Haynes Johnson and Bernard M. Gwertzman, *Fulbright: The Dissenter* (New York: Doubleday, 1968), pp. 12-41.

4. Johnson and Gwertzman, *Fulbright: The Dissenter*, pp. 41-50; Allan Gilbert, *A Fulbright Chronicle* (Fayetteville, AR: Fulbright Investment, Co., 1980), pp. 135-40; Mary Lynn Kennedy, "Politics in Academe: Roberta Fulbright's Role in Her Son's University Presidency" (Paper in possession of author, Fayetteville, AR., 1975), pp. 1-15.

5. Johnson and Gwertzman, *Fulbright: The Dissenter*, pp. 53-58.

sworn into the House in 1943, and inexperienced in politics, Fulbright became the most conspicuous freshman representative. In his maiden speech he outpointed the sharp-tongued Clare Boothe Luce for her deriding as "globaloney" the foreign policy of the administration of President Franklin D. Roosevelt. Winning a seat on the Foreign Affairs Committee, Fulbright became engrossed in the subject of postwar planning: how to wage a "creative war" in order to secure a "creative peace." He repeatedly spoke about America's new role in the world, advocating U.S. membership in a United Nations with a strong peacekeeping military force.

For this freshman, "the first time [he] got any notice" came when the House overwhelmingly passed the one-sentence Fulbright Resolution, which urged creation of and American participation in "international machinery with power to prevent further aggression." When the Senate followed suit with a similar resolution, a giant step was taken toward formation of a United Nations with American membership. While maneuvering the resolution through the House, Fulbright learned a great deal about how to get legislation passed. Purposefully, he skirted the Democratic Foreign Affairs Committee chairman who acted, said Fulbright, in a "pompous" and "very dictatorial and extremely contemptuous" manner toward "junior members." Instead, Fulbright quietly lobbied key House members and worked with Democratic and Republican leaders, the two top officials in the State Department, key White House staffers, and even President Roosevelt.

Secretary of State Cordell Hull then appointed Fulbright to chair the American delegation to a 17-nation ministerial conference on postwar education in London. Unanimously selected chair of the conference, Fulbright lunched with Prime Minister Winston Churchill and addressed the British people on the radio. "I live in an old log house on a small farm . . . and am sometimes called a Hillbilly," the "egghead from the Ozarks" began his BBC broadcast.[6]

Even before the London conference, Fulbright declared his candidacy for the U.S. Senate. Stiff competition in the Democratic primary would come from the incumbent, the ineffectual Hattie Caraway, and the man reputed to be the state's wealthiest citizen, Colonel T. H. Barton, who hired the Grand Olde Opry, including Minnie Pearl, Jam-up, and Honey, to draw crowds for him. But Governor Homer Adkins would prove to be Fulbright's major opponent. In one of the most vicious campaigns in Arkansas history, the other contenders denounced Fulbright as "British Billy," a "Lord Plushbottom," and a draft dodger, a pet of the Congress of Industrial Organizations labor unions and Communists, a "nigger lover," and a legislator whose votes helped to induct hard-working chicken farmers into the armed forces. However, Fulbright's record aided him in turning back these slurs. As newspapers such as one in

6. Ibid., pp. 59-76, 79-81; J. William Fulbright, "A Creative War," 1 Feb. 1943, Papers of J. William Fulbright, Special Collections Mullins Library, University of Arkansas, Fayetteville, (hereafter cited as Fulbright Papers); idem, "Sunday Postscript," 30 Apr. 1944, ibid.; Harry P. Jeffrey, "Interview with J. William Fulbright, August 28, 1984"(Manuscript, Oral History Program, California State University, Fullerton, 1985), pp. 2-3, 15-22; Oscar Cox to Harry Hopkins, 6 Oct. 1943, Oscar Cox Papers, Franklin D. Roosevelt Library, Hyde Park, NY; Fulbright to Cox and Cox to Fulbright, 23 June 1943, ibid.; Diary of Oscar Cox, 30 Sept. and 4 Oct. 1943, ibid; Beverly Smith, Jr., "Egghead from the Ozarks," *Saturday Evening Post,* 2 May 1959, pp. 31 ff.

Little Rock stated, "Congressman Fulbright, in his first term in Washington, has gained more favorable publicity than any other Representative we have ever sent to the Congress." After finishing first in the primary, the freshman congressman trounced Adkins by 32,000 votes in the runoff campaign. "Miss Roberta" Fulbright could not resist mocking the governor's ungrammatical style in her newspaper column: "Homer Adkins has came and went."[7]

In his early years in the Senate, Fulbright's interest in international affairs grew. As a freshman he failed to win a Foreign Relations Committee seat, but he did secure a position on the Education and Labor panel. Working closely with Republicans in early 1945, he initiated a round-robin letter by the 16 new members urging vigorous action by the administration to create a United Nations. A resolution introduced by Fulbright, and passed by the Senate and the House, advocated American participation in an international office of education and encouraged "the exchange of students and scholars."[8]

THE PROBLEM OF THE LACK OF GOVERNMENT INVOLVEMENT IN INTERNATIONAL EDUCATION

As Fulbright well knew, the scholarship program bill he was formulating would be the first large-scale effort by the U.S. government in the field of international education. Nineteenth-century American activities in this area involved private groups and individuals, not the government. This reflected traditional isolationism, the belief in limited government, the feeling that education should remain a local concern, and a certain distance of the State Department from the people of the United States. Philanthropic foundations, religious missions, institutions of higher learning, and private societies carried out some international educational activities. During the early years of the twentieth century the role of the government increased slightly. Boxer Rebellion indemnities to the United States of $16 million built up a Chinese college and helped send 2000 Chinese to study in America. After World War I, left-over relief funds for Belgium, allocated to the Belgian-American Educational Foundation, a group led by Herbert Hoover, were used to educate 700 Belgians and Americans in each other's country.

Only after World War I did Americans studying abroad reach significant numbers; however, the U.S. government remained indifferent to scholarly exchange. Indeed, when the director of the Institute of International Education inquired why the State Department neglected to answer his letter, he received the reminder that the "department paid attention only to communications from other governments." Under provisions of the 1936 Buenos Aires Treaty the United States pledged to exchange two professors and two graduate students yearly with other Latin American signatories; however, no provision for federal funding was implemented. To counteract Nazi and Fascist activities in Latin America the State Department established a Cultural Relations Division in 1938. The division asked American universities to offer scholarships to Latin American

7. Johnson and Gwertzman, *Fulbright: The Dissenter*, pp. 64, 77-79, 81-85; Allen Drury, *A Senate Journal* (New York: McGraw-Hill, 1963), pp. 19, 35, 49, 62, 224; *Little Rock Arkansas Democrat*, 20 Oct. 1943; *St. Louis Post-Dispatch*, 9 July 1944.

8. Johnson and Gwertzman, *Fulbright: The Dissenter*, pp. 89-106; Fulbright to John Gunther, 24 May 1945, Fulbright Papers.

students, but provided little money for this activity.

During World War II the division ran a small-scale educational program including scholarly exchanges in China, Africa, and the Near East. In the war years the State Department Office of the Coordinator of Inter-American Affairs, using presidential emergency funds, provided for a limited exchange of students and professors. However, after the war both bureaus were terminated, although educational programs did become a part of the American occupation efforts in Japan, Germany, and Austria.[9]

THE PROBLEM OF WAR DEBTS

Senator Fulbright also spent a good deal of time pondering the question of debts that the wartime allies owed the United States. He had first considered this subject in an Oxford paper he wrote, and later he encountered the problem during House Foreign Affairs Committee hearings on lend-lease. Controversy over repayment of similar war debts had disrupted international relations and the global economy after World War I, and it threatened to undermine Fulbright's creative peace

efforts as World War II ended. The Arkansan introduced a bill, which failed to pass, to repeal the act that barred credits to nations that had defaulted on their World War I debts.[10]

THE PROBLEM OF
SURPLUS PROPERTY

Linked to Fulbright's concerns about war debts and the lack of governmental involvement in international education was the thorny question of surplus American war property. Over 4 million items remained scattered in warehouses and storage depots around the globe after World War II. No one knew the value of this property; estimates varied from $60 million to $105 million. This excess material included planes, trains, tanks, and bulldozers as well as food, tools, clothing, telephones, and hospitals. Items ranged from agricultural implements and air pumps to zippers and zwieback. A surplus-property law passed in 1944 prohibited sending them back to the United States. Transportation costs would have eaten up most of the value of the goods anyway.

Nevertheless, American special interest groups clamored to have the law changed. They maintained that their special interest affiliation, whether veterans, business, farmers, or educators, be given the first chance to buy the surplus, or even that it be given to them free. These groups pointed out that when American troops left an area abroad they abandoned, destroyed, or left the goods under questionable guardianship.

9. Walter Johnson and Francis Colligan, *The Fulbright Program: A History* (Chicago: University of Chicago Press, 1965), pp. 15-20; Henry Kellermann, *Cultural Relations as an Instrument of United States Foreign Policy* (Washington, DC: Department of State, 1978), pp. vii-viii, 3-6, 9-13; Wilma Fairbank, *America's Cultural Experiment in China, 1942-1949* (Washington, DC: Department of State, 1976), pp. vii-xiii, 4-6; Committee on Educational Interchange Policy, *Twenty Years of United States Government Programs in Cultural Relations* (New York: Institute of International Education, 1959), pp. 1-12; Manuel Espinosa, *Inter-American Beginnings of United States Cultural Diplomacy, 1936-1948* (Washington, DC: Department of State, 1976), pp. vii, 1-17, 79.

10. Jeffrey, "Interview with Fulbright," pp. 2, 4-5, 23; Johnson and Gwertzman, *Fulbright: The Dissenter*, pp. 107-9; *Report from the Committee on Education and Labor, Report No. 286, 25 May 1945* (Washington, DC: Government Printing Office, 1945).

Also, the interest groups reiterated that often armed services personnel remained in a region merely to watch over excess material.

Racked by wartime devastation and unsettled economies, foreign nations pleaded for some of the surplus. However, they lacked the currency or even the goods, much less the dollars, to pay for the materials. "They were all broke, you know," claimed Fulbright years later. If the United States took the dollar exchange available when selling the surplus to other countries, future American export trade would suffer and the debtor nations would be less likely to repay their war debts. Thus this excess equipment spread around the globe really meant that the United States had substantial amounts of currency, or the equivalent of currency, frozen abroad.[11]

OBTAINING EXECUTIVE BRANCH APPROVAL

As Fulbright declared, all of his concerns about surplus property, war debts, international education, a creative peace, a strong United Nations, and America's new and larger role in the world "converged at that moment" after "the atomic bombs had just been dropped" and "the war was just over." Therefore he introduced in September of 1945 a seemingly innocuous bill to amend the 1944 Surplus Property Act. His short 30-line, somewhat vague bill authorized funds from the sale of overseas surplus equipment to be used for an international student exchange in the fields of science, culture, and education.

In November of 1945 Fulbright introduced a second and broader piece of legislation, which also was couched as an amendment to the Surplus Property Act, incorporating recommendations of various executive branch agencies. It made the State Department the sole disposal agency for surplus property located outside the United States and its possessions. Such property could be paid for in foreign currencies or credits. Agreements could be entered into by the secretary of state with foreign governments to finance educational activities for Americans in other countries, foreign nationals in overseas American institutions, and transportation of visitors from abroad to study in the United States. Funding for educational exchanges would be in money, other than dollars, acquired from selling surplus goods. This bill, Fulbright argued, would help cut the surplus property knot, prevent the war-debt question from becoming "a source of irritation" between nations, promote trade and commerce, strengthen political relations with other countries, build up goodwill around the world, help ensure "the future peace of the world," and aid the United Nations and the United Nations Educational, Scientific, and Cultural Organization by coordinating education programs with them.[12]

Fulbright then painstakingly lined up backing from the executive branch. He consulted with the Bureau of the Budget, the Office of War Mobilization and Reconversion, the Surplus Property Administration, the military, and the State Department. Because the State Depart-

11. Jeffrey, "Interview with Fulbright," p. 2; Army-Navy Liquidation Commission, "Statement," 26 Sept. 1945, Fulbright Papers; *Congressional Record,* 79th Cong., 1st sess., 30 Apr. 1945, pp. 3943-4.

12. Jeffrey, "Interview with Fulbright," pp. 1-3, 31-32; J. William Fulbright, "Statement," 27 Sept. and 30 Nov. 1945, Fulbright Papers; *Congressional Record,* 79th Cong., 1st sess., 27 Sept. 1945, p. 9044.

ment looked suspiciously at this rare congressional foreign policy initiative, Fulbright's second bill gave the secretary of state broad statutory power to dispense funds for matters other than education alone. State Department officials did not want any of the money designated specifically for education, but Fulbright insisted on it. The Arkansan agreed with the department on questions such as not specifying by law the age or other qualifications of candidates or a maximum dollar figure for scholarships or living expenses, and not having grants divided equally among the states. After a long struggle he overcame Budget Bureau contentions that money received from surplus property sales had to be submitted to the Treasury and that money could not be earmarked for education without specific congressional appropriations.

Finally, he secured the blessing of the new president, Harry Truman, although the chief executive, according to Fulbright, "didn't know anything" about the bill and did little to support it. Thus, incorporating revisions negotiated with the executive branch, Fulbright submitted a new bill before Senate hearings began. Because of the warning of a member of Congress, he placed a yearly limit of $2.5 million to be spent in any one country on educational exchange. The title of this revised second proposal deceptively read, "A bill to amend the Surplus Property Act of 1944 to designate the Department of State as the disposal agency for surplus property outside the United States, its Territories and Possessions, and for other purposes."[13]

SENATE PASSAGE

With great skill Fulbright piloted the bill around the legislative shoals. He cleared the first hurdle, the Subcommittee on Surplus Property of the Senate Committee on Military Affairs. While deferring to the subcommittee chair, Democrat Joseph O'Mahoney of Wyoming, Fulbright organized the hearing for the ill O'Mahoney, who was often back in Wyoming recuperating. Fulbright lined up an impressive array of witnesses who favored his bill, and he saw to it that no one testified in opposition. The subcommittee hearing lasted just one day, in February of 1946, with O'Mahoney and Fulbright the only senators present. Those testifying included representatives from the five most concerned executive agencies plus nongovernmental organizations interested in international education. William Benton, the new assistant secretary of state for public and cultural relations, asserted that the Veterans Administration already had been sent "several thousand" letters from American soldiers desiring admission to foreign universities; he noted that New York State alone had a 20,000-student "surplus."

Given to the subcommittee was a great body of supportive letters and articles. All of these documents had been asked for by Fulbright over a period of many months. Proponents of the legislation averred that the bill amounted to a unique "golden opportunity" to begin an international education program very "inexpensively" through

13. Jeffrey, "Interview with Fulbright," pp. 2-4, 10, 22-24, 31-34; Fulbright to Perrin Galpin, 28 Jan. 1946, Fulbright Papers; Fulbright to John Nason, 11 and 18 Feb. 1946, ibid.; Haldore Hanson to Mr. Reynolds, "Report on S. 1636," 30 Jan. 1946, ibid.; *Congressional Record*, 79th Cong.,

1st sess., 15 Dec. 1945, pp. 12123-4; U.S., Congress, Senate, Committee on Military Affairs, *Foreign Educational Benefits and Surplus Property: Hearing before a Subcommittee of the Committee on Military Affairs on S. 1440 and S. 1636* (Washington, DC: Government Printing Office, 1946), pp. 1-2.

the sale of surplus property largely unusable by Americans.

Working assiduously, Fulbright won the backing of key Republicans. Securing the support of the party patriarch, Herbert Hoover, was especially important. Ex-President Hoover, who had chaired the Belgian-American Educational Foundation, carried great weight among conservatives of both parties. In a letter Hoover reminded members of Congress that as secretary of commerce, president, and ex-president he advocated proposals for government-funded international education efforts. New Jersey Republican Senator H. Alexander Smith also had served on the Belgian foundation and had worked with Fulbright on the round-robin letter; he gave the bill his approval and quietly lobbied for passage. Proponents of this "cultural currency" legislation repeatedly stressed the precedents, initiated by two Republicans, Theodore Roosevelt and Hoover, of the Boxer indemnity and Belgian relief funds.[14]

The Surplus Property Subcommittee and the Military Affairs Committee both reported out Fulbright's revised second bill. Wisely, Fulbright let the first bill die. Noting that "politically" it would be "exceedingly dangerous," Fulbright talked O'Mahoney out of inserting in a draft an antidiscrimination clause.

14. Committee on Military Affairs, *Foreign Educational Benefits and Surplus Property: Hearing before a Subcommittee*, pp. 1-56; Jeffrey, "Interview with Fulbright," pp. 5, 10, 31-32, 39-40; George Zook to Fulbright, 16 Jan. 1946, Fulbright Papers; Fulbright to Perrin Galpin, 28 Jan. 1946, ibid.; Fulbright to O'Mahoney, 30 Jan. 1946, ibid.; Fulbright to James K. Smith, 27 June 1946, ibid.; Hoover to Fulbright, 8 Feb. 1946, Bureau of Educational and Cultural Affairs Papers, Special Collections Mullins Library, University of Arkansas, Fayetteville; Fulbright to Hoover, 8 July 1957, ibid.

"For the purpose of making it palatable" Fulbright did not include in the subcommittee bill federal funding of exchanges of students with countries having no surplus property credit. He realized, correctly, that once established the program would be popular and could be broadened to include more countries. Later on, when surplus property funding dried up, the program could be funded by other means. American government funds could be appropriated, and so could money from foreign nations once world trade recovered from the shock of war and once dollars had accumulated abroad. At Fulbright's urging, O'Mahoney discarded the idea of adding complete funding of foreign students' education in the United States, not just the transportation costs to America that they would receive in the draft. Thus some potentially explosive items never saw the light of day in the bill.

To make the proposal more popular Fulbright added clauses to the bill. One stated that no foreign student studying in the United States could deprive veterans of an opportunity of an education; later the Arkansan broadened this prohibition to include any American citizen. The committee bill also placed a $20 million limit on aggregate spending in any one nation. Fulbright incorporated a suggestion giving preference to American veterans of World Wars I and II, and another proviso calling for consideration for all geographical areas of the country in applicant selection. Still another revision required the State Department to make annual reports to Congress detailing agreements initiated that year, the names and addresses of all Americans attending school under the program, the names and locations of those schools, and the amount of credit or currency expended in each foreign country. Finally, Fulbright fended off another State Department effort to have all of its education programs funded by provisions of the proposed legislation.[15]

This revised and politically strengthened bill whisked through the Senate. In April of 1946, with one minor change and no debate, just six weeks after the subcommittee hearing, the Senate unanimously passed the Fulbright proposal without a roll call vote. Only a handful of senators were present—Fulbright had seen to that. Quietly he cleared the bill with the majority and minority leaders, announced their support, and late in the day presented the proposal as a routine measure under the unanimous consent calendar when the only suspected opponent, Kenneth McKellar, "just happened" to be off the floor.

"I didn't want him there. I didn't want any debate," conceded Fulbright. "A roll call vote, we'd have probably lost." Crusty old McKellar, the Democratic chair of the Appropriations Committee, worried about the surplus property funds being dissipated. Later the Tennessean told Fulbright that he would have killed this "very dangerous bit of legislation" if he had been on the floor: "Young man. . . . It's a very dangerous thing to send our fine young girls and boys abroad. They'll be infected with those foreign 'isms.'"

Thanks to the work of Fulbright and O'Mahoney the Senate bill appeared almost unassailable politically. Fulbright later recalled how he worked with O'Ma-

honey: "He was very important" because "I was as fresh as can be. I was very ignorant about the procedures." O'Mahoney, maintained Fulbright, "suggested certain provisions that were more in accord with the traditional practice of the Senate."[16]

HOUSE PASSAGE

Passage by the House of Representatives came even more quickly than in the Senate. Before House consideration of the measure Fulbright headed off serious opposition by a "patronizing" Democrat from Mississippi, William Whittington, a high-ranking member of the Committee on Expenditures in the Executive Departments, which considered the bill. Adroitly Fulbright used a fellow Southerner, William Clayton, an assistant secretary of state and long-time friend of the Mississippian. 'Well, if there's any money around for education, we need money for education in Mississippi,' Fulbright quoted Whittington as saying. 'We're not interested in educating foreigners.' Later Fulbright recalled that Whittington considered him "a young whippersnapper" and "frowned upon" the Arkansan as "too obstreperous." "I tried to explain [to him that] there's a difference between a non-convertible German mark and a dollar that could be used in Mississippi," Fulbright remembered, "but he wouldn't listen to me." But he "listened to Will Clayton . . . and allowed it [the bill] to come out" of his committee.

The expenditures committee made only one major change in the measure. Because members distrusted the State

15. Jeffrey, "Interview with Fulbright," pp. 7, 13, 30, 32-35; Committee on Military Affairs, *Foreign Educational Benefits and Surplus Property: Hearing before a Subcommittee,* pp. 1-56; idem, *Foreign Educational Benefits and Surplus Property, Report No. 1039, 12 Mar. 1946* (Washington, DC: Government Printing Office, 1946), pp. 1-11.

16. Committee on Military Affairs, *Foreign Educational Benefits, Report No. 1039,* pp. 1-11; Jeffrey, "Interview with Fulbright," pp. 5-6, 29-30; Oberdorfer, "Noun," p. 82.

Department, they inserted a provision establishing a Board of Foreign Scholarships to supervise the program. Three other modifications were made: slightly changing the disposal powers of the secretary of state; striking out a proviso for the funding of State Department library operations; and limiting the amount to be spent in any one country to $1 million, not $2.5 million. In its report the committee stressed that "the appropriation of funds is not the subject of the instant bill."

On the House floor two Republicans and the Democratic committee chair advocated passage. Only one member raised an objection, saying in just two sentences that the measure appeared "detrimental to the best interests of the people of this country," but never explaining what he meant. Even though Fulbright claimed to be uncertain of the outcome a few days before the House debate, a debate that lasted less than ten minutes, the bill passed under suspension of the rules without a record vote with what one representative described as a "whoop and a holler."[17]

FINAL STEPS IN ENACTMENT

Just one day after the House approved the bill Fulbright asked the Senate to

concur with the House version. Only two senators other than Fulbright spoke, both asking what proposal they would be voting on. Then the Senate agreed to the measure unanimously.

President Truman signed the Fulbright Act, Public Law 584, on 1 August 1946, three days before Congress adjourned. Truman gave the pens he used to J. William Fulbright and Assistant Secretary of State William Benton, the key executive branch official supporting passage. The Fulbright scholarship program had come into being.[18]

CONCLUSION

Passage of the international education program came about because Fulbright shaped the proposal "to combine virtue and thrift in a single package." A national public opinion poll on the question of what "can be done that will give the United Nations a better chance of preventing wars" found that the overwhelming answer was to exchange students with other countries. And a magazine article on "cultural currency" brought a tremendously favorable deluge of letters from both general readers and "thought leaders." Clearly, international education seemed on the side of the angels. In addition, Fulbright hit upon a painless method of financing the exchange that required no congressional use of tax dollars. "I don't think we could have gotten to first base with a request for an authorization for appropriations at that time," Fulbright argued years later. Indeed, the sale of surplus property saved

17. Jeffrey, "Interview with Fulbright," pp. 3-4, 8-10, 28-29, 34-35; Clayton to Fulbright, 11 June 1946, Fulbright Papers; Fulbright to Henry S. Commager, 29 July 1946, ibid.; Fulbright to Clayton, 18 July 1946, Bureau of Educational and Cultural Affairs Papers; *Congressional Record*, 79th Cong., 2d sess., 7 July 1946, p. 9284; ibid, 26 July 1946, pp. 10214-5; U.S., Congress, House, Committee on Expenditures in the Executive Departments, *Disposal of Surplus Property Abroad, Report No. 2546, 17 July 1946* (Washington, DC: Government Printing Office, 1946), pp. 1-11; *Pathfinder*, 28 Aug. 1946, in Fulbright Papers.

18. *Congressional Record*, 79th Cong., 2d sess., 27 July 1946, p. 10237; J. William Fulbright, "Statement," 1 Aug. 1946, Fulbright Papers; Francis Colligan to Mrs. Williams, 10 Oct. 1967, Bureau of Educational and Cultural Affairs Papers.

the public's tax dollars. Years after enactment of the measure President John Kennedy referred to the program as "the classic modern example of beating swords into plowshares."[19]

The second reason for passage of the bill came from Fulbright's shrewd tactics. Don Oberdorfer, a reporter, summarized Fulbright's role in securing approval:

In 1945 there was no pressure from educators or anyone else to launch the exchange-study program. Fulbright conceived it, pushed it through Congress, [and] sold the doubters in the executive branch. . . . Senator Fulbright consulted and convinced a few vitally important lawmakers that educational exchange was a worthwhile way to employ these funds. . . . Wisely, he kept in the dark everyone who didn't need to know what his proposal was all about.[20]

"I was such a junior member, having been in the Senate such a short time— less than a year—that no one took notice of this legislation at all until it was passed," Fulbright stated. "The bill was allowed to pass," he wrote, "because influential senators who might otherwise have opposed it deemed it insignificant. I was content to have them believe that." "It didn't involve a lot of money," he said, "So what the hell? Nobody paid any attention to it."[21]

In retrospect, the scholarship program came into being because of the efforts of one man. Fulbright's experiences as a student abroad, a traveler absorbing other cultures, a professor, and a university president convinced him that international educational exchange would promote tolerance and understanding among all peoples. As a member of Congress during and immediately after a devastating global conflict, the Arkansas senator became engrossed in attempting to establish, via a larger American role and a potent United Nations, "world peace and international community." Realizing that the mushroom cloud of nuclear Armageddon hung over all states, Fulbright creatively tried to use the quandary about war debts and surplus property to institute a mechanism to dampen hostility between countries. His strategy involved formulating a politically palatable measure that appeared to be an innocuous revision of a minor bookkeeping act. Drawing on his acquired political skills, he employed the tactic of rushing a bill through Congress by stealth. Fulbright quietly shepherded its passage through the iron triangle of interest groups, Congress, and the executive branch. That is why Webster's *Dictionary* now lists "ful-bright" as a common noun, a synonym for the scholarly exchange grant.[22]

19. Oberdorfer, "Noun," pp. 79 ff; Jeffrey, "Interview with Fulbright," pp. 3-4; Committee on Military Affairs, *Foreign Educational Benefits and Surplus Property: Hearing before a Subcommittee*, pp. 31-34.

20. Oberdorfer, "Noun," pp. 80, 82.

21. Jeffrey, "Interview with Fulbright," pp. 10-11; J. William Fulbright, "The Legislator as Educator," *Foreign Affairs,* 57(4):722 (Spring 1979); Douglas Cater, "World Progress through Educational Exchange: The Story of a Conference" (Pamphlet, Institute of International Relations, 1959), p. 9.

22. Jeffrey, "Interview with Fulbright," pp. 1-36; Avery Peterson, "Senator J. William Fulbright," *American Foreign Service Journal*, p. 18 (Feb. 1951); Fulbright to Frank Aydelotte, 6 May 1955, Bureau of Educational and Cultural Affairs Papers; Dean Albertson, "Reminiscences of J. William Fulbright" (Manuscript, Oral History Research Office, Columbia University, 1957), pp. 8-11, 32, 100, 112-28; Oberdorfer, "Noun," p. 79.

Academic Exchange and the Founding of New Universities

By WARREN F. ILCHMAN and ALICE STONE ILCHMAN

ABSTRACT: A major aspect of the Third World's higher education scene in the post-1945 period has been the expansion of the number and size of universities. Often approaching a tenfold growth, this development was also marked by a remarkable worldwide similarity of curriculum and structures of governance. A factor in the growth and character of these institutions has been the Fulbright program, in concert with the role of the United States as the educator of choice for Third World academic personnel. The contributions of the Fulbright program have been both direct and programmatic, and indirect and incidental, to the process of academic exchange.

Warren F. Ilchman is provost of Rockefeller College of Public Affairs and Policy, State University of New York, Albany, and director of the Rockefeller Institute of Government for the entire State University of New York system. He received his B.A. from Brown University and his Ph.D. from the University of Cambridge. From 1976 to 1980 he was program adviser to the International Division of the Ford Foundation.

Alice Stone Ilchman, president of Sarah Lawrence College, received her B.A. from Mt. Holyoke College and her Ph.D. from the London School of Economics. From 1977 to 1981 she served as assistant secretary of state for education and cultural affairs and associate director of the International Communication Agency, with the responsibility for the Fulbright program.

NOTE: The authors wish to thank Ms. Cassandra Pyle and Ms. Anne Carpenter of the Council for the International Exchange of Scholars and Dr. Elinor Barber of the Institute of International Education for their assistance in providing data and their reflections on the authors' interpretation. They also wish to thank Mr. Frederick A.C. Ilchman for assistance in the basic research.

ANNIVERSARIES are often an opportunity for exaggeration. In whatever is being celebrated, achievements are usually stressed and failures minimized. The sum is frequently more than what reality bears out. So with the anniversary of the Fulbright program. There is, however, an achievement that can only be asserted and impressionistically supported, but that we believe is part of an unrecognized reality of the program's record. It is the post-1945 contribution of the Fulbright program, along with the role of American higher education, to the development of higher education in the Third World, the non-European and non-North American world. We believe that contribution to have been quite substantial.

THE DEVELOPMENT OF HIGHER EDUCATION

Cultural historians of the next century will surely note what we take quite for granted. One of the most ubiquitous developments of the post-World War II era has been the increase and diffusion of universities throughout the world. So striking has this movement been that one needs a cultural analogue fully to understand it. Such an analogue can be found in the Cistercian monastic order. At the beginning of the twelfth century, there was but one Cistercian monastery; by the end of the century there were more than five hundred. Monasteries, it would seem, embodied values that were widely held to be useful and were worthy objects of personal and collective resources. More particularly, they represented a social technology that was relatively easy to replicate.

So with universities. At the beginning of the twentieth century there were but 81 universities outside of Europe and North America. These included the 11 Spanish colonial universities founded in the sixteenth and seventeenth centuries to provide for Spain's imperial civil service and the 3 Indian universities established in response to the social demands of the 1800s. By 1985 there were more than 1500 universities in the Third World, over 600 having been founded in the period between 1961 and 1975 alone.

In this quite extraordinary increase is a story that should someday be told in its fullness. For our purposes, however, we need only to outline that growth. In Table 1, the institutional development by region and era is displayed.[1] The period after 1945 witnessed the greatest growth; fully 80 percent of the universities of today in the Third World were established in the last forty years. This can be seen graphically in Figure 1, where the regional and the total growth are depicted.

The development, however, was not only in numbers of institutions. It can be seen as well in the increase in the number of faculty and students. Figures 2 and 3

1. The data for Table 1 and Figures 1, 4, 5, and 6 are taken from *The World of Learning, 1984-85* (London: Europa, 1984). Institutional types were determined from entries; where three or more professional schools were listed in addition to arts and science faculties, the institution was termed "comprehensive." "Specialized" institutions contained one or more professional programs, but no degree programs in the humanities or social sciences. The authors have confidence in the dates provided for the foundation of institutions and in the universality of the sample. Only Vietnam, North Korea, and the People's Republic of China are questionable. It was decided to exclude Vietnam and North Korea, and the People's Republic of China contains the bulk of "not availables" in the East Asian category. All regional categories are consistently used and are those pertinent to the Fulbright program.

TABLE 1
THIRD WORLD HIGHER EDUCATION: NUMBER AND DATE OF
ESTABLISHMENT OF UNIVERSITIES AND COLLEGES

	Africa	East Asia and Pacific	Latin America and Caribbean	Near East and South Asia	Total	Percentage
Pre-1900	6	13	41	21	81	5.38%
1901-45	13	50	66	50	179	11.89%
1946-60	43	117	116	83	359	23.85%
1961-75	154	78	212	163	607	40.33%
1975 to the present	46	12	33	72	163	10.83%
Not available	31	65	12	8	116	7.71%
Total	293	335	480	397	1505	
Percentage	19.47%	22.26%	31.89%	26.38%		

SOURCE: Data derived from *The World of Learning, 1984-85* (London: Europa, 1984).

portray increases often approximating a factor of ten.[2]

Individual institutions increased many times, such as the University of Madras—from 59,000 in 1958 to 165,000 in 1984—or the National University of Mexico—from 53,000 in 1958 to 327,000 in 1984. In South Asia, where the affiliating college system is the norm, India alone saw the creation of 4600 non-degree-granting but teaching colleges.[3] Often universities in the Third

World doubled every decade in students and faculty, and university attendance became an increasingly common experience for the Third World's young people.

Certain kinds of institutions of higher education became more common. Not only did degree-granting colleges decline relative to universities, but comprehensive universities, where degrees from faculties of arts and sciences and at least three professional schools were offered, became the dominant mode. Needless to say, to call many of these institutions comprehensive is to exaggerate their present and future, but the adjective does not exaggerate what they intend to become.[4] The general trend may be seen in Figure 4.

2. Data for Figures 2 and 3 are derived from various editions of the *Statistical Yearbook* (Paris: United Nations Educational, Scientific, and Cultural Organization, 1965, 1980, and 1982). The authors believe that the numbers for students and faculty in Latin America overstate the case through an inevitable double-counting of students and part-time faculty, while the numbers of both faculty and students are understated in South Asia and East Asia. The regions used are those pertaining to the Fulbright program. The fall in number of faculty and students in the 1960s in East Asia is entirely due to the Cultural Revolution in China.

3. Data are from *The World of Learning, 1984-85*. In Bangladesh, 373 teaching colleges were created, while Pakistan had 167 affiliating colleges added. *The World of Learning, 1984-85* refers to "82 colleges of higher and professional education" and "60 Factory (Engineering) Colleges" for North Korea, lists 46 "colleges" for Vietnam, and for the

People's Republic of China it mentions "about 170 institutions of higher education [that] have been reestablished"; see pp. 787, 1700-1, and 282, respectively.

4. A superior determination would have been by degrees conferred, reserving "comprehensive" for institutions offering the whole range of higher degrees. As that was impossible from the data available, the more liberal definition was used. This provided anomalies, such as the Universidade Estadual de Londrina in Brazil, with seven faculties, 38 departments, 10,000 students, 1000 faculty, and only 64,000 books, all having come into being since 1971, being called "comprehensive."

FIGURE 1
THIRD WORLD HIGHER EDUCATION BY PERIOD ESTABLISHED

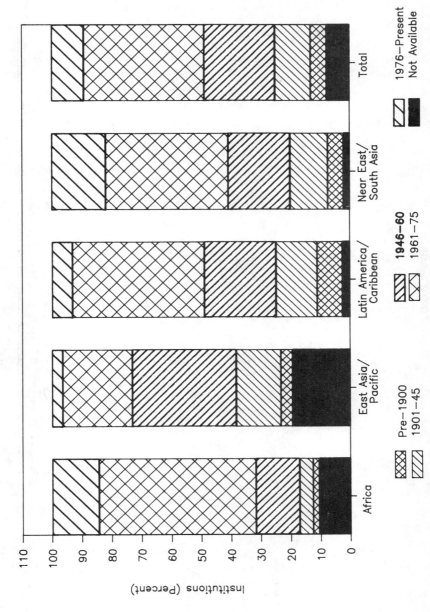

SOURCE: Data derived from *The World of Learning, 1984-85* (London: Europa, 1984).

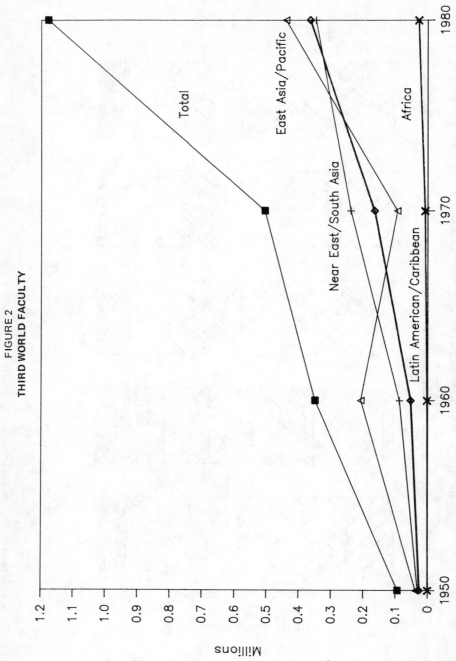

FIGURE 2
THIRD WORLD FACULTY

Total

East Asia/Pacific

Near East/South Asia

Africa

Latin American/Caribbean

Millions

1.2
1.1
1.0
0.9
0.8
0.7
0.6
0.5
0.4
0.3
0.2
0.1
0

1950   1960   1970   1980

SOURCE: Data derived from *Statistical Yearbook* (Paris:: United Nations Educational, Scientific, and Cultural Organization, 1965, 1980, and 1982).

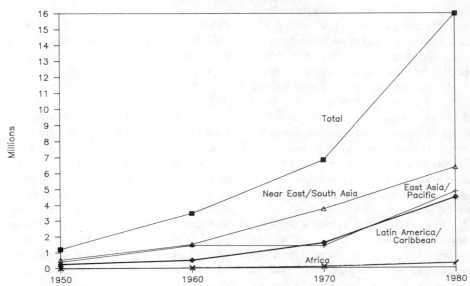

SOURCE: Data derived from *Statistical Yearbook* (1965, 1980, and 1982).

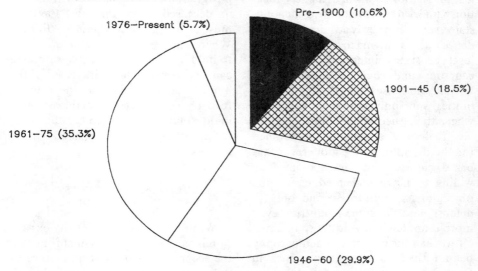

SOURCE: Data derived from *World of Learning, 1984-85*.

The period since 1945 also saw the rise of specialized institutions. These institutions, focusing as they do on such subjects as engineering, agriculture, and management, became common features of the educational scene. Their establishment over time can be seen in Figure 5.

Universities, of course, cannot stand alone. To support the quality control that higher education requires, as well as to ensure the ability to participate in the international generation of knowledge, a considerable infrastructure of national academies, professional associations, and independent research organizations had to be created. The record of Third World countries in developing universities is matched by their efforts to create—or allow to come into existence—the necessary support systems for universities to improve. Figure 6 demonstrates this effort by region.

Why so much wealth, energy, and commitment went into this development is hard to specify in an article of this length. The development of higher education paralleled the development of nation-states, some with newly acquired independence, others moving to a more complex level of statist intervention into the economy and social life. Above all, virtually all those with official responsibilities saw universities as the place where their successors—more specifically, their children—would be groomed for the disciplines of a modern urban-based culture. They were more than willing to make higher education the object of expenditure second only to defense and in some countries even more than defense. And these national efforts had the pressure of demography behind them. Just as universities in Germany, Japan, France, Great Britain, and the United States increased in size and number in the post-World War II era to accommodate the baby boom and a greater commitment to public access to higher education, the Third World had the need to accommodate a growing cohort of young people and the growing participation rate born of the increase in expenditures on primary and secondary education.

In these developments, there are patterns. The late 1960s saw an international reexamination of higher education and its capacity to cope. With each reexamination, there was expansion. Across Latin America, the work of these national commissions can be seen in the dates of expansion of the number of institutions. And when one expands the number of institutions, there is a multiplier effect. Now, every province requires an institution; the commemorating of one regional hero begets the need to commemorate others. If the state creates a new institution in Latin America, then the Church must do likewise, often in the same city. If India establishes a postgraduate university in the name of its deceased prime minister, Pakistan must do the same in honor of Jinnah. Where nations such as India have tried to hold back the tide of expansion, one can find periodic large increases in the number of institutions as the pent-up forces have found political release. As a middle class increased and as the needs for an official sector expanded, so did universities.

CULTURAL INFLUENCES ON UNIVERSITY DEVELOPMENT

While the story of university expansion is as dramatic as it is unchronicled, the second most interesting feature of this development is that all the universities created and developed were remarkably alike. Indeed, in the Third World

FIGURE 5
INSTITUTIONS OF SPECIALIZED HIGHER EDUCATION
BY DATE OF ESTABLISHMENT

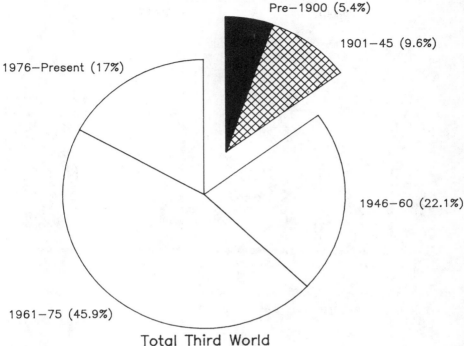

Total Third World

SOURCE: Data derived from *World of Learning, 1984-85.*

there is hardly an institution where, from face characteristics, there is evidence that its founders rethought the structures of knowledge so as to relate the new institution better to its setting or to be, for its own sake, an institution of distinctiveness. The hundreds upon hundreds of universities founded since World War II accepted the international conventions about the divisions of knowledge. While individual programs, undoubtedly, made an effort to fit, it was mandatory that each university have at least four kinds of social science, four kinds of humanities, five kinds of science, four kinds of engineering, and so forth. Whenever one found, for example, a department of social relations—where the social sciences were interdisciplinarily mixed—it would turn out to be a temporary arrangement until more faculty returned to the country from their foreign training. Nowhere in the Third World does one find the urge to experiment that characterized Evergreen State, the University of Wisconsin at Green Bay, the University of Sussex, or the University of Tsukuba in Japan. Whether steak or hamburger, meat-and-potatoes higher education, without sauce, became the Third World's fare.

Not only was there great similarity in the Third World regarding the structures of knowledge, but there appeared two contrasting models of university organization that began to prevail. Each drew on the country's tradition regarding parastatal organizations and, where appropriate,

FIGURE 6
ACADEMIC INFRASTRUCTURE

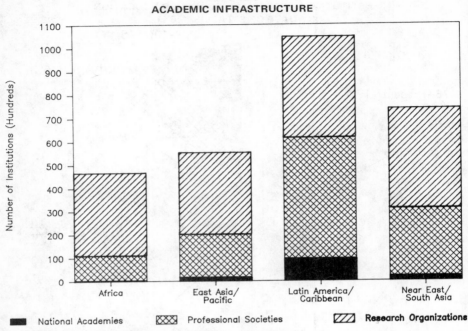

SOURCE: Data derived from *World of Learning, 1984-85.*

the institutional forms and relationships long established in the colonial power. The adoption of one model usually set into play forces for the alternative model. The intra-university and intergenerational disputes that characterize higher education everywhere more often than not in the Third World took the form of contests between opponents and proponents of features of these contrasting models.

For purposes of their preliminary consideration, the two models might be called American and Continental, and their chief characteristics are arrayed in Table 2. While there are probably few national examples approximating the pure models, there is a sufficient clustering of these attributes to attest to the utility of considering the models as polar.

Why the basic international similarity of higher education occurred, however, is a story in itself. A major reason, of course, was the need to expand rapidly and the propensity to turn to what was established and known as the mode of doing so. There was little pressure to experiment, though there was pressure to shift at the margin to a mode unlike what prevailed in the former colonial power. Moreover, if the West set the standards for higher education generally, then one had to simulate—in terms of structure and content—what was going at the time these institutions were so quickly increased in number and size. Another factor was the explicit efforts to assist the process of expansion, differentiation, and quality control by such organizations as the Rockefeller Foundation—in its program in education for

TABLE 2
CHARACTERISTICS OF WORLD UNIVERSITY MODELS

American Model	Continental Model
Central administration and trustees are dominant in governance	Faculty organization is dominant vis-à-vis central administration
Research occurs in universities	Research occurs more often in independent institutions outside of universities
Course examinations, rather than field exams, denote progress toward degree	Progress toward degree is by field, not course, examinations
Assessment is by instructor	Assessment is by outside authority
Full-time faculty is favored	Part-time faculty is common
Organization is according to department and discipline	Organization is according to faculty
Professional education usually follows initial degree	Professional education is coequal with arts and science education
Doctorate is expected of professoriat	Doctorate is not prerequisite for professoriat
State and institution are considered separate	Institution derives from the state

development—the Ford Foundation, the U.S. Agency for International Development, the United Nations Education, Scientific, and Cultural Organization, the international and national professional associations, and the many national foreign aid efforts of Europe and Japan.[5] Each reinforced the norms of its own country, and the countries were in themselves increasingly homogeneous with respect to an international standard of how knowledge was organized and purveyed.

We believe that a further force in university development in the Third World and a factor in stimulating similarities in these new universities was the Fulbright program, working in concert with the dominant position of the United States in providing education and hence role models for the Third World's scholar-teachers and institutional models for their university builders.

5. The impact of the United States and other world powers on Third World universities is a story well worth telling. An initial effort at this was undertaken by Kenneth W. Thompson and Bar-

SCHOLARLY EXCHANGE AND THE ROLE OF THE FULBRIGHT PROGRAM

To experience an almost 700 percent growth in numbers of institutions and more than a tenfold increase in numbers of faculty and students had to presuppose a larger international capacity not only to provide higher educational opportunities while the home institutions were being built, but also to provide their new professors. In addition, as basic credentials for membership in a faculty increased, this dependence on an international system of higher education persisted. While today it is possible to study to the highest degree in all four regions that comprise the Third World, the capacity and presumption for quality remain wanting, thus perpetuating this dependence.

bara R. Fogel, eds., *Higher Education and Social Change* (New York: International Council for Educational Development, 1976). See also Laurence D. Stifel, Ralph K. Davidson, and James S. Coleman, eds., *Social Sciences and Public Policy in the Developing World* (Lexington, MA: Lexington Books, 1982).

Where beyond the shores of one's own country higher education is pursued is very much affected by the international fortunes of the host country. A reason for the success of the fellowship exchange most often spoken of in the same breath as the Fulbright, the Rhodes, is that the Rhodes sent young men deemed special by their countries to be educated in what was then the world's most powerful nation. The equation of powerful education with the global power of Britain was not surprising. This same propensity is with the Third World today.

Whether higher education in the United States was or is truly superior to what could be achieved elsewhere or whether America's economic and military role in the world conferred a presumption of efficacy to its education that may or may not have been substantiated in reality, there can be no doubt that the United States has been the chief educator to undergird the development of higher education in the Third World since 1945. This role paralleled, and even facilitated, the substantially expanding capacity of higher education in the United States itself in this period. As credentialing faculty positions became more stringent in the Third World, the relative advance of the United States as regards post-bachelor's education further consolidated this status. The early faculty received their master's degrees in the United States more frequently than they did elsewhere in the world, though the pioneer faculty were usually educated in the universities of the colonial power and these institutions continued to play an important though abating role. The successors of the early faculty now receive their doctorates predominantly in the United States.

While the evidence for this assertion is primarily personal, deriving as it does from our visiting over one hundred universities in the regions in the last twenty years, the general statistics bear out the contention. The United States is overwhelmingly the educator of choice for Third World students. The United States receives well over a third of all students who leave their own country to study elsewhere. Its universities and colleges receive more students from abroad than the next five countries— France, Germany, the USSR, the United Kingdom, and Canada—combined. And the students have been increasingly from the Third World, from 71.0 percent of the total foreign student population in 1954 to 85.5 percent in 1984-85. The percentage of foreign students nearly doubled—from 1.4 percent to 2.7 percent of all students—in a university system that rose from a total of 2.5 million to nearly 12.5 million in the same period. Those imputed as having been at the graduate level and pursuing specialized education increased more than tenfold. Table 3 presents this growth and distribution of foreign students over time.

Within the larger community of international exchange of scholars, of which foreign students constitute a subset, there is a further subset in the Fulbright program. It is important to have a sense of the dimension of this exchange with the Third World. Table 4 details the number and distribution by time, region, level, and purpose of exchange with the Third World.

While there has been a historical emphasis on Europe and Japan in the Fulbright program in terms of numbers, the role of the Fulbrighter has been very important to the development of the new and expanded systems of higher

TABLE 3
FOREIGN STUDENTS IN THE UNITED STATES, 1954-85

	Total Foreign Students	Third World (percentage)	Total Third World	Graduate Level, Total Foreign Students (percentage)	Graduate Level, Third World*	Specialized, Total Foreign Students (percentage)	Specialized Third World*
1954-55	34,232	70.9	24,270	38.8	9,417	53.8	13,057
1959-60	48,486	74.7	36,219	42.9	15,538	52.8	19,124
1964-65	82,045	76.0	62,354	47.9	29,868	45.5	28,371
1969-70	134,959	73.3	98,925	48.3	47,781	51.2	50,650
1974-75	154,580	83.9	129,693	46.5	60,307	56.4	73,147
1979-80	286,343	86.6	247,973	35.3	87,534	59.5	147,544
1984-85	342,113	85.5	292,507	38.3	112,030	55.4	162,049

SOURCE: Data derived from Marianthi Zikopoulos, ed., *Open Doors, 1984/5* (New York: Institute for International Education, 1985), pp. 3-26.

*Assumes constant proportion of Third World to non-Third World.

education in the Third World. This function has seldom been an explicit public objective of those with responsibility for the Fulbright program in Washington, but we know from the record and personal experience that it has been a goal of those administering the program in the field.[6] Unlike Europe and Japan, the Third World candidates would come disproportionately from expanding and new universities; their candidacy would often be part of a vice-chancellor's or department head's plan to develop various areas or levels of learning, and the selection committees everywhere in the Third World took this into account when awards were made. Why various Third World countries had Fulbright programs in the first instance is hard to

know. They were often started in, say, Mali or Malaysia or Ecuador because their neighbors had programs or America's competitors had offered scholarly exchanges, or as the accident of an energetic cultural affairs officer or the gift to a head of state when more valuable resources were too scarce and the visitor politically could not leave empty-handed. Whatever the reasons, the Fulbright program was an important factor in the developments we have described.

How important is the question? Extrapolating from personal evidence and without systematic quantitative substantiation—though we consider such substantiation possible—we believe that a high proportion of heads of institutions and departments, pioneers in new subjects, chairs of commissions to reorganize and expand university education, and scholarly mentors for subsequent generations of national scholars had themselves been Fulbrighters. In being so, they were in residence in the United States in better-established universities where international norms of university development were more strongly kept. We also

6. For official Washington positions on the Fulbright program, see U.S., Department of State, *Swords into Plowshares* (Washington, DC: Government Printing Office, 1956); Board of Foreign Scholarships, *A Quarter Century: The American Adventure in Academic Exchange* (Washington, DC: Department of State, 1971); Robert J. Armbruster, ed., *A Process of Global Enlightenment* (Washington, DC: Board of Foreign Scholarships and the International Communication Agency, 1980).

TABLE 4
EXCHANGE OF FULBRIGHT SCHOLARS WITH THE THIRD WORLD

	Africa		East Asia and Pacific		Latin America and Caribbean		Near East and South Asia		Total	
	US-R*	V-US†	US-R	V-US	US-R	V-US	US-R	V-US	US-R	V-US
Senior Fulbrights										
1949-70	278	68	1,930	2,276	1,360	703	2,206	1,206	5,774	4,253
1970-75	123	133	447	286	386	294	282	220	1,238	933
1975-80	205	221	556	462	368	223	297	438	1,426	1,344
1980-85	248	195	621	611	487	308	491	595	1,847	1,709
1985-86	84	53	172	167	196	68	65	98	517	386
Total Research	938	670	3,726	3,802	2,797	1,596	3,341	2,557	10,802	8,625
(percentage)	11.94	87.02	33.71	81.88	10.27	71.00	21.89	83.85	22.52	81.00
Junior Fulbrights										
1949-70	86	1,685	842	6,977	999	3,911	677	4,958	2,604	17,531
1970-75	14	76	105	946	161	840	39	290	319	2,152
1975-85	109	841	271	1,622	395	1,989	116	771	891	5,223
Total	209	2,602	1,218	9,545	1,555	6,740	832	6,019	3,814	24,906

SOURCE: Data derived from reports of the Council for International Exchange of Scholars and Board of Foreign Scholarships, 1949-85.

NOTE: As regions changed in their compositions over time, the numbers were recalculated to reflect a consistency with the present composition of the four regions.

*"US-R" stands for U.S. scholars teaching and doing research in the region. "V-US" stands for region's scholars teaching and doing research in the United States.

60

believe that in subsequent years these Fulbrighters were part of national and international scholarly networks that further sustained these norms. In their national and intra-university discussions about standards and procedures, these returned scholars were more likely to be proponents of the close coupling of research and teaching, assessment by instructors, progress in course examinations rather than in field examinations, full-time faculty, doctorates as prerequisite of the professoriat, and the university's being separate from the state—those attributes we describe as comprising an American model for universities.

The Fulbright program, of course, is two-way, not only receiving in the United States but also sending young and more senior scholars to the Third World to do research and teaching. Table 4 describes their number and destinations. These individuals carried some of the burden of developing the structures of knowledge that constituted the curriculum in new and developing institutions and certainly carried with them the norms of how universities are thought in this country to function best and what the citizenly roles of academics should be.

Much of the contribution to university building by Fulbrighters was the deliberate objective of the countries' binational commissions. Commission members tried to develop certain subjects by having American progenitors until their local product could finish his or her graduate education, usually in the United States. In Pakistan through the 1970s, for example, there was a deliberate effort to build anthropology, while in Thailand the social sciences and educational administration became the objective for development in the provincial universities. A Fulbrighter even helped the Thais plan the expansion of their system of higher education. In country after country, one finds deliberate efforts to use American Fulbrighters to build the indigenous system.

Many of these contributions, however, were not planned, but were the product instead of the ordinary day-to-day actions of Fulbright scholars as researchers and teachers. End-of-tour reports by Fulbrighters are replete with unintended contributions: sustaining a campus research organization, teaching a new subject, being available for office hours in a system where faculty are conspicuous by their absence, offering a seminar at other institutions or a national conference, developing a system of peer review for a new journal in an old subject, expecting to attend committee meetings and to support efforts at curricular reform, hiring a young faculty member or a would-be academic to be part of a research team working on a project for which empirical research was required, supporting a central administration when the norm was to bash the vice-chancellor, questioning a promotion that appeared to be justified only on political grounds, and so forth. Typical of these contributions is a 1981 report of a Fulbrighter who had been in Nigeria, where he claims that he had been "given a free hand in program development" in devising the provincial campus's M.B.A. program. While few made contributions like that of one Fulbrighter to Liberia—who within the year 1973-74 was asked to revise the curriculum and be interim dean and later acting president—the uncompiled annals of the 14,000-plus Fulbrighters to the Third World will provide a future cultural historian some of the evidence for the diffusion of norms and structures of knowledge that were available at the critical time when their status was most problematic.[7]

7. We are grateful to the Council for Interna-

CONCLUSION

The world of higher education expanded substantially after 1945. Those countries that constitute the Third World were an important site for this expansion both absolutely, in total number of institutions and participation, and in relation to the paucity of their pre-1945 experience. Lacking strong internal models, the Third World countries adopted internationally sanctioned structures of knowledge and found themselves variously attracted to the prevailing

---

tional Exchange of Scholars for the opportunity to examine a sample of end-of-tour reports from Fulbright scholars for the period 1960-85 from Africa and East Asia.

modes of university-society relations and internal organization. In the process of this development, the capacity of the United States to educate foreign nationals and to prepare faculty for an increasingly credentialed professoriat in the Third World became important. A critical aspect of this capacity was and is the Fulbright program, where both deliberate programmatic design and daily experience of the exchanged scholar-teachers contribute to building the intellectual and organizational structures of Third World universities. The fortieth anniversary of the Fulbright program should celebrate this achievement as well.

ANNALS, *AAPSS*, **491**, May 1987

Research Access: Scholarship
versus National Interest

By ELINOR G. BARBER

ABSTRACT: Research access to foreign countries has become increasingly problematic. Because research is seen as potentially damaging to national interests or the interests of local researchers, foreigners' access to research sites may be restricted. Claims to rights to carry out scientific endeavors come into conflict with claims to rights to make access conditional or to deny access. The following issues or sticking points have provoked conflicting interpretations of rights: where, within a foreign country, research may be done; what topics may be studied; what types of research are acceptable; who shall study a given problem; who shall be supporting the research; and who shall benefit from it. In the absence of clear-cut agreement about rights, access has to be negotiated, by governments or organizations or individual researchers. Different kinds of reciprocal concessions are necessary, depending on the relationships between the countries involved, for example, between the United States and the Soviet Union or between the United States and Third World countries.

Elinor G. Barber is director of research at the Institute of International Education. Previously she was a program officer at the Ford Foundation and an associate editor of the International Encyclopedia of the Social Sciences. *She holds a B.A. degree from Vassar College and a Ph.D. from Harvard University, both in history. Her major piece of research is a study of the bourgeoisie in eighteenth-century France. She has also written on international studies and international education.*

I N recent years, scholars in Western countries have become increasingly aware that they cannot take research access to other countries for granted. "Research access" is widely used as a short-hand term to designate the freedom researchers in one country have to study the topic of their choice in another country. To the extent that scholars in any academic discipline prefer research sites outside of their country of residence or even consider such research sites essential, research access may become problematic.[1] The scholars for whom the problem may come up are, therefore, those humanists and social scientists who specialize in countries other than their own, as well as such natural scientists as zoologists, geologists, and botanists.

The increasingly problematic character of research access has to do, in part, with changing relationships between the countries of the West and

1. The reader may be interested in the following volumes: Ralph I. Beals, *Politics of Social Research: An Inquiry into the Ethics and Responsibilities of Social Scientists* (Chicago: Aldine, 1969), esp. chap. 2, "Evidence from Foreign Research"; Tom L. Beauchamp et al., eds., *Ethical Issues in Social Science Research* (Baltimore, MD: Johns Hopkins University Press, 1982), esp. chap. 3, by Donald P. Warwick, "The Types of Harm in Social Research"; Robert T. Bower and Priscilla de Gasperis, *Ethics in Social Research: Protecting the Interests of Human Subjects* (New York: Praeger, 1978); Edward Diener and Rick Crandall, *Ethics in Social and Behavioral Research* (Chicago: University of Chicago Press, 1978); Irving L. Horowitz, *The Rise and Fall of Project Camelot* (Cambridge, MA: MIT Press, 1967); Paul Davidson Reynolds, *Ethical Dilemmas in Social Science Research: An Analysis of Moral Issues Confronting Investigators in Research Using Human Subjects* (San Francisco: Jossey-Bass, 1979); Gideon Sjoberg, ed. *Ethics, Politics, and Social Research* (Cambridge, MA: Schenkman, 1967), esp. Sjoberg's chapter, "Project Camelot: Selected Reactions and Personal Reflections."

those of the Third World, as well as with the perennial tensions, since World War II, between the United States and the Soviet Union. Thus, in earlier times, researchers from Western countries were free to carry on their studies on their own terms in the regions of the world that were either actual colonies or economically and politically dependent on the West.

In part, also, the problem of research access has its source in new and worldwide awareness of ethical issues related to medical and social research on human subjects. In the context of this new awareness, countries may be regarded as individual human subjects writ large. In the case of individual human subjects, the potential harm that may be done by research is physical, as may occur in biological research; psychological, such as risk in certain psychological experiments; or social, incurring embarrassment or legal difficulties as a consequence of the invasion of privacy. Harm alone is not the issue; the researcher has no right to experiment with human subjects if informed consent has not been obtained. The absence of informed consent is *ipso facto* evidence of the violation of autonomy and dignity. With respect to countries, research may be damaging to national security or internal political stability; or it may do violence to the cultural integrity of the local community; or it may seem to be a usurpation of the research domain of insiders by outsiders. To avoid such potential damage, countries are disposed to control the access of foreigners to research sites, either of all foreigners or of foreigners from particular countries. And in the case of countries also, research, whether harmful or not, is intrusive on autonomy and dignity if it is carried on without prior consent.

Research access has become problematic not only because of the fear that foreign researchers may do direct harm to the host country—the country where the preferred or essential research site is located—but also because of the sense that these foreign researchers produce nothing positive for the country they wish to visit. Whether they are natural scientists or social scientists, they are or appear to be in search of empirical data to further their own scholarly objectives or, worse yet, the national ends of their home country, rather than contributing to the economic development of poor countries or the professional development of local researchers.

Although both visiting researchers and their host-country counterparts share a commitment to the advancement of science—an endeavor that is highly esteemed and has broad legitimacy in virtually all countries—foreign researchers are necessarily also involved in producing knowledge that is directly or indirectly useful toward ends not shared by host-country nationals. Such knowledge may have either quite remote or quite immediate applications to the political or international interests of a foreign government or to the economic interests of foreign corporations, and inevitably it is intended to further the career of the individual foreign scholar. Insofar as the research is perceived to be useful toward ends that are not shared by host-country nationals and visiting researchers, it may also be perceived to be exploitative. The subjects of research, whether they are individuals or countries, resent being used—that is, exploited—and if they can muster the necessary resources, they take steps to protect themselves from abuse. As the richest and most powerful country in the world and the country with the largest number of researchers

and research resources, the United States is especially vulnerable to charges that it is taking advantage of less powerful countries and their scientific communities to further its own objectives. Recent measures taken by the U.S. government to protect the United States against the transfer of valuable technologies to other countries can only serve to exacerbate the resentment toward U.S. researchers seeking research access overseas.

The universal commitment to science is, to be sure, an important asset to researchers as they confront the subjects of research. In principle, at least, researchers and their subjects share both this commitment to science and a concern about possible harm to the subjects, but in practice, these two values often are not shared in equal measure. In some instances, judgments about priorities seem easy and obvious: it is relatively easy to deplore, on the one hand, the denial of research access by powerful organizations within the United States—presumably, they are hiding something—or to accept, on the other hand, the reciprocal limitation of research access established as a component of generally unfriendly relations between the United States and the Soviet Union. But it is much more difficult to come to judgments about the extent to which Third World countries are violating the common commitment to science when they assert the priority of their political interests and cultural integrity and the interests of their own scholars over the rights of foreign researchers, just as the legitimacy of U.S. export-control legislation is somewhat dubious. In any event, it is difficult to sustain simple arguments to the effect that all researchers are part of an international community of science in which national boundaries should never present obstacles.

In order to establish the legitimate limits to the rights claimed by U.S. researchers in foreign countries and the corresponding legitimate limits to the rights claimed by those countries to make access conditional or to deny access, it is necessary to understand more clearly the issues that have provoked conflicting interpretations of these rights. These issues might be called sticking points, and they include the following:

— where, within a foreign country, research may be done; this often involves security issues or internal political problems, but it may also have to do with the safety—or comfort—of foreigners in certain border areas or rural areas;
— what topics may be studied; sensitive topics often include particular subgroups of the population, political attitudes, corruption, ancient artifacts, anything in the military area; and the reasons for sensitivity are typically national security, political stability, cultural integrity, or the image of the country;
— what types of research are acceptable; any of the following kinds may be permitted or rejected: archival research, excavation, ethnographic research, biological experimentation, observation, surveys, statistical studies; the types of studies most likely to be permitted tend to be those that do not involve direct contact with the local population and that do not represent intrusion on the cultural heritage, political interests, or the integrity of small communities;
— who shall study a given problem; this issue may involve academic turf problems or sensitivity about interpretations by foreigners of local phenomena; also, there may be resistance to particular researchers because of gender, political stance, or ethnic or racial background;
— who is sponsoring or supporting the research; concerns in this area range from fear of political or economic espionage to uneasiness about restriction of academic freedom and scholarly objectivity; and
— who shall benefit from research. This issue involves control over or use of the results of research; the extent to which research represents shared needs for knowledge or is perceived as exploiting foreign research sites for economic, political, or individual ends; the participation of local schools and institutions; collaborative arrangements; and the locus and language of publication.

Yet other sticking points might be identified. Close examination of the emergence of these various sticking points in connection with research in different disciplines and in different countries facilitates the understanding of what needs and rights of access are being asserted by foreign researchers and questioned or denied by those who control access to the research sites in question.

PERSPECTIVES ON RESEARCH ACCESS

To a considerable extent, where one sits determines what one sees with regard to the problem of research access: those seeking access tend to share one perspective and those granting access share another perspective.[2] Those in the first

2. The perspectives on access that will be discussed in this section emerged in two conferences, one held at the Smithsonian Institution, 18-19 November 1985, and attended primarily by

category tend to stress the rights and needs of scientific efforts, while those in the second category tend to stress the rights and vulnerabilities of the subjects of research. Yet to divide all of those involved in the problem of research access into only two categories is to oversimplify the situation.

In the United States, at least, there are those who lean toward a hard line, demanding, on the one hand, that access to research sites in other countries be freely granted in the name of the universal commitment to science and insisting, on the other hand, that access to U.S. sites or facilities be governed by strict principles of reciprocity. There are also those in the United States who take a softer line, acknowledging the rights of other countries to impose constraints on access and waiving strict reciprocity so far as access to U.S. sites and facilities is concerned. In their postures toward countries of the Third World, those who advocate a soft line are liable to be charged with suffering from postcolonial guilt, while those who take a hard line may be excoriated as ugly Americans. And in their postures toward the Soviet Union, the soft-liners on the access issue are likely to lean more generally toward détente, while the hard-liners on access tend to assume a generally more antagonistic posture. It seems likely, though evidence is scarce, that in the countries to which Western scholars seek access, these harder and softer positions are mirrored, that is, that there are those, on the one hand, who give higher priority

to the support of the international scientific community and lower priority to national interests and those, on the other, who reverse those priorities.

Clearly, there is no widespread consensus, either within the United States or within a larger set of countries, about the very existence of rights to obtain research access or rights to restrict or deny access. In the absence of clear-cut agreement about rights, access necessarily must be negotiated, the negotiators being either governments or organizations—public or private—or individual researchers. The framework within which negotiation takes place must be established at one or another of these levels. The effectiveness of negotiations depends on many factors, as will be indicated later, some related rather directly to the circumstances of particular projects and some, like the broader politics of East-West and North-South relations or considerations of long-term United States-China relations, casting large shadows from the outside.

The process of negotiating access cannot be properly understood unless the fundamental fact is accepted that access is a problem both for those seeking and for those granting it, but not the same problem. For those seeking access, the problem is a matter of identifying and overcoming obstacles—sometimes irksome and occasionally outrageous—to valuable research; for those granting access, the problem is a matter of devising mechanisms that will, at best, keep the research by foreign scholars in line with their nation's political, cultural, and economic interests and the professional interests of local academics, and, at the very least, prevent damage to these interests. Each side in the process of negotiation must make concessions or take risks, explicitly or implicitly; and

---

U.S. scholars and administrators, and one held at the East-West Center, 11-14 December 1985, attended mainly by scholars and administrators from the countries of Southeast Asia, as well as some U.S. administrators. Lists of the participants at the two conferences are available from the author on request.

though the concessions or risks are different, each side has to yield a certain amount of autonomy. Those seeking access must yield some of the autonomy that Western researchers customarily have in selecting research topics, while those granting access must accept some degree of intrusion on their political or cultural autonomy.

Reciprocity of different kinds, then, is involved in making possible research that crosses national boundaries. Depending on political or historical circumstances, reciprocity may be more direct or less, or more formal or less. Thus in negotiations of research access between the United States and Soviet Union, in which the power of the two countries is roughly equal, direct and formal reciprocity is central to the exchange of scholars and the scholars' license to do research in the host countries. Rejections or restrictions imposed by one side meet with appropriate retaliation on the part of the other, and each side is ultimately prepared to jeopardize the continuation of research access. But reciprocity of this kind hardly exists in the relationship between the United States and the People's Republic of China: scholarly relations with China are deemed by many in the United States to be so important that, in spite of various restrictions imposed on access by the Chinese, the United States persists in turning the other cheek. In between these extremes are reciprocal relationships with countries that have more power or less vis-à-vis the United States and more—or less—cordial foreign relations. In the case of India, for example, it is at least arguable that the United States should insist on a greater degree of formal reciprocity.

The reciprocal relationships established between Western scholars and relatively weak Third World scientific communities often follow the development model. Access to research sites is exchanged for contributions on the part of the Western scholars to the nation's development. Such contributions may take various forms. They may consist of focusing research on problems that the host-country government defines as essential for the practical improvement of the conditions of life or for the generation of a sense of cultural or historical identity. Contributions may also involve, in one way or another, enhancing the quality of the local scientific community: by training researchers in fields in which little advanced training is locally available, like archaeology, forestry, or survey research; by entering into collaborative research arrangements with local scholars; or by drawing these local scholars into new networks, through the exchange of publications, the arrangement of visiting appointments, or invitations to participate in international professional meetings.

In many or most efforts to obtain research access to developing countries, successful negotiations entail some adjustment of the research priorities of the visiting scholars in terms of the priorities of the host-country government or of the local research community, as well as some transfer of resources—training, data, professional status—to the local researchers. It may be necessary to sacrifice some degree of the individualism or autonomy prized by scholars in the United States, and in the West more generally, by accepting collaborative arrangements created not so much to bring together complementary competences, but to symbolize joint participation in the research at hand. At the same time, the host-society government or research community may have to abandon certain preconceptions about equitable relationships in light of the impracticality of implementing viable collaborative projects. Basically, a good deal of negotiation involves trade-offs between equity and scientific autonomy, with national interest entering into the equation on both sides.

The extent to which research access is obtained in an amicable or antagonistic atmosphere depends considerably on the quality of the personal relationships between the visiting researchers and the local academic community, and often also on the kinds of relationships between these same visiting researchers and those members of the host-country bureaucracy who are empowered to provide necessary visas or research clearance. Good personal relationships are most likely to emerge over a long period of time, and in this respect, the natural scientists, with their well-funded, long-term projects, have a considerable advantage. Continuity is relatively easily achieved by them. Yet social scientists also can win the trust that is based on long-term interaction. The personal factor is not just a matter of familiarity; it has to do with such things as evident concern for the interests of local counterparts and for the difficulties under which they work, as well as appreciation for the scholarly contributions they have made. Acknowledgment of the importance of personal relationships is not entirely congenial to U.S. academics, who fear that departures from universalism in science may entail the blurring of distinctions between high-quality and lesser work and who worry that relationships built on personal ties may disappear along with those who created them.

The highly decentralized character of the U.S. academic system, which enhances the real or apparent autonomy of individual researchers, is in sharp contrast to the more integrated systems of other countries, in which the interests of individual scholars tend to be superseded by national interests and national policies. This disparity between the two types of systems is a factor in the emergence of difficulties in the negotiation of research access, since researchers from these different systems—from scientific communities with different basic values—operate with different assumptions of what is right and equitable.

While U.S. scholars do accept the intervention, on both sides, of official and quasi-official agencies in arranging their interactions with such countries as the Soviet Union and the People's Republic of China, they prefer to avoid establishing a role for U.S. governmental agencies in the relationships between themselves and the scientific communities of more democratic and/or less powerful countries. Not surprisingly, in the negotiation of research access to these latter countries, U.S. academics tend to question the legitimacy of the involvement of host-government agencies in reviewing their projects and making decisions about their acceptability. Rejections of projects, however few, cause considerable dismay, to the surprise of the host-country bureaucrats, and when bureaucratic delays and/or rejections are more frequent, as has been the case in India, frustration runs high. Yet from the perspective of the countries that are exercising what they consider to be legitimate control over research access, U.S. scholars appear to be lacking in appreciation of the many projects that are approved. Moreover, because a U.S. national interest in overseas research is rarely fully explicit, U.S. researchers are often not prepared for the ways in which international politics and political differences along the right-to-left spectrum can and do affect their reception overseas, while host-country governments and academics, who are more likely to take intersections between the worlds of academia and of politics for granted, see nothing unusual about applying political tests to visiting researchers and their work. Clearly, the ability of U.S. scholars, and of Western scholars more generally, to understand the conditions under which research access may be successfully negotiated is limited by scientific individualism and academic decentralization.

The structure of Western scientific communities leads to the assumption that sensitive, ethical, considerate individuals are key factors in establishing good relationships overseas and obscures the importance of systemic factors. There are access problems that may be rectified through the correct actions of individual researchers, but there are also those that are entirely beyond the control of individuals. In some cases, researchers do things right and all is well; in others, researchers also do what they think is right, and things do not work out for them. Good behavior by individuals is important but not sufficient.

Among the systemic factors are, as mentioned already, political relationships between the countries of the West and the countries of the Third World and the Eastern bloc. Political tensions between countries inevitably affect relationships between scientists, with natural scientists vulnerable especially in the area of military security and social scientists in the area of ideology. Other systemic factors are funding structures that preclude, for Western social scientists and humanists especially, long-term projects that make it possible to develop solid relationships with local scholars; more appropriate funding struc-

tures would make possible the short-term investments in the training of individuals from developing countries that produce valuable longer-term cooperation. These systemic factors include the changing conditions of U.S. academia, in which the diminishing security of faculty, especially nontenured faculty, enhances the difficulty of sacrificing individual professional advantage in the pursuit of knowledge to the interests of potential collaborators among scholars in other countries. These factors include the differences in the priorities of science between Western countries and developing countries; in the West, theoretical science is valued over applied science, while the contrary is the case in developing countries. And the systemic problems include, finally, such vast obstacles as the catastrophic decline in international communications that has resulted from the international debt problem.

POLICY IMPLICATIONS

Policies that would serve to reduce the tensions created by the need for research access and the reluctance to grant such access are, to a considerable extent, implied in the foregoing analysis of the access problem, yet it may be useful to spell out certain policy implications.

First, while individual scholars tend to believe that they are well aware of access issues and of the nature of proper conduct while carrying on research in a particular foreign country, there is reason to believe that these scholars are not as sophisticated as they think they are. Universities and professional organizations might well make it their responsibility to inform prospective petitioners for research access of the possible obstacles they may encounter in particular countries and about the history of research activities by Western scholars in these countries. It is not the case that every scholar simply knows what the various sticking points are, especially since these sticking points vary from country to country. Nor is it the case that behavior that is unquestionably ethical in the researcher's home country may not be open to challenge elsewhere. Many researchers have learned, through their own or others' painful experiences, about behavior that risks provoking resentment, but they may see these experiences in isolation rather than as part of a whole set of interrelated interactions. Careful orientation of those seeking and obtaining research access would be useful, as would the inculcation of a sense of responsibility to the entire community of Western researchers who are dependent on relations of amicability and trust in carrying on their work in particular countries.

Second, animosity and disappointment in the relationships between visiting scholars and host-country scholars might be avoided if certain assurances of mutual benefit were clearly spelled out as part of the process of seeking and granting access. What may be needed is the equivalent of prenuptial agreements between prospective spouses. If local scholars expect or hope for collaboration that is not possible, disappointment would be avoided if the scope of the actual feasible relationship between visiting and local scholars is specified in advance. Appropriate advance agreements should be encouraged and perhaps even required by funding agencies, on the one side, and by host-country agencies that grant research clearance, on the other.

Third, insofar as it is possible, it would be desirable to insulate the activities of researchers who need access from the politics that affect relationships between the researchers' country and the host country. The optimal way to do this is to remove the sphere of research from the sphere of government, but this is not altogether easy even in the countries of the West and harder yet in the more centralized countries to which research access is sought by Western scholars. In the United States, at least, sponsorship of overseas research should be either private or, if it is governmental, under the auspices of agencies like the National Science Foundation, the Smithsonian Institution, or the National Endowment for the Humanities, which are not directly identified with either foreign policy or domestic politics.

Fourth, as the nation with the most favored intellectual community in the world and a research enterprise based on the belief that openness is crucial, the United States must play a complicated role. On the one hand, the United States must strongly assert the value of the openness of research and refrain to the greatest possible extent from erecting its own barriers against foreign researchers. On the other hand, the United States should respond appropriately to the resistance of other countries to permitting research sites within their borders to be used by researchers from abroad. Sympathetic responses are in order in the case of less powerful countries, along with efforts to make the necessary intrusions more acceptable, while in the case of powerful countries and/or highly developed scientific communities, insistence on quid pro quos is in order.

Finally, the statisms that exist in the world are more and less blatant, and it is best to deal with them in appropriate terms. If government-to-government relations need to be carried into the arena of science and research, as is the case in dealings between the United States and the Soviet Union, so be it; but other kinds of relationships are possible, mediated by such entities as the overseas research centers—such as those in India and Egypt—or the joint committees of the Social Science Research Council and the American Council of Learned Societies, which include, insofar as resources permit, members from the region that is the focus of each committee's concern. Another organizational route is exemplified by the International Council of Scientific Unions, which permits bilateral arrangements in the context of multilateral structures. In general, it is important to maintain as much private and academic control over international research as possible, since the expansion of the domain of the state and the backwash from international politics are among the principal threats to research access and the valuable knowledge that results from access.

In focusing attention on the problem of research access it is important to remember that access is not an end in itself but a necessary means to the advancement of knowledge in certain academic disciplines. Successful negotiations of access are not triumphs in foreign diplomacy but agreements that the advancement of knowledge is sufficiently important that it warrants certain concessions on the part of the foreign scientists and of the host society.

ANNALS, *AAPSS*, **491**, May 1987

A Host Country's View:
The Federal Republic of Germany

By ULRICH LITTMANN

ABSTRACT: The Fulbright program is evaluated from a host country's perspective. The transition from a program in occupied Germany in 1952 to a truly binational program with sharing of funding and supervision since 1964 is shown in the historical setting, added responsibilities, and the Fulbright Commission's contributions in four areas: cultural foreign relations, academic cooperation, educational reforms, and bilateral cultural consultations. The dual goal of the Fulbright design—to advance academic knowledge and to promote mutual understanding—is pursued in binational and regional cooperation. The role of the Commission, the Board of Foreign Scholarships and the contracting governments places emphasis upon true partnership rather than the image of the Fulbright as being an American government program.

Ulrich Littmann studied history, economics, and physics in Göttingen and, in the United States, at Haverford College and Ohio University. After holding positions in industry and managing Fridtjof Nansen House in Göttingen, he began working for the Fulbright-Kommission in 1958 and has been its executive director since 1963. He also serves on the boards of several organizations concerned with international exchange and is the author of several publications.

73

E VEN though binational programs are sui generis, they do not operate by themselves but rather are, or have become, part of the national structure in each country. This is particularly evident when not only supervisory and planning functions but also funding commitments are shared. National conditions and procedures inevitably affect developments in bilateral cooperation and vice versa. A statement in Parliament by State Minister Karl Mörsch reflects this point.

The Federal Government assigns great importance to the jointly sponsored German-American academic "Fullbright Program" [*sic*] for the further development of our close relations to the United States. This program has rendered outstanding proof as the most important instrument of educational and scholarly exchanges as mutually agreed upon between the governments of both countries. The pertinent executive agreement provides a wide frame of activities that facilitates flexible approaches and thus consideration of a variety of target groups relevant for German-American exchange in academe and scholarship. Both the wide spectrum of target groups . . . and the conceptual implementation of the program—such as the promotion of German and American Studies, the priority given to projects of present needs and contemporary significance in research . . . — offer the guarantee that this program for student and scholar exchanges will also substantially contribute to promoting better knowledge of the general political situation in both countries.[1]

The Federal Republic of Germany is presented as a case study in order to depict some general features that may exist in Fulbright countries around the world and to analyze characteristics and developments specific to Germany.[2]

Germany became a member of the Fulbright program in 1952 when the young republic had not yet attained full sovereignty; in 1962 it signed the first cost-sharing agreement. Today it has one of the largest Fulbright programs, and the program has attained a most remarkable position as a binational institution—neither American nor German, but both sides claim credit for its achievements and both sides utilize its potential in maintaining bilateral cooperation and goodwill. The original setting in occupied Germany and the active involvement of the Commission in developments ever since would actually call for a biography rather than a history of the U.S.-German program,[3] and the present article can only indicate highlights. I shall not consider what the 9316 grants to U.S. nationals and the 9761 grants to Germans between 1952 and 1986 have made possible in personal careers or scholarly research, and I shall not list all the activities that the Fulbright Commission has been, and still is, pursuing. I will rather discuss some of the political and structural implications that the concept of Fulbright exchanges and their implementation have had from the perspective of a participating country.

In a broader context, this study will test the thesis of Henry Kellermann: "it is . . . the political and social benefits rather than the personal gains that will have to serve as the principal yard-sticks

1. State Minister Karl Mörsch, MdB, statement in the German Federal Parliament, 19 Dec. 1974, *Deutscher Bundestag, Stenographischer Sitzungsbericht 7/139*, p. 9609.

2. The terms "Germany" and "German" refer to the Federal Republic of Germany.

3. For the first years a comprehensive account has been rendered by Henry J. Kellermann, *Cultural Relations as an Instrument of U.S. Foreign Policy: The Educational Exchange Program Between the United States and Germany 1945-1954*, pub. no. 8931 (Washington, DC: Department of State, 1978).

in measuring the accomplishments of the [exchange] programs."[4] At the same time, there is no doubt that individual experiences and achievements as results of grants also contribute to the long-range goals of the exchange program. We usually find that an excellent grantee would probably have entered a most successful career without having been abroad, but the foreign experience does have an impact upon the direction of career activities. Similarly, not all teachers who conduct regular classes within an interchange will become textbook authors or policymaking administrators—although quite a few have—but the aggregate of experience and goodwill will be palpable when they become school principals or heads of departments and transmit their knowledge and insight to generations of students and young teacher colleagues. These examples may serve to illustrate the dilemma of all administrators of educational programs, in which short-range principles of accountability collide with long-range planning.

In a programmatic address in March 1986 the state minister of the Foreign Office, Jürgen Möllemann, observed:

I am not sure whether Senator Fulbright was aware of the extraordinary impact which the document that became known in 1946 as "Public Law 584" or the "Fulbright Law" was to have; it is in fact doubtful, considering the dry and legalistic language of the law.[5]

It is, indeed, not certain that the potential of this new instrument was fully recognized at the time when its structure and operations were molded into a legal design and moved into its early stages of implementation. It is even less certain

that the various segments of U.S. political life or the academic community have fully comprehended the entire range of the impact that the Fulbright design has had, and still has, upon developments abroad. Many factors have helped determine this impact. Here we mention three.

The first originates from a characteristic of America and the Americans: the multitude and variety of activities in which the public and the private sector share burdens and responsibilities. Contemporaries of the immediate postwar years will remember and cherish the help that the Americans offered to all those nations that suffered severe losses from World War II. When we talk about the relief work—and its concomitant spiritual uplift—of religious groups, of private foundations, or of institutions of all kinds, or when we look at the opportunities offered by the European Recovery Program under the Marshall Plan, or—last, but not least—when we point to the many programs conducted for exchange of persons, it appears as if the Fulbright program was only one of many efforts to mitigate the pains and wants that the war had left behind.

A second factor probably originated from a misunderstanding between the partners abroad and the sponsors in the United States. While the design that Senator Fulbright and the Board of Foreign Scholarships (BFS) had in mind clearly aimed at a true partnership and equal opportunities, the financial burden rested entirely upon the United States and the operational coordination was left to the BFS and its administrative arms in the U.S. Department of State or the cooperating agencies. Inadvertently, in quite a few participating countries and in many circles within the United States, the image of the exchange pro-

---

4. Ibid., p. 4.
5. Speech at Harnack House Berlin, 15 Mar. 1986; press release, Foreign Office, Bonn.

gram is one of a U.S. government program. Even the Fulbright-Hays Act of 1961, which stressed the idea of partnership through the new concept of cost sharing and shared supervision or responsibilities, could not prevent a certain image of or identification with American control or domination from developing, although this had not been the intent of the sponsors and consuls of the Fulbright program. This identification as a U.S. government program may well weaken its impact abroad where partner governments are providing funds for and creativity in program planning to promote common, rather than unilateral, interests.[6]

A third major factor follows from the first two. American government-sponsored programs have to compete with other beneficiaries of public funds and with programs of the private sector, some of which blend well into public diplomacy. The original conditions of the Fulbright program have been reversed. The Fulbright Act of 1946 disposed of funds that were or became available, and a program could be designed around those funds. When war surplus properties had been exhausted and funds under the Fulbright-Hays Act of 1961 became available from regular allocations—or from partner governments—the quality of program proposals had to justify mainly U.S. funding. After all, in the aggregate it is still the United States

that keeps the partnership of the Fulbright exchanges going. In cost-sharing countries the peculiar formal requirements for designing programs and compiling budgets according to American specifications place a particular burden upon the commission officers to interpret the U.S. requirements to the host-country administrations.

Even though there are other factors causing the particular American image of the program—such as the necessary bureaucratic tasks performed by embassies and the United States Information Agency, inevitable auditing of records, the common language, and, of course, the name "Fulbright" itself—this analysis may suffice. But, to reemphasize, all the factors just outlined have not altered the principles of the Fulbright design since 1946 nor do they constitute a dominance of the United States in any of the binational programs or commissions. This becomes all the more visible when we add views from abroad.

As we look at the concept of Fulbright exchanges we note several features that still make the exchanges unique, although certain portions have been adopted by, or transformed into, other programs in the United States as well as abroad.

Its most striking feature is that a worldwide net of bilateral exchanges has been established by executive agreements with one nation, namely, the United States. It permits, under the umbrella of a fairly simple set of guidelines, the policy statements of the BFS, the inclusion of nations of all kinds, big and small, highly industrialized or still in earlier stages of economic and academic development. It accommodates needs and interests of a broad variety as visualized by both partners to each executive agreement. It leaves room for

6. It is true that Section 102(b)(6) of the Fulbright-Hays Act leaves incentives for one-sided American programs. The more recent increase of programs that are operated out of Washington directly—regional grants, Scholar-in-Residence program—seems to point in the same direction. But cf. Advisory Panel on International Educational Exchange, "Final Report" [to United States Information Agency], mimeographed (New York: Social Science Research Council, 1986).

the partner countries to find the optimal form of bilateral cooperation, be it in the form of binational commissions or through direct governmental contact, be it by sharing fully or partially the burdens and functions in the conduct of the program. It integrates public diplomacy and private sector activities and has been remarkably free from any partisan political influence, although the very nature of educational exchange across borders always involves politics. It is a highly selective program based on competition, and yet it performs very well in promoting mutual understanding, establishing personal ties, and furthering academic cooperation. Not only is it solidly committed to binationality in programming and implementing exchanges, but it also insists upon mutuality of exchanges, that is, a two-way traffic of exchanges. It facilitates regional cooperation between host countries abroad. Finally, it has branched out far beyond its own exchangees or grantees into serving their constituencies, institutions, governments, and the public-at-large both in the United States and in the participating countries.

EXCHANGES WITH GERMANY

In Germany the impact of exchange programs has a variety of dimensions. We shall consider the historical setting, the instruments, and the impact.

The exchange programs of the early postwar years until 1954 have been described and assessed in the most comprehensive manner by Henry Kellermann. His account covers the pre-Fulbright period and the beginning of bilateral programs in occupied Germany, and by hindsight it may explain the long-range effects that the Fulbright program and the binational Commission have had since their inception in 1952. It is essen-tial to remember that the division of Germany into four occupation zones placed heavy burdens not only upon the German population, but also upon the military governments. The challenges were numerous. The country and its infrastructure lay in total destruction, refugees and millions of people expelled from their homes in Poland, eastern Germany, and Czechoslovakia had to be accommodated and fed, the economy had to be developed, and the programs to reeducate the German population to the principles of democracy—as understood by each occupation power in its own terms—were launched also in the American zone of occupation as an integral part of the total military, economic, and political operation under the auspices of the Office of Military Government (U.S.) (OMGUS). An exchange program was started for civic leaders in 1947. Compared to the humanitarian relief projects, these early exchanges were associated in the view of many Germans with occupation and reeducation efforts.

When in 1949 the Federal Republic of Germany emerged and OMGUS was changed into the High Commissioner's Office, Germany (HICOG), the principles of occupation and reeducation were transformed into the policies of reconstruction and reorientation. Reorientation programs paved the way for the new republic's integration into the Western community of nations. The cold war, the Berlin Airlift, the Marshall Plan, and the emergence of a new political structure had created the paths for new beginnings. This period also coincided with the implementation of the Smith-Mundt Act of January 1948 (Public Law 402, the Information and Educational Exchange Act of 1948), which was intended to spread information about the United States, its people, and its policies and which—unlike the Fulbright Act of 1946—operated with hard U.S. currency under regular appropriations. Exchanges between Germany and the United States became part of the worldwide exchange program that the American government has been conducting ever since, under varying authority and with almost unchanged objectives. In the young Federal Republic this HICOG program not only was the largest and probably the most effective measure to develop close political ties with the West (*Westbindung*), but it also provided established and potential leaders with firsthand knowledge of the United States and with personal friendships that facilitated cooperation in many societal and professional areas. The bulk of these exchanges were earmarked for the so-called Leader Program, to bring young German professionals and specialists to the United States. Between 1949 and 1953 HICOG programs brought 9837 visitors to the United States; of these 6470 were leader grantees and trainees, 1492 were students in various projects, and 1875 were participants in programs for teenagers. During the same period, 736 U.S. specialists were brought to Germany to serve as advisers or teachers there.[7]

Interestingly enough, the German federal government has adopted a very similar structure in its own visitors' programs and group programs (*Themenreisen*), and the objectives are similar.

A significant change in approach to educational or academic exchange occured with the U.S.-German Fulbright Agreement of 18 July 1952. It created an independent institutional identity and funding structure, thereby establishing a

7. Kellerman, *Cultural Relations*, p. 261.

separation from HICOG programs and from any notion of reeducation or reorientation.

The executive agreement and the beginnings of the Commission's work— even before the first groups of Fulbrighters traveled in 1953—laid the foundation for patterns of bilateral academic exchanges that continue into the present-day operations of many programs. Five major aspects can be identified:

1. The objectives under the agreement were summarized in the preamble: "Desiring to promote further mutual understanding between the peoples of the United States of America and the Federal Republic of Germany by a wider exchange of knowledge and professional talents through educational contacts..." the agreement supplanted the OMGUS and HICOG exchange and their objectives to familiarize Germans with the United States, its people, and its policies. The Fulbright program was clearly understood as a two-way street toward mutual understanding.

2. The program, as stated in Article 1 of the agreement, was designed for American scholars and students to come to Germany as well as for German academics to go to the United States. A balance of grants to Germans and Americans not only has been a tradition of the Fulbright program, but it was most readily adopted by the German Academic Exchange Service and in university partnerships. To this extent the agreement implied that German scholarship was returning to academic standards without ideological limitations and that it deserved to be re-accepted in the international academic community as an equal partner.

3. The Commission itself became a unique body. The agreement stipulated

in Article 4 that "the Chief of the Diplomatic Mission of the United States of America . . . shall have the power to appoint and remove the [five] citizens of the United States of America on the Commission. . . . The [five] members of the Federal Republic of Germany shall be appointed and may be removed by the Federal Republic of Germany." Under this provision the Commission became the first board on which the representatives of the still occupied Federal Republic had equal rights with the U.S. members. Notwithstanding the clauses that necessitated American privileges in appointing the chairperson and approving the budget, German board members embarked upon their new role as partners from the first Commission meeting, held 19 September 1952, on. The name "United States Educational Commission" was immediately translated into "Fulbright Commission," and its credibility and reputation as a truly binational institution has since been enhanced by ensuring trust and partnership.

4. One of the outstanding features of the agreement for the binational Commission and the academic community has been the role and position of the BFS, described in Article 2. The very fact that neither the U.S. Department of State nor the United States Information Service in Bonn but rather the BFS was to become the partner of the Commission in planning exchanges and in assuring the quality of the program and its grantees has been, and still is, the basis for cooperation and for maintaining the integrity of the Commission's efforts.

5. Funding and expenditures, under Article 8 of the 1952 agreement, could be arranged in local currency only, that is, in deutsche marks. Therefore the Commission could pay for transporta-

tion for all its grantees, and it could also pay for maintenance and tuition of American grantees in Germany. But it had to rely on other outside funds to provide for the German grantees in the United States, and HICOG, the Institute of International Education, American foundations, private donors, and colleges or universities cooperated in the pragmatic American spirit. This in itself was a new experience for Germans, who were accustomed to the tradition of state dominance in funding and controlling educational activities. In fact, the success of the early years of Fulbright exchanges depended largely upon the cooperation and interaction between the government and the private sector, and this interaction has now become so evident in a large number of other bilateral exchanges that occasional withdrawals of funds or services from the U.S. private or public sectors are regarded—or, rather, misunderstood—as an expression of political reorientation.

The Fulbright Agreement of 1952 facilitated cultural cooperation in several respects. The general Cultural Agreement between the U.S. and the Federal Republic of Germany, which had been under consideration since 1951, was effected by an exchange of notes in April 1953 signed by Chancellor Adenauer and Secretary of State Dulles.[8] The German state secretary, Walter Hallstein, at the opening ceremony of the Fulbright program in September 1952, expressed the hope of the German government that the implementation of "this activity should constitute a [first] stage in the efforts to bring both peoples closer together."[9] In retrospect, Dr. Hans Arnold, former assistant secretary

8. Ibid., pp. 159 ff., 266 ff.

of state for cultural affairs in the Foreign Office, noted the two characteristics of bilateral cultural relations: "In our cultural relations towards overseas regions U.S.-German cooperation has priority over the other activities; and within German-American cultural relations the academic and scholarly relations rank highest because they provide the strongest impulses for the overall relations."[10]

Because in Germany foreign cultural relations are regarded as the third pillar in foreign policy, next to political security and economic relations, it is not surprising that German politicians assess the Fulbright program not only as an educational opportunity but also as a trendsetter in foreign policy.

The German federal president, Dr. Richard von Weizsäcker, in addressing American Fulbright grantees from all programs in Europe at the Fulbright Berlin Week in March 1986, observed that the basic ideas of the Fulbright Program—partnership by common goals and mutual concern—have assumed worldwide dimensions. On the same occasion the state minister in the Foreign Office, Jürgen Möllemann, emphasized that the biblical motto "to beat swords into plough-shares," which symbolized the Fulbright Act, has seized peoples in East and West, and a few weeks later the deputy assistant secretary of state for cultural affairs, Dr. Karl Heinz Neukirchen, referred to the confidence-building nature of the Fulbright design as a forerunner to the Helsinki negotiations. A few years ago a major event in Germany's cultural relations, in particular with Third World countries, the Symposion '80, under the leadership of Dr. Hildegard Hamm-Brücher, then state minister in the Foreign Office, showed that the concept of Fulbright exchanges had deeply affected all educational programs of development aid.

In contrast to the United States, where the political impact of the Fulbright program upon domestic affairs is marginal, the program in Germany exerted considerable influence upon organizational involvement and upon educational policies.

In contrast to the more flexible, individualized practice of appointments on the American side, German membership on the Commission's board reflects organizational interest and constitutional considerations. Each of the five German members represents either a federal ministry, the 11 states of the Federal Republic, or a body of academic self-administration.[11] This structure facilitates cooperation with all major organizations of higher education and research such as the Alexander von Humboldt Foundation, the German Academic Exchange Service, the German Research Society, the Max Planck Society as well as with all state ministries and institutions of higher learning, and it permits coordination of questions of bilateral concern far beyond the Commission's own exchange program.

9. Minutes, First meeting of the United States Educational Commission in Germany, 29 Sept. 1952, p. 2.

10. Hans Arnold, *Auswärtige Kulturpolitik; ein Überblick aus deutscher Sicht*. (Munich, Vienna: Carl Hanser Verlag, 1980), p. 79.

11. At present these are the Foreign Office, the Federal Ministry for Education and Science, the State Secretary for Higher Education and Research in Lower Saxony, the West German Conference of University Rectors and the German Academic Exchange Service; since the new agreement of 1964 the States' Commission on International Treaties has to concur before the foreign minister can appoint his nominees to the Commission.

Because of the composition of German membership on the Commission, the Fulbright program offered major contributions to educational reforms in Germany, where the entire educational system is supervised and funded by the state. As samples we mention early university linkages, professional exchanges such as the so-called Cleveland Program[12] and teacher interchanges, the inclusion of new types of educational institutions, and many pilot projects.

A TRULY BINATIONAL PROGRAM

With the advent of the Mutual Educational and Cultural Exchange Act (the Fulbright-Hays Act of 1961, Public Law 87-256), new perspectives were offered for continuing the principles and structure of the Fulbright program. The most important innovations were in financing, allowing dollar allocations and contributions from host countries and the reconfirmation of shared responsibilities with the partner government.

The German federal government immediately considered how it could contribute to establishing a truly binational program. In December 1961, only weeks after Public Law 87-256 had been signed into law, informal discussions began in the Foreign Office.[13] On 20 November 1962 a cost-sharing agreement was signed—the first among Fulbright countries—but it took another 14 months before the German side obtained parliamentary approval and the agreement went into force, on 17 January 1964.[14]

As specified in Article 1 of the cost-sharing agreement, the Commission emerged with the legal status of a "binational organization" with certain privileges and immunities granted to U.N. specialized agencies. This principle served as a model for the Agreement on Franco-German Youth Exchange of 5 July 1963, although the scope of these exchanges is somewhat different from the U.S.-German Fulbright program. There are two honorary chairpersons, the German foreign minister and the U.S. ambassador. Approvals of budgets and special services, appointment of the auditor, who also functions on behalf of general auditing offices of each country, and other supervisory responsibilities are equally shared by the secretary of state of the United States of America[15] and the minister of foreign affairs of the Federal Republic of Germany.

Today the national identity of the program has become somewhat ambiguous. While its binational character is recognized and stressed in legal matters, its administration is frequently viewed

---

12. This program eventually has become an exchange jointly sponsored by the Federal Ministry for Youth, Family and Health, U.S. Information Agency, and the Fulbright-Kommission; it now operates under the name of "Council of International Programs."

13. Several German Commission members met informally on 12 December 1961 to discuss the internal conditions and factors for an amendment of the then existing agreement or for an entirely new agreement; the author was informed by Min.-Direktor Dr. Dieter Sattler the next day. Official negotiations, however, did not commence

until after the Executive Order of 25 June 1962 had delegated specific functions and responsibilities to the various branches of the U.S. Administration.

14. *Bundesgesetzblatt*, 1964, pt. II, no. 2, pp. 27-32.

15. The transfer of the administrative functions from the Department of State to the United States International Communication Agency and its subsequent redesignation as United States Information Agency did not require an amendment to the agreement itself.

as a German institution in Germany and as an American program in the United States. At bilateral meetings, which the Commission is sometimes asked to attend as adviser to both sides, it is referred to as the "third delegation." Although the name "Fulbright" does not appear in any of the agreements, the Commission, with a complicated official name in English and German, adopted the designation of "Fulbright-Kommission."[16]

But the funding of the program from both sides and its diplomatic immunity permit long-range developments and promote innovative and experimental projects.

The Commission interacts with the private sector and various public sectors in both countries, and it serves as a model for other exchanges such as the Youth Exchange Initiative and the U.S. Congress-Bundestag Program. As American Ambassador Richard Burt pointed out in 1986, this spirit has fostered "private initiative and individual creativity—people, not governments, have intensified contacts between the United States and the nations of Western Europe as never before."[17]

The ten U.S. and German members and their deputies on the Commission's board deal with questions of equivalences of degrees and curricula, student counseling, study-abroad programs generally, guaranteed student loans for study abroad, and other topics. Their relations to the academic world in the United States and the Federal Republic of Germany are quite different.[18] In the

United States the public sector constitutes just one element in the concert of educational institutions, associations, and foundations, and the government can exercise only limited influence upon higher education. In Germany, however, the government, together with the appropriation committees of the federal or state parliaments, has considerably more authority to support or limit the international activities of the academic community. At the same time it has to guard the autonomy of academe, the arts, and culture. It is the government that has to maintain the balance between its political mission and the interests of its frequently critical cultural constituency. Dr. Barthold C. Witte has characterized this situation as "external cultural policy in the tension between politics and culture."[19]

However, there are problems in developing fully the ideal of binational partnership.

The members on the Commission's board represent the American concept of public diplomacy on the one side and the German concept of educational and international policy on the other side. Internal factors of educational policy have played an important role for the German members. They must deal with the whole gamut of German educational policy and exchanges into which Fulbright is incorporated. The Americans are concerned only with the Fulbright program.

For the German side—that is, the Parliament, the government, the eleven states, and the academic community—

16. Minutes, Sixty-second meeting of the (German) Fulbright Commission, 28 Feb. 1962, p. 2.

17. Richard R. Burt, "The Fulbright Program: Moving toward an Open World" (Address at Harnack House Berlin, 15 Mar. 1986); press release, United States Information Service, Bonn.

18. Ulrich Littmann, "Academic Exchange

and Its Impact," in *America and Western Europe*, ed. Karl Kaiser and Hans-Peter Schwarz (Lexington, MA: Lexington Books, 1977), pp. 63-84.

19. *Universitas*, 27:17-28 (1985). Dr. Witte is the director of the Cultural Division of the Foreign Office.

the Fulbright program and its local administration clearly are a part of the fabric of the political, social, and cultural relations between the two countries. The financial or programmatic contributions from the German side are considered to be an international commitment. Hence, all administrative or financial issues raised by the American partners within ordinary budget reviews in Washington are examined carefully in Bonn as a possible indication of an American shift in overall bilateral relations.

The need to harmonize national requirements becomes apparent in the administration of the program itself. Seemingly simple procedures such as compiling the budget, financial reporting, and rendering accounts must follow the standards of both countries, and one side's procedural guidelines easily clash with the legal requirements of the other; that solutions to conflicting regulations have been found in each instance is no small achievement of the program. As a somewhat strange by-product of the Fulbright program, its secretariat receives numerous requests from administrations and courts to explain legal differences, and its expertise in comparative bureaucracy benefits mostly non-Fulbrighters.

It is in the context of its broader role that the Commission has been requested by both governments to review developments in bilateral academic cooperation over and beyond Fulbright exchanges.[20]

CONCLUSION

The Fulbright program in Germany has never been static. It has responded

20. "German-American Exchanges: A Report on Facts and Developments" (May 1980), prepared and published as mimeographed document at the request of both governments, has become the best known of such activities.

to changing needs and changing conditions and has promoted changes when they were in the common interest of its constituencies. Today, changes in the political culture and in bilateral and international relations are bringing forth important new challenges. The dual goal of the Fulbright design, the promotion of academic knowledge and mutual understanding, has been placed in a new context. The founding generation did not need a definition of either goal. Today, with the emphasis on new learning opportunities—continuing education and midcareer training may serve as examples—and with the diversified and often critical attitudes of the successor generation toward their own and other societies, the term "mutual understanding" is no longer self-evident and no longer describes common interests. The perception of the host country today is much more influenced by mass media before prospective exchanges even apply. This does not render the Fulbright program obsolete, but it requires a new look at cooperative efforts. The goals remain as basic as they were in 1946.

The new generations claim their own mandate in new contexts, and a host of exchange opportunities have appeared—some structured, others loose. The demand for financial aid remains high because of the high expectations that are associated with international exchange. We have to see to it that unsuccessful applicants—that means 90 percent of applicants in some categories—do not turn against the idea of international education as such and against the host country that seems to reject them.

The Fulbright program cannot and should not become the only or the largest force of contact between the United States and its many partner countries. But only a strong, viable, and flexible grant program will lay the foundation upon which the governments and the private sector can build the variety of opportunities that the future demands. Hence the Fulbright program must retain its integrity and selectivity. To use terms from genetics, even if the Fulbright program's phenotype seems to blend in with many other programs, its genotype will provide a hope that the coordinated efforts will serve the interests of the society at large.

Regional cooperation between Fulbright commissions, especially in Europe, has added a new dimension to the bilateral concept. Grantees are shared through the Interfoundation Lecturer Program, which invites an American Fulbright scholar to give occasional lectures in another country, European Seminars are conducted by the Commission in Belgium and Luxemburg for U.S. Fulbrighters from all European countries, and a midyear Berlin Week is conducted for American Fulbrighters. The German government has considered the feasibility of a consolidated European-U.S. Fulbright program. At the same time, there is no question that the European developments, cooperation, and the search for the promotion of European internal programs may affect the transatlantic dialogue. On a broader scale, it is conceivable that demographic developments in Europe, with declining numbers of students, may attract more Third World students to Europe and thereby ignite a keen competition between the institutions of higher learning on both sides of the Atlantic. This will add a new role to the binational Fulbright commissions and their partners in the United States.

The partnership and the national component were best expressed by Senator Fulbright himself when, at a convocation at Bonn University, where he is one of three Honorary Senators, he observed:

The purpose of international education transcends the conventional aims of foreign policy. This purpose is nothing less than an effort to expand the scope of man's moral and intellectual capacity to the extent necessary to close the fateful gap between human needs and human capacity. We must try, therefore, through education to realize something new in this world . . . —cooperatively rather than competitively.[21]

Professor Dr. Karl Carstens, then president of the Federal Parliament and later president of the Federal Republic, encompassed the same theme from a German perspective:

Those among us who are familiar with the general discussion of cultural foreign policy will perceive . . . that the work of the Fulbright-Kommission is based on a concept of cultural politics that is closely tied to the terms of an "expanded definition of Culture" from which our current cultural foreign relations are formed. In this context culture thus understood embraces, as noted in the report of the Reform Commission of the Foreign Service, "the entire range of living reality; extends from literature to technology, from issues of social policies to problems of environmental protection; it includes the past and present with a view towards future challenges."[22]

However, we must not forget that, as in other matters, it is the people—the grantees and hosts, the landladies and the university presidents, and, last but not least, the taxpayers—who make this unique program viable.

21. Quoted from "The German-American Fulbright Program 1970-1977," mimeographed (Bonn: Fulbright-Kommission, 1978), p. i.
22. Ibid., p. ii.

ANNALS, *AAPSS*, 491, May 1987

Multiple Cost Sharing:
The Japan Experience

By CAROLINE A. MATANO YANG

ABSTRACT: Among the approximately 120 countries with Fulbright programs, Japan's Fulbright program is the only Fulbright program where cost sharing by the United States and the host society is on a fifty-fifty basis and where the Fulbright alumni contribute approximately 15 percent of the program's budget. This article analyzes the factors behind this unique multiple cost-sharing of the Fulbright program, particularly the strong support from the Japanese alumni. Among the contributing elements are the historical relationship between Japan and the United States, the rapid economic development of Japan, cultural factors peculiar to Japan, timing, and the right leader. These factors converged in 1982, the thirtieth anniversary year of the Japan program, and resulted in the organization of nine regional alumni associations within a period of two months and the launching of a fund-raising campaign to invite more Americans to Japan. The campaign developed a momentum of its own and evolved into the establishment of a permanent alumni Fulbright Foundation in 1986 through which contributions to the regular program are made. The entire alumni movement has served as a catalyst to the expansion and dynamism of the Fulbright program in Japan and may offer some lessons for other programs.

Caroline A. Matano Yang (B.A., Smith College; M.A., Michigan State University) first came in contact with the Fulbright program in 1967-68 as a Fulbrighter's spouse. She joined the Japan Fulbright program in 1972 and was appointed executive director a year later. In 1984 she was awarded the Japanese minister of foreign affairs award for her contributions to a better international understanding of Japan, the first foreigner and woman to be so recognized. She has previously worked at the United Nations in New York and at the International Center of Michigan State University.

AUTONOMY from national poli- tics, binational administration, and cost sharing are concepts that have been central to the Fulbright program. The implementation of these concepts, however, has been uneven during the first 40 years of the program. While funding for the program has ebbed and flowed according to the administration in power, the value of the program itself has never become a political issue. In Japan during the violent anti-U.S. demon- strations of 1960 over the Japanese-U.S. Security Treaty that forced President Eisenhower to cancel his visit to Japan and led to Prime Minister Kishi's resig- nation, the Fulbright program was totally unaffected and continued with business as usual. Its reputation as a program free from U.S.-Japanese poli- tics was firmly established even during the first 28 years of unilateral U.S. funding. Iran and other countries, how- ever, demonstrate that this perspective is not universal.

The implementation of binational administration and cost sharing have also not progressed in 40 years as much as one might expect, since even today only 40 out of 120 countries with Ful- bright programs have some form of direct or indirect cost sharing, and only 41 have binational commissions estab- lished by treaty or executive agreement between the United States and the host country. Among these, Japan's program is unique for two reasons: it is the only program where cost sharing between the two governments is based on the princi- ple of equality, and it is the only one where the alumni contribute roughly 15 percent, or close to half a million dollars, annually to the cost of the total program. Even though West Germany and Spain have larger programs, those programs do not include such cost-sharing ele-

ments. In West Germany the government bears over half the costs with no private sector support, while in Spain the gov- ernment and a consortium of banks are the major supporters of the program. Japan's program integrates binational and alumni cost sharing in a unique way that reflects historical and cultural factors.

THE PRINCIPLE OF EQUALITY

Fifty-fifty cost sharing by the two governments reflects the historical rela- tionship between Japan and the United States, especially since World War II. When negotiations on cost sharing began with the Japanese government, the United States had not expected that the Japanese would offer to share half the burden. This offer undoubtedly was a reflection of the political and economic ethos of the 1970s, when the economy spiraled upward, the yen grew in strength as the dollar was devalued, and Japan regained its political and psychological confidence especially vis-à-vis its big brother, the United States. The new agreement covering the Fulbright pro- gram signed on 24 December 1979, replacing the original agreement of 1951, embodied this principle of equality not only as an ideal but as a reality. With the 1979 agreement[1] the Fulbright program

1. The 1979 agreement, in fact, does not even mention the Fulbright program. The Japanese concept of *tatemae*, the surface appearance, and *honne*, the true base or reality, comes into play here. Thus the agreement reflects the *tatemae* of a new program supported on a fifty-fifty basis, although the *honne* is the continuation of the Fulbright program, which is recognized as a U.S. program. The Japanese government could not logically agree to support half of what is essentially a U.S. government program; thus there is no mention of Fulbright exchanges. After the agree- ment was signed, resulting in a change of the

in Japan became the only program in any field between the two governments founded and administered on a fifty-fifty basis. In one year the budget doubled, and through 1986 it has increased annually as each side has striven to fulfill its 50 percent obligation, if not for a given year, then at least through the medium and long term.

As any business executive will testify, however, any binational fifty-fifty joint venture is fraught with management problems. Since neither side can push through its will, much time must be devoted to building consensus and shaping compromise. In the long term there could have been a debilitating effect on the program since bold, new initiatives tend to be discouraged or watered down by compromise.

The entry of the Japanese alumni as an additional pillar of support for the program beginning in 1982, the thirtieth anniversary year of the Japan program, contributed to softening this potentially negative effect. The alumni, with their fund-raising campaign to invite more Americans to Japan under the program, have added a new dimension to the principle of cost sharing and have enabled a significant expansion of the program on the American side. From the very beginning in 1951, the Japanese grantees— whose total number of 6000 is almost five times that of the 1300 Americans —consisted of graduate students, professors, young journalists, government officials, young businesspersons, graphic

and performing artists, and other bright, ambitious Japanese from all fields and professions. The American side of the program, however, has been overwhelmingly academic. Alumni involvement has enabled American journalists, lawyers, government employees, and businesspersons to receive Fulbright grants, giving the program a new breadth in keeping with the current state of Japan-United States relations.

What are the factors that motivated the alumni and the Japanese public to respond so enthusiastically in support of the program? The program's founder, Senator Fulbright, and others have wondered why other countries with equally mature programs and with as many or more alumni could not carry out a similar fund-raising campaign in support of the program. The following analysis of the Japanese experience may provide part of the answer.

THE TIME ELEMENT

In 1982, 30 years after the establishment of the Fulbright program, many of the early alumni had reached their late fifties and early sixties, an age when, in Japan, one is at the peak of one's career whether in business, government, or academe:[2] (Table 1 gives a sampling of the key positions occupied by alumni.) It was a time in the alumni's lives for

---

commission's name from "U.S. Educational Commission in Japan" to "Japan-U.S. Educational Commission," the Japanese agreed that for practical—*honne*—purposes, "Fulbright Program" in paranthesis could be used after the name of the commission since it was widely recognized in Japan. In this way, both the *tatemae* and *honne* of the situation have been served.

2. Included among the alumni are approximately 1000 Japanese who received scholarships between 1949 and 1951 under the occupation. These scholarships are referred to as GARIOA (Government Aid and Relief in Occupied Areas) grants. With the signing of the Japanese-U.S. Peace Treaty in 1951, the agreement establishing the Fulbright program was signed on 26 August 1951, superseding the GARIOA grants. The Japanese public identifies these two programs as essentially the same although GARIOAns take pride in being the first to go to the United States.

looking back, a time when the desire to contribute something to society was coupled with the economic means to do so. Looking back meant recollecting the stark, hungry days of the early 1950s, when many were still struggling to recover from the war, when America was the land of opportunity for the defeated but bright, ambitious Japanese, when three meals a day was far from assured—a sharp contrast to their current comfortable status as leaders of society. The thirtieth anniversary therefore coincided with what could be called the golden period in the professional and personal lives of the Fulbrighters of the 1950s who became the natural leaders of the alumni movement.[3]

THE CULTURAL FACTOR: *ONGAESHI*

As important as the time element was the Japanese sense of *ongaeshi*, the concept of returning a favor that has been received. In a society where human relationships take priority over all else, receiving favors and returning obligations permeate all aspects of life. Japanese speak of their *on-jin*, a person to whom one is particularly obligated for personal or professional reasons. Gift giving is one manifestation of *ongaeshi*, which pervades all sectors of society. One always gives a gift whether for an

3. Had the anniversary occurred five or ten years later, many of these leaders in various sectors would have retired from their leadership roles, losing access to the staff support that they were able to utilize for the fund-raising campaign. As alumni have become younger, their perception of the Fulbright grant has changed, reflecting the political and economic changes in Japan and the political and economic differences between Japan and the United States. The younger alumni perceive the grant as the most prestigious among grants now available, and the economic benefits, while appreciated, are not as crucial as they were to the grantees of the 1950s and 1960s.

informal or formal visit. An office colleague always returns from a business or pleasure trip with a box of sweets for co-workers. There are two formal periods during the year, summer and the year-end, when gifts are sent to those to whom one has been obligated, not only during the past year, but during one's life up to that point—a teacher, doctor, supervisor, business associate, or a marriage go-between. The fund-raising campaign was the perfect vehicle for grateful alumni to reciprocate the gift of the Fulbright grant they had received from the United States. "*Ongaeshi*" became a major slogan of the campaign and was readily grasped by the alumni and the public. It may have been the strongest single factor in the success of the fund-raising campaign.[4]

POLITICAL AND ECONOMIC FACTORS

Beginning in the 1970s, Japan's economic growth leaped forward, with the yen rising as an international currency. Japanese began to travel abroad freely as businesspersons, tourists, and honeymooners and for short-term study. By 1980 the trade imbalance with the United States had grown to the point where daily newspapers were dominated by articles on economic frictions between the two countries. Many of the stories were American criticisms of Japan for the trade deficit, which was attributed not only to closed markets but to Japa-

4. This strong *ongaeshi* feeling resulted in what alumni called the Sentimental Journey to the United States, in 1984, when approximately 100 alumni and their families traveled to Washington, D.C., to express their appreciation to the U.S. government for the generosity bestowed on them as citizens of a defeated nation. They visited the White House and the Capitol, held a discussion with Senator Fulbright, then dispersed to the universities that they had attended as Fulbrighters.

TABLE 1
KEY POSITIONS HELD BY JAPANESE ALUMNI, 1982-86

Supreme Court, including chief justice	4
Diet members	7
Government officials	
Vice minister of foreign affairs	2
Vice minister of education	2
Vice minister of finance	1
Ambassadors	35
Senior officials, including councilors, director-generals, directors	27
University presidents, including six of the nine former imperial universities	23
Business executives, including presidents, vice-presidents, managing directors	45
Media, including presidents, editors, editorial writers, television newscasters	27
Writers, critics, commentators	14

nese working too hard, saving too much, and not doing enough for developing countries. Such assertions were often put forth with disregard for the facts. Many of the stories reflected the wide perception gap about Japan held by the United States and by Japan itself. The United States regarded it as an economic giant, and Japan still regarded itself as a resource-poor, vulnerable country. The alumni were concerned by these developments and believed that a fund-raising campaign to invite more Americans to Japan would be a concrete gesture of their concern that would contribute in the long term to better mutual understanding.

THE INTERNATIONALIZATION OF JAPAN

Together with Japan's emergence as an economic power was the growing— and peculiarly Japanese—concern with the necessity for Japan to international-ize, whether in business, government, or academe. The meaning of "international-ization" varies according to the source, but frequently it refers to increasing the number of foreign students and scholars at Japanese universities, serving as a host family to foreigners, hiring foreign

employees, liberalizing or opening up the financial market to foreign firms, and for cities other than Tokyo, building an international center and attracting international conventions. This concern with becoming more international reflects the Japanese belief in their basic homogeneity and uniqueness going back to the days of the Tokugawa era when Japan closed itself off from the world for over 200 years. This belief in the necessity for Japan to internationalize, in accord with its economic status, in order to be respected by the world has been another element in the success of the fund-raising campaign, especially in regions outside Tokyo such as Fukuoka, Hiroshima, Sendai, and Okinawa where funds raised locally have been used to invite American Fulbrighters to that prefecture, a tangible sign of becoming more international.

THE RIGHT LEADER

Bringing together these diverse elements was the right leader. The alumnus designated in 1982 by the Fulbright program commission and a group of representative alumni as the organizer of the alumni movement embodied all the factors described previously. He was a 1954 Fulbrighter at the University of Illinois who had served in the war and had worked for general headquarters during the occupation. At age 59 he was the chairman and chief executive officer of the Japanese subsidiary of a major American corporation that was known for its philanthropic activities in education in the United States and that gave him its blessings for Fulbright activities. He was an alumnus who believed the Fulbright grant had made a direct contribution to his successful career as an international businessman. Beyond this serendipity was an atypical—for Japanese—personality: dynamic and persuasive, he also had the ability in a status-conscious society to quickly befriend either a secretary, the president of a bank, or a university president, coupled with a keen sense of timing. The Japanese found this Fulbright salesman irresistible while the Americans found him comfortable.

This organizer or "head of the working committee" was teamed with a titular chairman whose position as the president of a major newspaper was instantly recognizable throughout Japan and who provided valuable publicity for the Fulbright program and the alumni movement. As a 1952 Fulbrighter at the University of Wisconsin, he bridged the gap between the last group to receive grants under Government Aid and Relief in Occupied Areas (see footnote 2) and the first Fulbright class in 1952. The alumni naturally rallied round these two complementary leaders.

OTHER FACTORS

Finally, the role of the commission and its secretariat must be mentioned. No extra staff were hired at any time. The same number of staff dating back to 1972 carried on the expanded grant program and educational advising services while taking on the new tasks of organizing the alumni into nine regional associations and conducting the fundraising campaign. As an American, I firmly believe that this was possible because of the conscientious and devoted Japanese staff, who embody the Japanese work ethic that continues to puzzle the world.

The commission took a relatively minor role in the entire movement, one that could be described as acquiescence rather than active encouragement. Again, this reflects cultural differences and the equal cost sharing of the program by the two governments. Historically, philanthropy in general and participation by the private sector in government activities have been actively encouraged in the United States. In Japan, philanthropy is very new and began taking hold only in the 1970s with the establishment of many foundations. It is still discouraged, however, by the tax laws. Similarly, the government, which has historically been paternalistic, and the private sector have been clearly separate with little overlapping. Given this background, the Japanese government members of the commission seemed occasionally to view the alumni involvement in the program as somewhat of an intrusion that had to be tolerated because of the American government's enthusiasm and encouragement, emanating not only from American commission members but from Washington, D.C., as well, and because of the Japanese government members' realization of the intrinsic worth of alumni support for the program.

FULBRIGHT FOUNDATION ESTABLISHED

On 31 March 1986 a new alumni Fulbright Foundation, formally named the Japan-United States Educational Exchange Promotion Foundation, was established to institutionalize permanently the alumni's fund-raising for the Fulbright program. Since 1982 the alumni have received over $2.5 million, and they plan to fund 10 to 12 awards to Americans each year, with an approximate value of $500,000. Beginning as a thirtieth-anniversary event in 1982, the fund-raising developed a momentum of its own, due to the crucial factors described, until it evolved into a permanent foundation.

After five years, U.S. government funding for the program is again on the wane because of the Gramm-Rudman deficit-reduction bill. In Japan, too, budgets have ceased to grow because of the administrative reform movement. Therefore support for the program by the alumni's Fulbright Foundation takes on an even more significant role. The two governments, however, cannot afford to become complacent about this support, for erosion of government support for a program to which the alumni have devoted so much effort may well have a negative impact on future fund-raising.

The applicability of the Japanese experience in multiple cost sharing to other Fulbright programs will depend on the nature of the host country's relationship with the United States and the unique national environment in which each program operates. What can be concluded, however, is that alumni involvement in the Fulbright program of any country can only have a positive catalytic effect on the program as a whole.

The Fulbright Program
in Africa, 1946 to 1986

By ADELAIDE M. CROMWELL

ABSTRACT: The history of the Fulbright program in Africa is one of slowly growing political and economic interest in the continent and an ongoing adjustment to radical political and social changes. The program has followed the directive of avoiding all appearances of cultural imperialism and keeping apart from political or bureaucratic interference. Responding to the growth of universities in Africa and the expanding interest and expertise of American students and scholars, the program grew rapidly in the 1970s and was strengthened in 1978 with the addition of the Hubert H. Humphrey North/South Fellowships for midcareer civil servants and in 1980 by the University Affiliation Program and the African-American Issues Center Program. The Fulbright has been largest in the largest countries or those of greatest interest geopolitically to the United States—Nigeria, South Africa, Kenya, Tanzania, and Liberia. The Republic of South Africa presents the greatest challenge to an exchange program founded on academic excellence and free intellectual inquiry.

Adelaide M. Cromwell is director of the Afro-American Studies Program and professor emerita of sociology at Boston University. She holds an A.B. from Smith College and a Ph.D. degree from Radcliffe. Her most recent books are The Dynamics of the African/Afro-American Connection from Dependency to Self-Reliance, *which she edited, and* An African Victorian Feminist: The Life and Times of Adelaide Smith Casely Hayford, 1868-1960.

NOTE: I am most appreciative of the assistance on this article from Dr. Curtis E. Huff, chief, Africa Branch, Academic Exchanges Division, members of his staff, and Ms. Linda Rhoad, executive associate of the Council for International Exchange of Scholars.

IN addressing the concluding luncheon commemorating the thirtieth anniversary of the Fulbright program, Senator Fulbright clearly articulated the rationale for its existence:

As World War II was ending . . . in order to create a consistency for the concept of a United Nations we needed a program of this kind in which people from all over the world would come to know one another and to understand and respect the traditions and cultures and values of other people.[1]

At this meeting, Davidson Nicol, executive director of the United Nations Institute for Training and Research, reminded the group that "for the first time in modern times, the small nations of Africa and Asia have acquired membership in the community of nations with a voice in all matters of concern to them. . . . The Afro-Asian states," he felt, "have introduced flexibility into world affairs and have helped to reverse the trend toward global bi-polarity."[2]

It is apparent that the Fulbright program would have its greatest challenge in implementing the expectations of Senator Fulbright within the context described by Dr. Nicol. For at the time of its conceptualization, most of Africa, except Liberia, Ethiopia, and the Republic of South Africa, was still colonized and therefore not free to enter into such meaningful relations with the United States. However, a cautious inquiry into the opportunities for such a program was initiated in the 1950s by Alan Pifer, then executive director of the British Fulbright Commission, who made a long survey trip to Africa on behalf of the commission to see how the Fulbright program could best serve the then British territories in Africa.[3]

But, understandably, in the United States Africa had not been viewed as an important concern for foreign policy.[4] In 1939, for example, when World War II began, the United States had only three legations, three consulates general, eight consulates, and one consulate agency in all of Africa. It was not until 1943 that a separate office of African affairs was organized within the Bureau of Near Eastern, South Asian and African Affairs. In 1950, Assistant Secretary of State George C. McGhee made the first high-level declaration of American policy toward Africa—and five years later when, as a spin-off of World War II, programs of African studies were under way in American universities, the Department of State began to send from one to four foreign service officers a year to these universities for a year of academic study of Africa.

The history of the Fulbright program in sub-Saharan Africa is one of slowly growing political and academic interest in the continent and an adjustment to the radical political and social changes occurring there, with the emergence after 1960 of 26 independent political entities.[5] The challenge of Africa for the

---

1. Robert J. Armbruster, ed., *A Process of Global Enlightenment, International Education: Link for Human Understanding* (Washington, DC: Board of Foreign Scholarships, 1976), p. 5.

2. Ibid., p. 22.

3. Fulbright Alumni Association, *Newsletter,* 9(1):1 (Winter 1986).

4. Vernon McKay, "American Interest in Africa," in Vernon McKay, ed., *Africa in the United States* (New York: MacFadden-Bartell, 1967), pp. 10 ff.

5. As the subsequent data will verify, the Fulbright program in Africa adjusted to the political demarcations of the continent then followed by the Department of State, beginning with an endeavor to include the entire continent—except for Egypt, which was considered a part of the Near East and Southeast Asia—and gradually altering the lines to suit practical and political

cultural programs of the United States is, therefore, that although Africa has rapidly minimized its political and economic ties to Europe and Great Britain and is ostensibly outside the orbit of a direct East-West conflict, it remains a factor to be counted both politically and economically in foreign policy and uniquely as the original home of a large and increasingly vocal sector of the American public.

A review of the Fulbright program in Africa reveals the endeavors to face these changes, intensified by the desire of the United States to recognize each political entity, no matter how young or fragile, as worthy of its attention and friendship—an expectation reciprocated by these small, fragile African countries. Almost every innovation in the implementation of the Fulbright program, deliberately or coincidentally, has been designed to address the changes in Africa as well as in much of the so-called Third World while at the same time following its own directive of avoiding all appearances of cultural imperialism and keeping the program free of either political or bureaucratic interference.[6]

As the sine qua non of a meaningful academic exchange program is the existence of a university or institution of higher learning, Africa has presented a formidable problem. Other than Fourah Bay College in Sierra Leone, started in 1827, and the Liberia College of Liberal and Fine Arts and Science, started in 1862 and acquiring university status in 1951, there was no university in Africa south of the Sahara and north of the Republic of South Africa before 1946. At that time the Universities of Khartoum in the Sudan and Makerere in Uganda were established.[7] During the next few years universities were rapidly established in Africa—in Ghana, Nigeria, the Belgian Congo, and Southern Rhodesia. But to a large extent the professors were expatriates whose citizenship and long-term careers lay in the metropoles from which they came. Within these strictures, the Fulbright program for Africa has functioned as have other sections of the program.

The grantees to and from Africa are also processed through the Institute of International Education for the exchange of students; through the Council for International Exchange of Scholars in the preliminary selection of American lecturers and research scholar candi-

---

reality. Consequently, it was possible to confine a discussion of Africa to Africa south of the Sahara—further divided into Anglophone, Francophone, and Lusaphone countries—though this did violence, perhaps, to the reality of geography and alignments on the continent as expressed in the United Nations or the Organization of African Unity. Independence aside, 47 countries including the Malagasy Republic and excluding Egypt and the Canary and the Seychelles Islands constitute Africa today, foreign policy objectives often dictating which country will or will not be included in the Fulbright program.

6. Board of Foreign Scholarships, *A Quarter Century: The American Adventure in Academic Exchange* (Washington, DC: Department of State, 1971), pp. 25-26.

7. In the Republic of South Africa, higher education for nonwhites had been under the control of the English-language universities. Therefore, many nonwhites enrolled in the Universities of South Africa, Cape Town, Witwatersrand, Rhodes, and Natal. Fort Hare, started in 1916 and incorporated in 1923, was for Africans from any tribe. In 1951 it was annexed to Rhodes. In 1959, all non-Europeans not registered by 1 January 1959 were barred from entering any white institution except the Medical School at Natal and correspondence classes at the University of South Africa. In March 1960, the first Bantu college was opened. Fort Hare was now exclusively for Xosa-speaking students. See Martena Sasnett and Inez Sepmeyer, *Educational Systems of Africa, Interpretations for Use in Evaluations of Academic Credentials* (Berkeley: University of California Press, 1966), p. 1070.

dates, and in the day-to-day operation and administration of the exchange program for research scholars and lecturers from abroad; and through the Office of International Education within the Department of Education for the Exchange of Teachers Program.[8]

Academic exchanges with Africa are managed internally by the Africa Branch of the Academic Exchanges Division of the Bureau of Educational and Cultural Affairs. This branch has four program officers and two program assistants who function under a chief and whose responsibilities are programmatically rather than geographically assigned.[9]

8. The Department of Education administers the Foreign Area and Language Training Program through the Office of International Education. The program is designed "to promote and improve foreign language training and area studies in American universities. . . . Grants available under this program include doctoral dissertation research abroad, faculty research abroad, group projects abroad and grants to bring foreign curriculum consultants from Africa to the United States. . . . These programs are different from other Fulbright-Hays activities in that their objective is research and training with no provisions for lecturing assignments overseas or for direct exchanges." The Teacher Exchange Program was moved to the United States Information Agency about a year ago.

9. Currently, the staff responsibilities are allocated among the following programs: UCLA-Somalia Project; University of California (Berkeley)-University of Nairobi Project; African-American Issues Center; U.S. Lecturers Program; U.S. Senior Research Scholars Program; Junior Staff Development/African Student Program; American African Educational Foundation Program (South African Students); American Studies Research Fellowship Program; University Affiliations Program; Francophone/Lusophone Africa Summer EFL [English as a Foreign Language] Institute; South Africa Long-Term EFL Training Project; Georgetown University's South African Lawyers Program; U.S. Student Program; African Senior Research Scholars Program; African Scholars-in-Residence (Lecturers) Program; Teachers, Technology, Texts Program.

At the outset, the Fulbright program included the entire continent exclusive of Egypt. But beginning in 1974, the countries of North Africa—Morocco, Libya, Tunisia—have been part of the Near East and South Asia branch of the Bureau of Educational and Cultural Affairs. In the earlier period, between 1949 and 1971, 565 U.S. citizens went as Fulbright grantees to 38 countries in Africa, the largest number—85—to Nigeria, 58 to Uganda, 52 to Morocco, 41 to Liberia, 34 to Ghana, 32 to Zambia, and 30 to the Republic of South Africa. The Canary Islands, the Central African Republic, Equatorial Guinea, Gabon, Portuguese Guinea, Mauritania, Mauritius, Niger, South-West Africa—or Namibia—Togo, and Upper Volta had no U.S. academic exchange grantees during this period. However, each African political entity, with the exception of St. Helena and the Seychelles Islands, sent at least 1 citizen for research, teaching, or practical experience. The largest number, 242, came from Kenya;[10] Nigeria sent 163; Uganda, 163; the Republic of South Africa, 156; and Morocco, 137.

Between 1964 and 1976, the Foreign Area and Language Program awarded grants administered by the Fulbright program to African nationals and U.S. citizens to pursue educational goals not necessarily requiring a university affiliation. Accordingly, grants to pursue research for doctoral dissertations were made for 16 students working in Morocco, 13 in Kenya, 11 in Tanzania, and 9 in Nigeria. Grants were also made for faculty members to work in Africa; the largest numbers of faculty, 7 and 5, worked in Nigeria and Ethiopia, respectively. Group projects of shorter dura-

10. This number represents those students brought in 1957 to the United States on a highly publicized and accelerated program by Tom Mboya, a labor leader and politician in Kenya.

tion, such as seminars and workshops, were conducted in Ethiopia, Ghana, Kenya, Lesotho, Nigeria, and Tunisia. Twenty awards to curriculum consultants from Africa to come to the United States were made, the largest number, 11, to Nigerians.

The availability of federal funds did much to facilitate the growth of African studies programs in the United States from two universities, Northwestern and Boston, in the 1950s to 20 or 25 major universities today, thereby expanding the pool of students and scholars eligible for and interested enough to seek an opportunity to study or work in Africa.[11]

Only one country in Africa, Liberia, has a binational commission to administer the Fulbright program.[12] Started in 1964 by an executive agreement between the governments of the United States and Liberia as the United States Educational and Cultural Foundation, this foundation determines the policies and programs through a binational board of directors composed of four U.S. and four Liberian citizens. The U.S. ambassador to Liberia serves as *ex officio* chairman of the board and appoints all U.S. members to it; the minister of foreign affairs of the Liberian government appoints the Liberian members. The day-to-day management of the foundation is handled by a board-appointed executive director who is a United States citizen and who is assisted by a small staff.

11. See Adelaide C. Hill, "African Studies Programs in the United States," in *Africa in the United States*, ed. McKay, pp. 65-88, for an early history of the development of these programs. Another twenty or so programs exist in the colleges and universities.

12. Other programs in sub-Saharan Africa are typically supervised by one-person United States Information Service posts rather than by commissions.

THE FULBRIGHT PROGRAM IN THE 1970s

The decade of the 1970s became a watershed for the Fulbright program in Africa. With North African countries no longer a responsibility of the African Branch, sub-Saharan Africa was given greater attention. A member of the Board of Foreign Scholarships, Mr. John H. Carley, attorney-at-law with Rogers and Wells, visited Liberia, Ghana, Nigeria, Ethiopia, Uganda, and Kenya in October 1971. Ethnic Heritage Seminars in Africa were added to the Seminar Programs of the Office of Education in 1972. In early 1973 a second member of the Board of Foreign Scholarships, Dr. Peter Sammartino, chancellor of Fairleigh Dickinson University, visited Liberia, the Cameroons, Gabon, Zaire, Kenya, Ethiopia, and the Sudan. In addition, as the second American Lincoln Lecturer of the Fulbright program, Mr. John H. Updike, the distinguished author, conducted seminars and informal sessions with groups in Ghana, Nigeria, Tanzania, Kenya, and Ethiopia. His lecture topics included "the art of fiction" and "the adequacy of the European form of novel to express either African or American forms of reality." According to the eleventh Annual Report of the Board of Foreign Scholarships, Mr. Updike's lectures stimulated interest in courses in American literature in African universities, which by then had become a priority of the Board.

In 1974 the Board expressed a desire to bring more Africans in the humanities to the United States as lecturers. As reported in the Annual Report of December 1976, for the first time emphasis on educational exchange with Africa was highlighted. Another member of the Board, Dr. Robert Osgood, dean of the Johns Hopkins School of Advanced

International Studies, made a trip to Liberia, Nigeria, Tanzania, and the Republic of South Africa in August 1976. Excerpts from Dean Osgood's report to the Board and included in the fourteenth Annual Report give testimony to the changing African scene as it affected the Fulbright program:

Education at all levels is viewed as a vital national resource in that it produces the people with the necessary skills and knowledge to validate the country's status as an independent nation on the road to modern development.[13]

Furthermore, he saw and reported the African universities as being

at the top or near the top of the institutional prestige ladder . . . able to retain their integrity as independent academic institutions with distinct and fairly high professional standards and a good measure of academic freedom. . . . To meet their academic needs the universities look to American higher education as a model and as a source of academic aid. . . .

The Fulbright-Hays exchanges between the United States and Africa . . . have been highly successful. Whether they have involved students or senior scholars, whether they have been short-term or long-term, . . . they have enriched the knowledge and comprehension of national cultures and societies on both sides and have created and consolidated personal and professional ties across national boundaries. They have preserved and enhanced the reputation of American education and indirectly of American society regardless of differences between political systems. . . . To have been a Fulbright student or scholar is a mark of distinction. The Fulbright-Hays Program in Africa has been an unqualified success by any reasonable standard . . . and has admirably fulfilled the central purpose of the Mutual Educational and Cultural Exchange Act of 1961.

Anticipating the concerns of the next decade, Dean Osgood also believed that

in spite of the importance of other kinds of unilateral aid programs, the Fulbright Program would play a unique role in Africa even in countries like Nigeria which are investing heavily in their own educational programs and in the utilization of foreign education and scholars.

It would have been instructive to know what weaknesses, if any, Dean Osgood saw in the Fulbright program in Africa or where it needed strengthening or alteration. Unfortunately, if he made such observations in his complete report, they were not, perhaps understandably, included in the excerpts of the Annual Report to the Board.

Africa did seem to be receiving greater attention. In 1978, when the Board of Foreign Scholarships was moved from the Department of State to the International Communication Agency, the latter had as its director John Reinhardt, a black American and former ambassador to Nigeria. Also, the newly formed Fulbright Alumni Association at its first national convention, in 1978 in Washington, included among its lecturers Francis A. Dennis, ambassador from Liberia, who expressed the hope that more Fulbright participants would choose to go to Africa. The same year, in May, Dr. J. Archie Hargraves, president of the Institute for International Development in Raleigh, North Carolina, and a member of the Board, visited Liberia, Nigeria, the Republic of South Africa, and Zambia and reported that "throughout Africa, returned exchange grantees are the new leaders and becoming very clearly so!"[14]

13. *Annual Report* (Washington, DC: Board of Foreign Scholarships, 1976), pp. 5-6.

14. *Report on Exchanges* (Washington, DC: Board of Foreign Scholarships, 1978), p. 4.

It was during 1978 that an important new initiative was introduced into the Fulbright program that would have a significant impact on African exchanges. The Hubert H. Humphrey North/South Fellowship Program was started in the Carter administration "to enhance the professional capabilities of midcareer public servants and managers from the developing world who are dedicated to careers in public service." The recipients were to study in small groups at institutions in the United States for one year of postgraduate work on problem-solving projects in order to reap the benefits of shared experiences. The program was to be administered by the Institute of International Education, with the final selection of candidates made by the Board of Foreign Scholarships. The average cost was $19,000 per fellow.

Selections were made in June 1979, and fellows began their study the following September. In all, 27 fellows representing 24 countries from Africa, Latin America, Asia, and the Middle East were enrolled in 11 universities; 5 of the fellows were from Africa. African fellows were chosen to pursue one of four fields—agriculture, health and nutrition, planning and resource management, or public administration. By 1986, the number of Humphrey fellows from Africa had grown to 53, or 36 percent, of a total of 147 fellows worldwide.

Beginning in 1979, data were given on the academic fields in which the various Fulbright grantees intended to work: the humanities, including the fine arts; the social sciences; education; physical and natural sciences. From the annual reports, it is impossible to extrapolate the specific African interest of the Americans, except in one or two fields, and virtually impossible to separate the Africans from other foreign nationals. But it is clear that two U.S. citizens received

grants in the field of African history, and five in African languages; four foreign nationals received grants to study African history and two to study African languages.

By the middle 1970s, with the geographical limits now encompassing 43 countries and two islands, 37 U.S. Fulbrighters went to Africa, the largest number—7—to Nigeria, the next largest—5—to Ghana, and 4 to Liberia. The same year, 1974-75, 125 Fulbright grantees came from Africa, the largest number, 19, from the Republic of South Africa, followed by Nigeria with 18, Ghana with 9, and Tanzania and Zaire with 8 each.

At the end of the decade the figures continued to increase, though the countries of choice reflected some altered political realities. In 1978-79, 52 U.S. citizens went to Africa as Fulbrighters; 8 went to Nigeria, 8 to Kenya, and 4 to Senegal. None went to the Republic of South Africa or Uganda and only 1 to Ghana. Coming to the United States the same year were 165 Africans, including 25 from the Republic of South Africa, 16 from Tanzania, and 12 each from Zambia and Liberia.

At about the same time—fiscal year 1978—under the Department of Health, Education and Welfare, 17 Americans went to Africa to work on dissertations, three faculty to do research, and 65 others on three group projects. Zaire was the locus for four doctoral projects and Kenya for three. Only five Africans came to the United States that year as curriculum consultants—three from Ghana and one each from Nigeria and Togo.

THE 1980s AND THE FULBRIGHT PROGRAM

In October 1980, the Board of Foreign Scholarships and the International Communication Agency sponsored a conference, "The Fulbright Program in the Eighties," at the Woodrow Wilson International Center for Scholars in Washington, D.C. During the meetings there was a clear expression of concern for issues relevant to Africa such as these: Could the Fulbright program be adjusted to reflect the new role of developing nations in international contexts or their new role as countries where development is the predominant goal? Could the program take a developmental orientation without distorting its first purposes? Should the program attempt to cover the entire world, or should it focus on a smaller number of countries and on the basis of what criteria?[15] Africa, particularly, with its great size, numerous countries, and still developing institutions of higher learning, underscored the need to consider additional mechanisms for implementing academic changes that would be mutually beneficial.

Some participants refused to recommend curtailing the program in Africa in spite of its many obstacles. On the contrary, they reasoned that the program would have to be the important means for "developing and sustaining the capacity of United States scholars to interpret societies other than their own."[16]

The 1980s, therefore, was not to be a period of retrenchment for the Fulbright program in Africa. Although the Africa Branch now could conceivably have programs in 46 political entities, it is possible to measure quantitatively, if not qualitatively, the impact the academic exchange program is having in Africa in the 1980s simply by identifying the countries from which the largest

number of Africans come and, conversely, the countries to which U.S. scholars most often choose to go.

It would be tempting to make a detailed correlation between the figures for specific countries and foreign policy directives. Some countries seemed never to have grantees. Others—Nigeria, South Africa—were favored continuously; still others once favored have not participated in the academic exchange during this period. But since the recommendations of the Wilson Conference, a certain pattern or trend is, in fact, discernable.

Until the 1980s, the Fulbright program extended to fewer than half the countries in sub-Saharan Africa. With significant increases in funds beginning in 1982, the program has expanded remarkably. In 1984, 35 countries were involved; in 1985, 36; and in 1986, 41. The program has been largest in those countries that are largest or of greatest interest geopolitically to the United States. In rank order, the total program—combining grantees from the country and American grantees to the country—has been largest in these countries: Nigeria, South Africa, Kenya, Tanzania, and Liberia. However, the structure of the program has varied quite significantly among these countries. A balanced program, with several grants in each category of programming, is found with Nigeria; this program includes U.S. lecturers, senior research scholars, and students in Nigeria and Nigerian lecturers, senior research scholars, and students in the United States. By contrast, the program with South Africa has been very one-sided, with 94 percent of the grants going to South African graduate students to study in the United States.[17] Finally, the program with Liberia has

15. "The Fulbright Program in the Eighties: Summary of Conference Proceedings" (Pamphlet, Board of Foreign Scholarships and the International Communication Agency, [1980?]), pp. 7-10.
16. Ibid.

17. After 1981 no grants were made to U.S. citizens to go to South Africa.

been larger than the size of that country would predict because of the bilateral agreement of 1964, which stipulated atypically large budgets for the program through 1999.

Another measure of the possible influence of the Fulbright program can be detected from the Hubert H. Humphrey North/South Fellowships. Since this program was inaugurated in 1978-79, the number of grantees has varied from 5 the first year to 51 in 1985. In 1983 there was a slight decline from the previous year, from 49 to 29. In all, 219 Humphrey fellows have participated in the program through the year 1984-85, the largest number—21—from Tanzania, followed by Ghana with 18 and Liberia with 16.

The pattern to date has consisted of 1 or 2 persons from a few countries—only 4 countries in 1979, but as many as 26 in 1984.

Since the Wilson Conference, three other potentially important programs have been initiated: the University Affiliation Grants Program for Sub-Sahaharan Africa, the African-American Issues Center Program, and the South African Higher Education Program for Politically Disadvantaged Students from South Africa.[18]

The University Affiliation Program was started in 1982 as a pilot program linking 13 universities in the United States with universities in Africa. The

18. The educational program for politically disadvantaged South African students is not a Fulbright exchange program and does not require that the Board of Foreign Scholarships select each student. It is coordinated by the International Institute of Education, but it is important to note because it is a special initiative responding to acute circumstances not unlike the airlift sponsored by Tom Mboya, mentioned earlier. In 1986, 250 students in the program were studying at 168 U.S. colleges and universities.

universities in the United States were selected on a competitive basis for a seed-money grant of $50,000 funded under the Fulbright program to be expended within three years. The grants were intended to promote and strengthen the international ties of universities, to foster a climate for collaborative research, and to support guest lectureships by faculty from abroad on American university campuses.

Some 24 universities in the United States have affiliated with 22 universities in Africa. Beginning in 1983, the University Affiliation Program became worldwide. And since its inception, 100 grants have been awarded to American colleges and universities and affiliated foreign institutions. It is important to note that what was started to strengthen the United States' ties to the academic communities in Africa is now seen to have comparable value in other parts of the world.

In 1983 the African-American Issues Center was proposed, as a response to the similar purpose of broadening academic ties to Africa. On the basis of a national competition, a grant of $250,000 was made to a consortium including Boston University, Harvard University, and the Massachusetts Institute of Technology "to foster collaborative research and policy dialogue between African and American scholars on critical issues in the areas of economic development, constitutionalism and communication."[19] Boston University's African Center was responsible for the overall management and for organizing activities in the area of economic development. The Harvard University Center for Interna-

19. Boston University, Harvard University, and the Massachusetts Institute of Technology, "A Proposal to the United States Information and Communication Agency for the Study of African-American Issues" (1983), p. 1.

tional Affairs' African Research Program was to be responsible for activities in the area of constitutionalism, and the Massachusetts Institute of Technology's Center of International Studies was to coordinate activities in the area of communications. An additional grant of $131,501 was made in 1985 to this consortium.

Since July 1986, three new programs have been launched for South Africa: the Georgetown University South African Lawyers Program, an M.A. degree program for black lawyers to develop their clinical and advocacy skills and therefore enhance their potential to qualify as advocates in the Supreme Court of South Africa; a summer institute for 25 high school teachers of English; and a full academic year of training for a smaller number of similar teachers.

THE PROGRAM AND
ITS PARTICIPANTS

As the Fulbright program was and in many respects continues to be evaluated according to the status of the scholars who have been grantees, it is therefore appropriate to apply this criterion to the program in Africa. Although distinguished black American scholars such as John Hope Franklin, the historian, and Andrew Brimmer, the economist, have been grantees, neither chose to go to Africa. The only nationally prominent American Fulbright alumnus, at this writing, who went to Africa is John Updike, the author. However, although precise figures are not accessible, it is more or less general knowledge that many outstanding American Africanists were able as students to acquire data for their dissertations and later as scholars to do further work in Africa under the Fulbright program.

Similarly, while it goes beyond the scope of this article to endeavor to identify Africans of national prominence who have been Fulbright grantees, the late Dr. Kenneth Dike, the outstanding historian and educator from Nigeria, and Dr. J.H.K. Nketia, the Ghanaian musicologist, come easily to mind. Others of prominence—all from the University of Abidjan—are the Rector M. Bakary Toure; dean of the Faculty of Medicine, Antoine Yangui-Angate; and dean of the Faculty of Science, Asseypo Hauhouot.

There are, it must be admitted, hurdles and handicaps facing the American scholar in Africa—beyond the general unfamiliarity with the continent. The inhospitableness of its climate in many areas, the hazards to health, the inadequacy of its housing, the uncertainty of its transportation, the frequent political turmoil, and the lack of resources for the scholar—books, library and laboratory equipment, and sometimes sufficient numbers of scholars with similar interests or leisure to provide a collegial environment—are deterrents to one's voluntarily seeking an overseas experience. But these liabilities must be seen in relation to the excitement of being on the ground floor, a pioneer, in the development of new countries: working with a nascent national theater or a new school of journalism, introducing educational television, advising on the utilization of audiovisual educational materials, or participating in important pioneering agricultural experiments. Some such projects include exploring the effects of seasonal fluctuations in Lesotho's food supply and work requirements on the health and productivity of its agricultural labor force; establishing a school of business administration, including an endowed chair in banking and finance, in Zambia or building the curriculum and popularizing the courses at the existing but still developing School of Education in Calabar, Nigeria; reconstructing a hospital in the war-torn city of Kampala; having one's own national art show in Senegal; experimenting with a wide variety of music and art forms; and on and on. There is often the mere joy of being needed and appreciated, which goes beyond the frustrations of bureaucratic red tape and environmental difficulties.

Most African grantees from graduate students to senior scholars return to their countries to centers of prominence, usually the capital or certainly an important city, and therefore are in a position to exert influence beyond their academic setting. At the same time, from their university base, they are in a position to play an important role in the development of the minds of the most promising students likely to be the future leaders of their countries. Indeed, one significant criterion for selection has been the potential multiplier effect, the probability that a grantee would share his or her experience with many others on returning home.

THE FISCAL PICTURE IN THE 1980s

Between 1982 and 1986 appropriations for Africa were allocated to three major divisions: (1) Country Programs, in Liberia and the Republic of South Africa; (2) Regional Programs, which include U.S. lecturers, U.S. senior researchers, U.S. students, African lecturers, African senior researchers, and African students; and (3) Institutional Programs, including the African-American Issues Center, the UCLA-Somalia Project, the University of California-University of Nairobi Project, University Linkages, summer institutes for teachers

of English as a foreign language, and Orientation Programs. With the theoretical focus still all of sub-Saharan Africa but excluding those countries that are not given formal diplomatic recognition by the United States such as Angola, the fiscal picture is as follows.

From 1982 to 1986 $34,787,299 was spent, the lowest amount—$5,450,898—in 1982 and the highest amount—$8,348,999—in 1986.

The Institutional Programs have varied as to type and year of funding. Allocations reflect an understandable but not exactly smooth adjustment to political reality, for Liberia and the Republic of South Africa remain the only countries with specific allocations. The rest of the continent is programmed regionally, permitting flexibility, on the one hand, and simultaneously addressing the worrisome question of concentration versus dispersal, on the other.

The largest sums are spent on bringing African students to the United States—$1,373,218 in 1982, rising to $3,794,630 in 1986—and on sending U.S. lecturers to Africa—peak funding of $1,924,555 in 1985, dropping slightly to $1,825,270 in 1986. There is a substantial gap between the amount spent to bring African lecturers and senior researchers to the United States—$430,000 in 1982, rising to $985,200 in 1986—and the amount spent to send U.S. lecturers and senior researchers to Africa—$1,444,870 in 1982, rising to $2,075,270 in 1986. While the allocations favor more U.S. senior scholars, African students far exceed the number of American students going to the continent. In 1986, for example, $3,794,630 was spent to support 326 African students in the United States, while $461,500 was spent on 36 American students in Africa.[20]

20. The higher figure of $3,794,630 can be

CONCLUSION

Some concluding observations are instructive in anticipating future developments. Academic exchanges have expanded significantly in recent years. Expenditures in fiscal year 1985 exceeded those in the previous year by 23 percent. In 1985, 36 of the potential 45 nations participated in the Fulbright program. Still, much more should be spent as the opportunities for expansion seem limitless in meeting the high priority now placed on education in Africa and because of its relative immunity from political interference. At the same time, greater effort must be made to recruit American candidates for all priority lecturing assignments in Africa—through expanded but still carefully targeted publicity. Efforts should be made to address some of the negative aspects of an African experience mentioned earlier—housing, transportation, and laboratory and library inadequacies. Younger American scholars whose availability might be greater than that of senior scholars should have the opportunity to participate in the program by way of more short-term assignments.

Today, the Republic of South Africa presents the greatest challenge to the credibility and potentiality of the Fulbright program in Africa as the clearest example of conflict between the scholarly concerns of the U.S. academic community and the foreign policy directives of the U.S. government. For as long as truth and freedom are denied in every political, economic, and social sphere of South Africa and, despite this, the U.S. government policy seeks to maintain an engagement with that country, it will be impossible to achieve even minimally the goals of the Fulbright program—to know, respect, and understand each other's values, traditions, and cultures. Almost 75 years ago, long before Senator Fulbright saw the wisdom and value of academic exchange in maintaining world peace, W.E.B. DuBois warned that the problem of the twentieth century was the color line.[21] In South Africa, where all colors clash, it is imperative that the integrity of the scholar and scholarly inquiry be asserted and protected—that no compromises be made—either for short-term or long-term political ends. To do otherwise would make a mockery of the Fulbright program and repudiate the value and power of the scholar in a world of conflict.

---

used for African students because this figure includes students from South Africa and Liberia added to the Regional Program for African students.

21. W.E.B. DuBois, *The Souls of the Black Folk* (New York: New American Library, 1969), p. 78.

Educational Exchange in Latin America

By MAURICE A. STERNS

ABSTRACT: Since its inception three decades ago, the Fulbright program in Latin America has aided individual students and Latin American educational institutions alike. The binational Fulbright commissions that select participants have earned a reputation for autonomy and fairness and have encouraged innovative programs such as cost sharing, state-of-the-art seminars, and flexible tenure provisions for U.S. scholars teaching in Latin America. As the U.S. and Latin American university systems have increasingly converged, Fulbright has also helped to introduce and promote such U.S. concepts as university-based research and decentralized higher education, as well as Latin American university commitment to social outreach. Yet some problems remain. These include competition from European and Soviet exchange programs, inadequate contact among Fulbright scholars now in the United States, and failure to maintain contact with Fulbright alumni once they have returned home. Further institution building in the Latin American educational sector also deserves greater support. The existing binational commissions provide an excellent model for the cooperation needed to address these problems, and they underscore the important role that Fulbright can continue to play in Latin America.

Maurice A. Sterns is executive director of the International Institute for Advanced Studies, an international training and consulting organization, in Cambridge, Massachusetts. He received his B.A. from Oberlin College, M.A. in political science and international development education from Stanford University, and Ph.D. in human development from the University of Chicago. He served as regional director of the Latin American Scholarship Program of American Universities at Harvard University, research director at the University Institute of Reserch of Rio de Janeiro in Brazil, and visiting professor at the University of Zulia in Venezuela.

SINCE its inception in the mid-1950s, the Fulbright program in Latin America has enjoyed a reputation for excellence. This reputation has a solid basis in fact. Among the Fulbright alumni now playing important roles in the political and cultural life of Latin America are Eduardo Rabossi, secretary for human rights in Argentina; Enrique Low Mutra, member of the Supreme Court of Colombia; Hugo Palacios, Colombian finance minister; and Maria do Rosario Cassimiro, rector of the Federal University of Goiás in Brazil, the first female president of a federal university in her country. The program continues to be considered one of the elite international awards in the region, even though a number of competing programs have come into existence since its founding. The ability to attract a consistently high level of applicants is testimony to Fulbright's continuing success.

In common with Fulbright exchange programs in other parts of the world, the program in Latin America has not only been distinguished by its high standards of selection, but also by a commitment to expose those whom it accepts to the experience of everyday life in the United States. Unlike some other programs, students are not assigned to a single university in a major city; rather, Fulbright scholars and students are scattered throughout the land in a vast range of settings. By and large, the majority of those who come here leave with good impressions. More important, they leave with a more sophisticated image of the United States, as they come to realize that issues that may have been previously presented to them in terms of black and white are in fact more complex. A recent Institute of International Education research report, based on interviews with Brazilian students regarding the impact of American higher education, concluded:

Perhaps the most gratifying feature of this high regard for America is that it is not the result of propaganda or illusion. It is exactly as Americans would wish it, the consequence of living among us. These shrewd observers left America well aware of its problems, mistakes, and contradictions, but remain enthusiastic advocates all the same for its free society, economic vitality, open and vigorous public debate, and demonstrated generosity.[1]

In looking back at the role that the Fulbright program of academic exchange has played in Latin America over the past decades, we thus have reason to be proud of its achievements. This does not mean, however, that no problems exist or that there remain no areas for improvement. There are both. In the pages that follow, I will sketch the background of Fulbright's initiatives in Latin America and their specific regional characteristics before investigating a few of these problems and, finally, suggesting some possible solutions.

During my twenty years of work in the area of Latin American higher education and educational exchange, I have benefited from the unusual advantage of experiencing Latin American education at the grass-roots level in many countries. The realities of Latin American education politics have been such that I was, over the course of six years as the Latin American Scholarship Program of American Universities (LASPAU) regional director, a stable observer in a

1. Craufurd D. Goodwin and Michael Nacht, *Fondness and Frustration: The Impact of American Higher Education on Foreign Students, with Special Reference to the Case of Brazil*, Institute of International Education Research Report no. 5 (New York: Institute of International Education, 1984), p. 44.

rapidly changing university world. My position required that I maintain contact with over one hundred universities in a dozen countries. Since many university presidents remained in office only for short periods, I would frequently visit an institution and know the two or three immediate predecessors of the university rector I was meeting, as well as several of his or her contemporaries—rectors at other universities in the country. Seen against the background of constant and disruptive change in Latin America, foreign academic exchange programs such as Fulbright possessed the simple virtue of longevity.

BACKGROUND

The Fulbright program came slowly to Latin America. Although the Fulbright Act of 1946 inaugurated educational exchanges with Europe, similar exchanges with Latin America did not commence for another decade. Not until foreign currencies from the sale of surplus agricultural products became available was a Fulbright agreement signed with a Latin American country. In 1955, the first such agreement was concluded with Chile. Seven others soon followed, ranging from Peru in 1956 to Uruguay in 1960. The climax of this early phase of postwar American interest in Latin America came in 1961, when the Alliance for Progress was announced. With the Alliance came increased economic assistance, with the stated aim of helping with the development of more equitable social structures. The role of improved education in bringing about these changes was clearly of great importance, and the Fulbright program was strengthened as a result.

One of the principal benefits of the Fulbright role in Latin America in the 1960s was to bring some hope of long-term continuity in educational assistance that could be counted upon year after year. This occurred despite the sharp reduction in financial support of the program that Congress mandated in 1968. Fulbright strengthened the binational, cooperative approach to exchange. Fulbright presence in a country meant an increased stress on continuous, year-round academic activities and thus an increase in steady contact with U.S. educators. It also swelled the number of Americans visiting those countries for regular studies and provided additional research opportunities for American scholars. Facilitating this two-way circulation of students coming north and professors traveling south has since remained the Fulbright program's primary function.

SOURCES FOR
EDUCATIONAL EXCHANGE

Well into the 1960s and even the early 1970s, the United States remained the sole significant actor on the scene of international educational exchange in Latin America. American education had for many years been admired, and many Latin American students who could afford to do so had begun coming to the United States to pursue advanced studies on their own. Thus U.S. government sponsorship simply strengthened an existing trend. But by the mid-1970s, the concept of educational exchange had gained currency among other countries both within and outside Latin America. Some of the relatively more developed countries in the region, such as Mexico, Venezuela, and Brazil, established their own scholarship programs to encourage students to continue studies both at home and abroad. France, Germany, and England increased attention to the provision of scholarships to Latin Americans. Italy and Spain also attracted increasing numbers of students, who found a special affinity for their educational systems and cultures.

The Brazilian government established Coordinacão do Aperfeiçoamento de Pessoal de Nivel Superior (CAPES) (Commission for Improvement of Personnel in Higher Education), a program to upgrade higher education that involved heavy investment in scholarships that enabled Brazilians to pursue advanced studies at home. This program also sent thousands of Brazilians abroad; many continue to come to the United States even today under Brazilian auspices. The Mexican government established Consejo Nacional de Ciéncias y Tecnología (National Council of Science and Technology) to promote scholarship opportunities for young Mexicans to undertake studies in areas determined to be of national priority. In Colombia, an aggressive country in terms of promoting study abroad, Instituto Colombiano de Crédito Educativo y Estúdios Técnicas en el Exterior (Colombian Institute of Educational Credit and Technical Studies Abroad) was founded, a vital educational credit arm of the Colombian government that provided educational loan opportunities to Colombians on favorable interest terms. The British Council, the Alliance Française, and the Deutscher Akademischer Austauschdienst of Germany all seemed to be stepping up their attention to opportunities for Latin Americans to study in Europe.

The major new foreign player to make its presence felt, however, was the Soviet Union. As I traveled through education and government offices in Colombia and Ecuador in the late 1970s, I soon became aware of the fact that a hundred five-year scholarships offering complete funding by the USSR were available in each of those countries. Typically, such scholarships included one year of language study, followed by four years of specialized training in the student's field of interest. The number of Soviet awards available stood in sharp contrast to the ten to twenty Fulbright scholarships awarded annually in each country. My general understanding is that Latin American students selected to study in the Soviet Union—like most other foreigners—were assigned to Patrice Lumumba University in Moscow, where they enjoyed little contact with their Soviet counterparts. Having had the opportunity to interview two Colombians who had spent a few years in the USSR on one of these scholarships, I was able to gain some additional, if anecdotal, insight into their experience there. I was told that they had been highly motivated to go to the United States, but could not get scholarship funding; when an opportunity to study in Moscow came along they had jumped at it as a substitute. In fact, their experience there had been largely negative. They reported feeling isolated, disappointed at the quality of their courses, and distinctly unimpressed with the quality of Soviet life.

It is ironic that in the late 1970s and early 1980s, as such programs began to compete with U.S.-sponsored attempts to attract able young Latin American scholars, the U.S. government's financial commitment to educational exchange with Latin America began to show a rapid decline. As two experts on educational exchange noted in 1984:

Perhaps the most significant paradox we encountered was that just at the moment when Brazilians and leaders in other [Latin American] countries have come jointly to recognize and accept the enormous success and value to all parties of the training of Brazilian students in the United States, American leaders seem to have developed doubts and lost conviction about the value of such experiences. We heard numerous accounts of how the Germans, French, Japanese and others were implementing substantial training programs just at the time when American programs were in decline.[2]

This situation has now, thankfully, begun to change, in part because of increased concern at the role of the Soviet Union in Central America and the Caribbean. Such concern is evident in the Kissinger Report of 1984, which specifically recommended a sharp increase in youth exchanges in the subregion. American fears concerning national security have now been translated into increased attention to international education and training. In response to President Reagan's Central American Initiative and congressional support for it, Fulbright exchanges in seven countries of the region were greatly expanded in 1985. One can only hope that such support will continue and, further, that it will be more evenly spread throughout the Americas. We should not reinforce programs for educational exchange merely as a response to crises, but should commit the United States to a long-term strategy that recognizes the permanent fruits of educational exchange.

THE LATIN AMERICAN UNIVERSITY TRADITION

One reason for Fulbright's success is a remarkable congruence between specific Latin American needs and the

2. Ibid., p. 46.

special possibilities inherent within the Fulbright philosophy of educational exchange. Fulbright has displayed interest in promoting reforms in the institutional structure of universities abroad as well as in bringing individual foreign students to the United States for study. In order to understand more fully Fulbright's innovative role in this domain, it may be useful first to examine some of the characteristics that set the Latin American educational situation apart from both its U.S. and European counterparts.

Like many university systems in the Third World, those of Latin America are perhaps best known to Americans as centers of political agitation and opposition to existing regimes. Yet universities in Latin America have also developed a rich tradition of reaching out to their communities in ways that have not been given the international attention that student politics has received. The net result is that many Latin American universities are branded as hotbeds of student radicalism when beneath the surface there exist numerous examples of university extension activities and related service efforts that bring university students into direct contact with their communities. These activities represent political commitment of a different kind—a desire to effect practical change on the grass-roots level within the existing structure of government.

University outreach programs in Latin America take many forms. One especially common aspect in countries the population of which is still largely devoted to farming is agricultural extension. University students and faculty alike go out and assist in the fields, meeting the small farmers and working with them, in some cases voluntarily and in other cases as an educational requirement. Agricultural schools that in the past had been criticized for not being relevant enough to the small farmer's needs now devote increased attention to understanding and responding to the local realities of the *campesino*.

Educational extension provides a second type of outreach. This appears to be the bare minimum for many universities that are developing outreach programs. If a university has any community orientation, it is likely to have some offerings in educational extension, usually a program to upgrade high school or primary school teachers.

Nonformal education constitutes a third outreach activity. One important example is the Open University in Colombia, founded with the aid of a Fulbright alumnus who studied the sociology of education at the University of Indiana, where he also became interested in nonformal education. As a result of his experience in the United States, he was asked by the Colombian Ministry of Education upon his return to head a pilot project at the Universidad de Antioquia that would serve as a basis for establishing a national open university.

Other outreach programs involve practical short-term training in health and nutrition, social service, and commercial and technical assistance. The health area is a natural one for university involvement in the community. At the Universidad del Valle in Colombia, the medical faculty began by assigning students to families and advising the students that they would be responsible for the family's health needs during their studies. This led to a larger commitment in the development of health centers, which in turn led to delivery systems. In the process, engineers were called in from the university's engineering school to construct some of the health facilities.

The president of the Universidad del Valle told me, "It is now impossible for a student to get a degree from this university without some participation in field work, without performing some kind of community service."[3]

Finally, there is the new field of applied research. Latin American universities have until recently been basically teaching institutions; there exists no Latin American tradition of university research. Instead, research has traditionally been conducted by national governments, foreign agencies, or international groups, in sharp contrast to the United States. This situation in Latin America wastes both human and institutional resources. It retards the growth of local universities' capability to do their own research, while at the same time prolonging technological dependence on research centers abroad. The United States' example of university-based research, transmitted through educational exchanges under Fulbright sponsorship, has been a major contributing factor in reversing this pattern and encouraging Latin American universities to develop their own research capabilities more fully.

As this example shows, features of U.S. higher education that may seem quite ordinary to North American observers take on a new relevance in the context of Latin American needs. The same is true in the growing regionalization that characterizes Latin American universities. Formerly, Latin American university structures were centralized, confined to the capital or a small number of other large cities, such as the Universidade do São Paulo in Brazil. Now, however, many large universities are

3. Interview with Alvaro Escober Návia, Cali, Colombia, 24 July 1977.

opening new campuses. Sometimes this means simply inaugurating branch campuses and offering university access to a larger number of students. But in other cases, especially in Central America, regionalizing the university means not just duplicating the main campus, but also setting up a variety of other learning centers that attend to the specific needs of each region being served.

The tremendous growth in university enrollments is based partly on the overall population explosion in Latin America. It is due also to the campaign to universalize primary education and to democratize higher learning. For several years, a movement has existed to promote the idea of free and mandatory education for all elementary- and secondary-age children; to the extent that it has been successful, many secondary school graduates are knocking on university doors. Part of the increase is due to universities developing more concrete programs. It is now legitimate to study mid-level technology in Latin American universities, where formerly the professions formed the core of the curriculum. University training is increasingly seen not just as a preserve for the privileged, but as essential for the effort to raise the standard of living and to transform the practical aspects of Latin American life.

In short, several trends in reshaping the Latin American university's structure have had the effect of bringing a traditionally very different conception of the university far closer to the American model. The presence of on-campus research, the efforts to develop strong outreach programs with the surrounding community, and the establishment of central campuses and a program of liberal arts education for entering students are all novel features in Latin American university life that owe their inception to a widespread feeling on the part of Latin American authorities that the best features of the U.S. model can be adopted to serve their needs. We, in turn, can learn something from the Latin American example of outreach and community involvement. Yet even with the explosion in student enrollments over the past two decades, students and graduates of Latin American universities still represent a small percentage of the population in contrast with the situation in the United States. This gives Latin American universities a special responsibility for the social needs of the countries where they operate, and the United States a special opportunity for aiding them in this role.

The direct contact with U.S. universities made possible by programs of educational exchange such as Fulbright has thus acquired a new importance for Latin America as the two systems have begun to converge. At the same time, however, the Fulbright program has made a signal contribution to rethinking higher education in Latin America through its process as well as through its content. The success of the Fulbright educational program in Latin America has been due in great part to the student selection process elaborated over the past thirty years. Attention to selection is peculiar to Fulbright among the various educational exchange programs. Others tend to rely on paper credentials alone, or simply honor nominations and confine their attention to the task of placement. With its binational commissions, personal interviews, and reliance on institutional as well as individual criteria in making awards, Fulbright is able to make a more accurate assessment of the candidates' potential and thus frequently makes superior choices.

In a conversation with a current

Fulbright student from Latin America, I learned that he had applied to Fulbright because "Fulbright was [his] only chance." He had gone through formal application to a government coordinating unit for scholarships and was in fact approved for the award, only to be rejected at the last moment due to lack of government funding. He was then invited to apply again in the succeeding year and once again became a finalist. He then learned, however, that due to political-military pressures, ten candidates who had not even participated in the selection process had been awarded the scholarships instead. Understandably, he was saddened and frustrated. He decided to apply to Fulbright, believing that he could at least count on getting fair treatment. His Fulbright application was reviewed, and he was invited to an interview that concentrated less on his field of specialization and more on his motivations and goals. He found this interview more serious and formal than the ones he had undergone for the government scholarship application. He won the award and is now a full-time graduate student in the United States.

This experience highlights the fact that it is not simply the experience of studying in the United States that affects students; the process by which they are selected also has an effect on their views. Fulbright's success in retaining its reputation for autonomy and fairness is due in no small measure to the binational commissions that supervise the selection procedure in South America. Commissions range in size from 8 to 14 members. A commission's membership consists equally of U.S. citizens and local representatives of government, industry, and education, who together determine priorities, review candidates, and support

programs. South America is unusual in having a majority of the Fulbright countries there guided by commissions. In Central America, by contrast, there are no commissions, and foreign service officers play a principal role in setting the program and reviewing candidates.

In 1985, of 42 countries worldwide with binational commissions, 27 shared the cost of exchange programs through direct financial contributions to such commissions. Among these were 2 Latin American countries, Brazil and Colombia. Brazil was last year the fourth largest host-country contributor among all countries with a Fulbright program, contributing more than England and some other European countries. Brazil and Colombia were 2 of only 5 Third World countries that shared Fulbright costs.

A key function of each commission is the drawing up of an annual program plan for exchanges, in consultation with participating universities and organizations in the host country. Another important function of the commissions is to provide counseling and advisory services to an increasing number of students wishing to study in colleges and universities in the United States under various sponsorships or with private funding. Other program responsibilities include screening, interviewing, and nominating to the Board of Foreign Scholarships qualified candidates for student and faculty grants under its exchange program; placing American students and scholars nominated for grants at participating host-country universities; monitoring the progress of grant participants during the academic year; and arranging for the orientation of arriving and departing exchange participants.

There has been an unusual degree of stability among the Fulbright executive directors in the region. Renee Abaracon in Uruguay, Rolando Picazo in Argentina, Francisco Gnecco in Colombia, and Marcia de Paredes in Peru are four examples of directors who have been in their positions for several years and who have thus provided valuable continuity in the programs of their respective countries. This is in sharp contrast, for example, to university rectors, who in some instances have been replaced as often as every six months.

INNOVATIONS IN LATIN AMERICAN ACADEMIC EXCHANGES

One welcome, though unexpected, effect of the commissions' work has been to introduce a number of innovations into academic exchange programs in Latin America that have subsequently been adopted in other regions of the world. Because they are binational, the commissions permit local representatives with expert knowledge of their countries' academic needs and possibilities to have direct access to American members who may be in a position to translate local needs into the realities of U.S. higher education and to secure prompt action.

One example of such innovation is the program to send Latin American professors to teach at American universities. Another is the State of the Art Seminars, first introduced in Brazil; these bring five to six American specialists on a specific topic to the host country at one time to conduct a conference attended by local experts. And in Peru, the Fulbright commission introduced the requirement that visiting researchers must also do some teaching to encourage them to share the fruits of their labor, which in turn elicits more

support among Peruvian counterparts.

The period and conditions of stay for visiting faculty from the United States were also made more flexible in a creative way. Traditionally the Fulbright program used to send a professor and his or her family abroad for an entire year. Latin American Fulbright programs switched to a shorter-term arrangement. This was especially important because, whereas elsewhere American faculty are permitted to teach abroad in English, in Latin America they were required to teach in Spanish or Portuguese; as a result of this policy, the pool of qualified applicants was naturally much smaller. Short visits helped to offset this problem, since more U.S. faculty could leave their home campuses for brief periods in Latin America.

The chief area of innovation, however, has been that of institutional development. Both Fulbright and LASPAU have helped Latin American universities to determine needs and priorities, then have selected staff members to receive advanced training in the United States as a prelude to returning to fill the need in the home university. The combination has both strengthened the effectiveness of the Fulbright program and increased the impact of the U.S. taxpayer's dollar devoted to academic exchange. The graduate studies pursued in these cases coincided precisely with the institutional needs of a Latin American university as they had been jointly defined, and the sponsoring Latin American university in turn contributed to the scholarship by providing salary in absentia to those LASPAU scholars accepted into the program.

In Brazil, for example, the Fulbright commission decided that faculty development and short-term study grants would be more appropriate than the traditional student-exchange program, especially since CAPES was already sending many students abroad.

The Brazilian Fulbright commission faced the handicap of being able to issue only a handful of awards in the 1970s, in comparison with the hundreds and even thousands being awarded by CAPES, the government faculty-development program. When Fulbright indicated interest in a LASPAU program in that country, I recommended on behalf of LASPAU that it would not be effective simply to add an additional six to ten physicists, engineers, or chemists to the thousands already being sent abroad for study by CAPES. Instead, it was decided to focus on two areas of study underrepresented and even overlooked by CAPES, namely, fine arts and communications. A small group of Brazilian universities that emphasized these areas was then identified so that with only a few scholarships at its disposal, Fulbright could still be assured of having a meaningful impact on Brazilian higher education. Some of the leading artists in Brazil were subsequently invited to participate in the selection process, which included personal visits for interviews with preselected candidates.

In the first few years, the program placed over 50 young Brazilian artists and art educators in a number of U.S. graduate programs in the arts with notable success. Then in 1981, the program doubled in size as a result of establishing a coordinated Fulbright-CAPES joint program for the arts. This was an important innovative step for the Fulbright program in Brazil in directing its resources toward promoting institutional development in a strategic area that complemented the efforts of a major Brazilian government program. This example also illustrates the important impact that a Fulbright program can have as its success leads to cost sharing and integration of the program into a host-government agency.

In Uruguay, LASPAU worked in the 1970s with the Universidad de la República to determine a series of fields of high priority for faculty development. Due to the earlier political climate, the university greatly suffered from a lack of mid-level staff. Many senior officials were older part-time professors who taught one or two courses, and most other faculty were very recent graduates. Fulbright entered as the first new opportunity for staff development and training abroad in several years. In Paraguay, the Catholic University was chosen as worthy of support as part of the reopening of the Fulbright dialogue in that country. A new interdisciplinary science faculty, which included Fulbright alumni among its leaders, was one of the special attractions, along with the discipline and seriousness of purpose that characterized this university.

In other countries such as Argentina, Colombia, and Costa Rica, the local Fulbright programs have also been increasingly involved in earmarking at least a portion of their small budgets for promoting institutional development through awards to faculty in priority fields who go on leave to pursue graduate studies in the United States.

BARRIERS TO ACADEMIC EXCHANGE

Despite the generally positive state of academic exchange programs conducted in Latin America under Fulbright auspices, there remain some problems that invite examination and reflection. In common with other regional exchanges, one serious issue is that of the brain drain that occurs when foreign students in the United States elect to remain rather than to return to their countries of origin once their studies are at an end. If the most able students are thus lost to more attractive careers in the United States, many Latin American nations understandably see little reason to support academic exchanges with *el gigante del norte*.

Related to this problem is the fact that Fulbright has traditionally paid little attention to alumni. Educational exchange should not simply end when a scholar returns home; some type of follow-up program should be available that can enable the scholar to remain in touch both with developments in his or her field of expertise and with the institution where he or she studied. Maintaining a link of this sort can clearly help to make the return less of a sacrifice in intellectual, though perhaps not in financial, terms. Active networks among alumni in the region would maximize the multiplier effect of studies in the United States and economize expertise budgets.

Traditionally, there has been little contact among scholars at different universities within countries or in different countries in Latin America. By fostering an alumni network, Fulbright could significantly increase ongoing and beneficial academic exchanges, which have heretofore been lacking. Alumni in general are an often overlooked resource; in the case of Fulbright the loss is all the more serious because so many alumni eventually go on to assume leadership roles in their homeland.

Opportunities for contact among Fulbrighters even while they are still in the United States have not been pursued as vigorously as they might be. Several Fulbright students currently studying in American universities have reported that they wish there was more contact with other Fulbrighters. They also missed the chance for interaction with the Fulbright office in Washington, from which they could have learned more about how program officers conceive of the Fulbright program's purpose and what their expectations of Fulbright students are. Especially for Latin Americans, such interaction would also make them much more comfortable, since a high value is always place on *personalismo*.

Orientation, especially for American scholars going south, continues to be inadequate. While more and more U.S. scholars to Latin America are now familiar with its history and culture to a degree that would have been unimaginable thirty years ago, this knowledge too often remains theoretical and abstract. There exists a need to orient individuals in relation to the skills they will be using in another cultural context. Teaching abroad, for example, involves much more than generic teaching skills—which, parenthetically, are themselves too frequently neglected in U.S. higher education—and researchers need to know the local culture in practical terms in order to be effective and culturally sensitive.

A further problem concerns the pressures exercised by the political climate. On the one hand, the military dictatorships of the 1960s and 1970s had a frequently disruptive effect on educational exchange, especially in discouraging the flow of American scholars south. During the height of political instability at Argentine universities, for example, few American Fulbrighters traveled to Argentina. In Uruguay during its period of political turmoil, a program that was small to begin with contracted to a bare minimum. In general, Fulbright commissions and posts have tried to follow the principle of keeping open the pipeline north, even when turmoil affects the southern flow. The least that can be said is that they have had to persevere in the midst of difficult circumstances and to argue unceasingly for the unpolitical nature of an exchange program that has aroused deep suspicions in some members of the political Right.

The shift toward more democratic governments in Argentina, Brazil, and Peru, among others, in the 1980s brings a promise of greater stability in maintaining an active program of educational exchange. At the same time, however, another political pressure has made itself felt in the demand to increase the tempo of exchange without adequate screening of participants. One fears that an unintended consequence of the strong push toward implementing the Kissinger Commission recommendations in Central America may be to force programs to sacrifice quality in favor of numbers.

The Venezuelan Gran Mariscal de Ayacucho Program, begun in the mid-1970s, should serve as a reminder of the potential problems that can occur when large numbers of students are dispatched for study abroad on short notice, without adequate attention to infrastructure, planning, or support. The program was inaugurated by President Andrés Pérez and his minister of intelligence, Hector Machado, with the aim of applying revenue from petroleum sales to upgrade the educational caliber of Venezuelan society. Almost overnight, a major government scholarship program came into being, sending thousands of young Venezuelans abroad for undergraduate studies. While certainly well intentioned, the Gran Mariscal de Ayacucho Program, especially in its early years, found its overall impact considerably reduced by the fact that many of its intended beneficiaries among the students were ill prepared to take full advantage of what it offered.

An analogous problem concerns the manner in which Latin American authorities select the U.S. institutions of higher learning that they wish their young people and scholars to attend. Latin American government offices—including scholarship program offices—demonstrate a general bias toward placing their scholarship recipients in only a few major U.S. universities, to the exclusion of all others. It has been very difficult to convince them that in the United States we have numerous lesser-known institutions that in many cases may be even more appropriate for a given candidate than big-name universities. In part, this situation derives from simple ignorance of realities in the United States and from the desire to interact on familiar terrain. In at least one instance, it has resulted from a program official having earlier been placed, while a student sponsored by the Agency for International Development, at a lesser-known institution that was not an ideal match, thus reinforcing a prejudice against further placement at institutions of that kind.

Let me cite one example of the pitfalls of this approach. I was helping to select a small group of scholars in nutrition and food technology in 1979. Some came from universities in major urban areas and others from small, rurally based institutions. Clearly, their needs for technical training and eventual delivery of advanced skills were quite different. Since much of the nutrition and food technology in U.S. universities was and is geared toward serving the needs of major metropolitan areas in the United States, that type of training is not most appropriate for the person who will be a nutrition specialist in a small, isolated rural community. After careful research we discovered a program in nutrition at Kansas State in Manhattan, Kansas, which had a reputable staff, including professors who had spent time in rural Latin America and were thus directly familiar with nutrition needs in the area. This, rather than the University of California at Berkeley or a similar large institution, was the ideal placement for the Latin American scholar from a rural pedagogical university. After considerable discussion, the Ministry of Planning was persuaded to accept this more practical, though less prestigious, choice. The results were fully warranted. The scholar gained exactly the type of expertise he most needed at Kansas State and returned to head a successful nutrition education program in his native region.

A final problem relates to reincorporation of students once they have finished their studies in the United States. In light of the pervasive instability among university administrations, frequently the scholar who studies abroad returns home to a changed institution. The new rector, for example, may not be willing to assign high priority to the same field as his or her predecessor and thus will not place as much importance on the reincorporation and proper use of a specialist who has just returned from the United States with advanced training. Here again, the political dimension of educational exchange programs becomes apparent.

THE EVOLVING ROLE OF EDUCATIONAL EXCHANGE IN LATIN AMERICA

If there is one direction in which the Fulbright academic exchange program should continue to evolve, it is in supplementing the education that Fulbrighters receive in U.S. colleges and universities, giving greater attention to what happens after the formal program of study is at an end.

It is my distinct bias that educational exchange programs among participants who are sponsored are much preferable to those merely oriented to upgrading the overall pool of human resources. This is a point upon which many foreign student advisers also agree. The sole exception is when students come from politically repressive countries; then it may be important to give support also to more democratically minded students against whom these governments are likely to discriminate by refusing them institutional sponsorship. Normally, however, international students with clear-cut plans and responsibilities awaiting them upon their return consistently use their time more effectively as students and scholars in the United States than those who have no such prospects. In part, this is because sponsored students are motivated by specific goals; it is also due to the fact that their U.S. academic advisers are in a much better position to assist them when they know what the ultimate aim will be. Sponsoring institutions become interested in the placement and monitoring of scholars and are often committed to sharing in costs. All involved are more deeply committed to a successful outcome, in fact, since they can see the end result and measure the student's performance accordingly.

Of all the students who come to the United States to study, the greatest number are nonsponsored and are undergraduates. A smaller number are graduate students, as are all in the Fulbright program. Fewest are those with institutional sponsorship. We should attempt to change this trend, so that limited U.S. resources are devoted more to sponsored individuals who possess a clear program of study and who have concrete roles to perform when they return home. Such a change in emphasis would simultaneously address the problems of a threatened brain drain and of reincorporation. We can also draw confidence from past Fulbright successes. Through the doors of U.S. universities have passed some of the leading agents for change in Latin American higher education today. It is U.S. university training that they carry to their home countries, and it is U.S. university education that has had an impact on educational patterns to the south that we want to continue.

Along with greater emphasis on sponsorship, we also need more attention to building a network of Fulbright alumni and to providing more contact among Fulbright scholars while they are still studying in the United States. Here enrichment programs devoted to teaching and communication skills—undertaken during the past two summers by the International Institute for Advanced Studies in Cambridge, Massachusetts, with Fulbright support—suggest a possible model for future efforts.

The beneficial results of binational planning on the Latin American commissions also suggest a second avenue to be explored in the future. This is the issue of institutional development in Latin America. It is my conviction that Fulbright could take an even stronger stand in favor of institution building in the educational sector, as well as in building centers of excellence for research. We should recognize that Fulbright will be most effective if it also promotes ongoing activity in Latin America on the part of institutions as well as individuals, working together at home in Latin America as well as in the United States.

A major opportunity exists to utilize the university as a vehicle for making a substantial contribution toward international understanding at the grass-roots level—an opportunity in which Fulbright should continue to play a leading role. In the fifth decade of its existence and the fourth of its presence in Latin America, the Fulbright initiative still has the power to inspire and to create in the field of educational exchange.

A Promising Future: The Fulbright Program with the USSR

By WILLIAM A. JAMES

ABSTRACT: This article offers a brief overview of the Fulbright program with the USSR by looking at the context in which this exchange of lecturers developed, its purpose, its achievements, some of the current critical issues facing it, and possible directions for future progress. Since its establishment during the 1973-74 academic year, this exchange has grown in size, range of academic disciplines, and geographic dispersion in the USSR. From the outset, this exchange has been a beneficiary of good U.S.-Soviet relations. Its current vigorous condition and future development are also dependent on these relations.

William A. James is currently academic exchange specialist for Czechoslovakia, Hungary, Poland, and the USSR at the United States Information Agency. He received his Ph.D. in history from the University of Washington in 1977, after spending an academic year in the USSR as an International Research and Exchanges Board grantee with Fulbright support. He was USSR program officer at the Council for International Exchange of Scholars for over five years, after which he served as assistant director of the Henry M. Jackson School of International Studies at the University of Washington.

T HIRTEEN may turn out to be a
lucky number for the Fulbright
program in the Soviet Union. Thirteen
years ago, during the 1973-74 academic
year, the first group of American and
Soviet scholars was exchanged under
the auspices of the program. It was a
significant development in the context
of U.S.-Soviet academic exchanges, for,
instead of simply adding to the existing
network of research programs, the new
exchange provided professors from both
countries with the opportunity to lecture
abroad. To this day, the Fulbright program with the USSR remains the only
exchange in the United States that enables American academics to lecture in
the vast majority of universities and
institutes under the auspices of the Soviet
Ministry of Higher Education.

Now, after years of gradual development, followed by a challenging period
when the U.S.-Soviet exchanges agreement was allowed to lapse, the Fulbright
program with the USSR appears to face
a promising future. A new U.S.-Soviet
exchanges agreement that provides better
benefits and guarantees for participants
was signed in November 1985 at the
Geneva summit. With the impetus given
by President Reagan and General Secretary Gorbachev, an additional category
of grants, known as Presidential Fellows,
is being developed in association with
the program. Finally, both sides show
signs of taking a more serious and
thorough look at how the exchange can
be refined and improved. Instead of
being a novelty, the Fulbright program
is now in the mainstream of exchange
activity between the United States and
USSR, with both sides concerned about
its progress.

The primary reason for this encouraging assessment is the interest that both
the United States and the USSR have in
improving their overall relations. Without this positive climate a new exchanges
agreement would not have been signed
and the momentum that exists in government agencies both here and there would
not be present. The state of U.S.-Soviet
relations, however, cannot adequately
explain the development of the Fulbright
program with the USSR. A clearer view
and better understanding of this academic exchange can be reached by looking
at the context in which the program
exists, the purpose of the exchange,
some of its achievements, the critical
issues its faces, and possible avenues of
future development.

CONTEXT

When the Fulbright program with
the USSR was established in 1973, official
U.S.-Soviet academic exchanges had
existed for 15 years. In 1958, the first
U.S.-Soviet exchanges agreement was
signed, which provided, among other
activities, opportunities for scholarly
research. These first research grants
between the United States and the Soviet
Union were administered in the United
States by the Inter-University Committee
on Travel Grants and were intended to
benefit predoctoral students and professors in Russian and Soviet area studies.
In 1968, this committee was reorganized
and assumed the name of the International Research and Exchanges Board
(IREX). IREX also gradually developed
contacts with the Soviet Academy of
Sciences for programs in areas of mutual
interest. The U.S. scientific community
had already established contacts with its
Soviet counterpart through an agreement signed in 1959 between the National
Academy of Sciences and the Soviet
Academy of Sciences.

The programs sponsored by the National Academy of Sciences and IREX shared two characteristics. They were sharply focused from a discipline perspective and had definite constituencies who were to benefit professionally from the exchanges. Perhaps the clearest instance of this latter point was the critical importance IREX had in enabling numerous students of Russian and Soviet studies to complete their doctoral dissertation research.

In contrast to these exchanges, the Fulbright program had a very broad mandate. Its constituency was almost the entire American academic community. Moreover, unlike a research exchange, the Fulbright exchange of lecturers could not provide a professional service. Although it could promise many rewarding personal experiences and even rare glimpses of Soviet society, it normally could not provide opportunities that were, strictly speaking, professionally productive.

Administratively, a central challenge was the fact that the Fulbright Program involved lectureships. Although research organizations have faced and will continue to encounter a variety of problematic issues in the course of finding appropriate repositories and adequate archival access for their scholars, arranging placements for lecturers is a much more complex business involving academic calendars, textbooks, and curriculum requirements. Both the American and Soviet sides had a great deal to learn about the many practical aspects of their counterpart's educational system.

Given the uneven fit of the new program into the existing exchanges network, there was some discussion initially about which agency should administer it. IREX was considered because of its experience in Soviet affairs. Until 1973, it was the only U.S. exchange

organization to deal with the Soviet Ministry of Higher Education. It also had a staff that could not only handle placement matters, but also develop publications and outreach activities that promoted greater U.S.-Soviet academic cooperation. Its strength was also its weakness, however, for IREX's primary contacts were with specialists in the field of Soviet affairs. The Council for International Exchange of Scholars (CIES), on the other hand, had a peer-review system in place and already had responsibility for Fulbright senior-scholar exchanges with the rest of the world. Its liability was the limited number and restricted area expertise of the staff it could assign to supervising the Soviet exchange. Put another way, at CIES the Fulbright program was placed within an international context, instead of a regional one.

Whether this difference in emphasis affected the progress of the exchange is difficult to determine. In the early years of the exchange, the number of grantees from each side was relatively small, falling between 5 and 11 annually, making it unnecessary to develop a large, specialized program staff. For its domestic constituency, the Fulbright program with the USSR functioned well at CIES, because of CIES's broad contacts across disciplines within the academic community and the new exchange's need for a variety of lecturers, exclusive of those with area expertise. If there was a negative aspect to the arrangement, it was in the area of relations with the Soviet Ministry of Higher Education.

Over the years, IREX had developed a manner of dealing with the ministry that was tailored to the Soviet situation. Essentially, it was built on frequent visits by members of the IREX staff, who could speak Russian and had academic backgrounds in some aspect of Russian area studies.

Introducing the Fulbright program into this context caused two types of difficulties. From the Soviet perspective, there seemed to be an initial discomfort in dealing with a system that was not similar to the IREX exchange. In fact, for many years it was not unusual for Soviet administrators and faculty to refer to grantees as IREX lecturers. From the American perspective, it was frustrating for Fulbright administrators to have a program that was continually requesting procedural exceptions, because of unique, local conditions.

One administrative detail that demonstrates this point was the matter of Fulbright staff travel. Travel abroad was a scarce commodity for both federal employees connected with the Fulbright program and CIES staff. Yet, apart from the powerful precedent of IREX's procedures, there were other factors that warranted exceptions for staff administering lecturer exchange with the USSR. For example, participation of the U.S. embassy in the administration of the Fulbright program was more limited in Moscow than elsewhere. At times, liaison with Soviet academic institutions was restricted, severely undercutting the embassy's ability to find out details relating to lecturers' appointments, university openings, and other practical features of an exchange. The embassy's staff was relatively small and extremely overworked. In these circumstances, a visit by a U.S. Fulbright administrator could help focus attention on abiding problems by having a fresh opinion brought into this discussion. It could also be the occasion for the embassy's staff to make visits to academic institutions that might otherwise be difficult to arrange. Thus staff travel to the USSR was a question with some special justifications that deserved attention.

Gradually, as the exchange grew,

some of these administrative procedures were adopted. In 1977, CIES hired a program officer with a doctorate in Russian history and fluency in the language. In 1980, the United States Information Agency hired a program officer for the USSR who also had language fluency. Travel by administrative staff was also initiated, although never reaching the level maintained by IREX. During this period the exchange not only grew in numbers, but promised an expansion of programs. A program was initiated with the USSR Ministry of Education, the organization responsible for Soviet elementary and secondary education, as well as the country's schools of education, in which two pedagogists from each side participated annually. There were serious negotiations with the Soviet Academy of Sciences about an exchange of lecturers, and a research exchange with the Soviet Ministry of Agriculture was planned. Both projects were shelved, however, following the Soviet invasion of Afghanistan.

Until the signing of the November 1985 agreement in Geneva, both sides seemed determined to keep the exchanges network operative. Although no new exchange initiatives were considered, the Fulbright program continued to function. Without an agreement, however, the exchange lost a legal basis for program management, making serious delays in nominations and confirmation of awards a common occurrence. Despite these difficulties, one positive development slowly took place. By the time of the Geneva meeting, the Fulbright program was considered a main component of U.S.-Soviet academic exchanges.

ROLE

There are two principal functions that the Fulbright program with the USSR serves. As has already been discussed, it complements the other research exchanges by providing lectureships. Second, it provides academic opportunities in the Soviet Union for the American scholar who is not a Russian or Soviet studies specialist. Until this exchange was established, only area studies specialists or scientists were able to receive research awards for scholarly work in the USSR. The Fulbright program opened the Soviet Union to the vast majority of the American academic community.

The breadth of the program's constituency can be appreciated by reviewing a roster of disciplines taught by Fulbright lecturers in the USSR, as well as a list of the U.S. universities with which these grantees are associated. The resulting directory would incorporate almost every discipline in the liberal arts curriculum, as well as a geographic dispersion among U.S. universities that would be truly representative. Equally impressive is the variety of Soviet academic institutions that have accepted Fulbright lecturers. With few exceptions Fulbrighters have taught in every constituent republic of the Soviet Union.

Beyond this professional definition of the Fulbright program's purpose is the broad mandate of increasing mutual understanding between the peoples of the United States and the USSR. Since Fulbright lecturers go to the USSR without a dissertation to research or a book to write, their stay in the USSR enables them to have a view of the Soviet experience that differs from that of other exchange participants. Lectureships also provide opportunities to meet with students and colleagues that are not available to research grantees. As a result, Fulbright lecturers usually develop an appreciation of the Soviet academic system that is based on their collegial experience, instead of their success in obtaining research materials.

For the purpose of gaining a broader appreciation of Soviet counterparts, therefore, the lecturer exchange seems to be uniquely appropriate.

ACHIEVEMENTS

The fact that the exchange still continues to exist today is a major accomplishment, given the difficult environment and obstacles that recently existed. After the U.S.-Soviet exchanges agreement was allowed to lapse in December 1979, neither the United States nor the USSR was obligated to continue the exchange. It is a testimony to the commitment of both sides to the exchange, as well as their estimate of its worth, that the exchange mechanism was kept intact during the early 1980s.[1] (see Table 1.)

Probably the most significant element of the exchange, as well as the most long-lived, is the annual lectureship appointment in American history at Moscow State University. Organized in 1974 by the late Nikolai Sivachev, a remarkable young Soviet historian who died suddenly four years ago, this lectureship has been filled consistently by an impressive roster of American historians. Over the years, a fine library of primary and secondary sources has been built up there through the generosity of the Fulbright program and Fulbright lecturers, providing students access to an unusual collection of titles.

Given the high caliber and future career paths of the Moscow State stu-

1. Although the number of grantees accepted and nominated by the Soviets diminished during the 1980s, it was not until the 1982-83 academic year that a serious drop in exchange activity occurred. At the time, this phenomenon was attributed not so much to the state of bilateral relations, but to a wholesale change in personnel in the Soviet Ministry of Higher Education's section concerned with U.S.-Soviet academic exchanges. Figures for all the years of the Fulbright program with the USSR are given in Table 1.

TABLE 1
PARTICIPANTS IN THE FULBRIGHT PROGRAM WITH THE USSR

Academic Year	Americans	Soviets
1973-74	7	5
1974-75	8	6
1975-76	8	11
1976-77	7	6
1977-78	12	5
1978-79	19	14
1979-80	14	14
1980-81	16	15
1981-82	15	6
1982-83	9	3
1983-84	8	1
1984-85	8	5
1985-86	6	4
1986-87	13	14

SOURCE: United States Information Agency, Washington, D.C.

dents, this lectureship has great importance for creating a better understanding of the United States among future generations of Soviet leaders. In order to provide a broad appreciation of the United States, a three-part survey is offered over a three-year period, starting with the U.S. Constitution and ending with World War II. Considering the usual emphasis in the Soviet curriculum on twentieth-century American history, with little emphasis on earlier periods, this schema is quite significant in itself.

In earlier years of the exchange, other attempts at establishing ongoing appointments in other fields had some success. Professor Rudolf Its, an anthropologist at Leningrad State University who taught as a Fulbrighter at Tulane University during the 1976-77 academic year, returned to the USSR with a desire to start an exchange of ethnologists. His efforts succeeded for a few years, as did a similar exchange of U.S. mathematicians requested by Novosibirsk State University. Later, the dedication of Professor Anatolii Martynov of Kemerovo State University and his American colleague, Professor Demitri Shimkin of the University of Illinois, resulted in the establishment of better contacts between U.S. archaeologists and their colleagues at Kemerovo and elsewhere in Siberia.

In a similar vein, Professor Eugene Trani, an American historian who taught at Moscow State University, was so impressed with the usefulness of academic exchanges that upon his return to the United States he endeavored to develop a program between his university, the University of Missouri at Kansas City, and Moscow State. Not only has an exchange been established, but through his efforts, as well as those of other American historians who taught in Moscow, a journal is being planned in cooperation with Soviet colleagues that will feature articles and critiques of these works by Soviet and American scholars. Now vice president for academic affairs of the University of Wisconsin system, Dr. Trani has started developing ties between Madison and Moscow, with the purpose of creating a Nikolai Sivachev chair of Russian Studies staffed by professors from Moscow State University.

CRITICAL ISSUES

Over the years, a number of aspects of the Soviet exchange have been of concern to American administrators of the Fulbright program with the USSR. A relative balance between grantees in the humanities and sciences has been a perennial topic of discussions. Assuring adequate accommodations for both grantees and spouses was another. Providing guarantees for the American scholars' professional travel in the USSR at rates charged Soviet academics, not the higher tourist charges usually expected from foreign scholars, also repeatedly figured in U.S.-Soviet negotiations. Fortunately, these and a number of other points have been dealt with successfully in the exchanges agreement signed in Geneva.

While exchange agreements are valuable documents, they are, in themselves, inadequate vehicles for administering an exchange of lecturers between two large, complex societies. Until the present, the primary concern has been to ensure the continuation of the exchange. Now might be the time for both sides to seek to improve the quality of the exchange.

As an interim measure, it might be worthwhile for American and Soviet representatives to meet at approximately the midpoint of the current agreement's duration. The focus of the discussions would be a review of the Fulbright exchange to date, improvements that can be made, and whether another administrative mechanism or regularly scheduled consultations might help to refine the exchange program's performance. For example, while the establishment of a Fulbright commission would not be warranted, some other type of administrative body, fashioned specifically for the lecturer exchange with the USSR, might

be appropriate. Even if the meeting did not result in the development of a concrete proposal, the discussions would assist in the renegotiation of the next exchanges agreement in 1988 and serve as a forum in which new exchange ideas could be presented.

This suggestion is based on a number of practical considerations. Better coordination is needed to determine where lecturers from both sides can teach in their native language. Discussions are also required regarding the role that language and literature should have in the exchange. The use of Soviet lecturers to teach a variety of languages used in the USSR would greatly assist a number of U.S. universities that want to start programs in Baltic, Central Asian, or other languages. The introduction of different resources from both sides and the growth and eventual size of the exchange should be considered. Finally, a whole range of topics that would increase the efficiency and efficacy of the lecturer exchange should be discussed.

At the present time, the bulk of the U.S. and Soviet lecturers teach classes that are usually described as enrichment courses, that is, noncredit classes that are taken in addition to the standard, required curriculum. It would be desirable for both sides to begin incorporating Fulbrighters into regular accredited courses. To date, the only required course taught regularly by a Fulbright lecturer is the American history survey at Moscow State University. Unfortunately, there is no reciprocal arrangement with an equally prestigious American university that is interested in accepting Soviet lecturers to teach a course on the history of the USSR on an annual basis. There is a great need for more thorough discussions and imagination about how to refine this exchange.

FUTURE DEVELOPMENT

Unlike other types of academic exchanges with the USSR, the potential desirability for future numerical growth in the Fulbright program would be considerable, if changes of the sort just outlined came to pass. In principle, the pool of qualified and available persons is quite large, encompassing not only the sciences or area specialists, but most of the American academic community. Before this growth could be considered, however, there is a need for more refinement and selectivity in the exchange to improve the quality of the experience both for grantees and their academic audiences.

One promising development in this direction is a proposal put forward by CIES through the Office of the Coordinator for the President's U.S.-Soviet Exchange Initiative. Known on the American side as Presidential Fellows, the program that has been proposed would retain the basic features of a Fulbright lectureship but add an outreach component, in which a grantee would spend the last part of his or her award period lecturing at other academic institutions in the area of his or her main affiliation. The intention of this new type of award is to expand the Fulbrighters' audience, in both the United States and the USSR.

For the immediate future, one factor could have a significant influence on the direction of the exchange. For the first time since the establishment of this lecturer exchange, the more experienced administrators are now located on the American side. Both within the U.S. Information Agency and at CIES there are staff members who have been associated with the Soviet exchange since its inception or from the early years of its existence, or who have served in the U.S. embassy in Moscow and worked on joint U.S.-Soviet projects. This combination of administrative know-how and professional familiarity with the USSR could be a significant component in the program's development in the next few years. The depth of experience on the American side is complemented by what appears to be a new openness and cooperative spirit of Soviet counterparts at the Ministry of Higher Education in Moscow and the Soviet embassy in Washington, D.C. There seems to be a genuine interest in improving communications and procedures that could lead to a more vital, rewarding exchange of lecturers.

In ten years, when the Fulbright program celebrates its fiftieth anniversary, another report on the exchange with the USSR will probably be requested. There is significant evidence that if circumstances in U.S.-Soviet relations permit, existing challenges will be met and overcome. In one sense, the next few years are a new test of both sides' commitment to the quality, as well as the value, of an exchange of lecturers. There is every reason to believe that when the results are available a decade from now, the outcome will be positive.

Research and Teaching
in the Middle East

By ANN B. RADWAN

ABSTRACT: Educational institutions and scholars in the Middle East and South Asia continue to produce world-class research despite the burdens imposed by the great number of students, inadequate libraries, and limited supportive institutional infrastructure. The challenges facing the foreign scholar are not dissimilar to those of the host-country academic with the exception of the entry formalities, including both the general permission to enter a country and specific permissions for access to particular libraries or sites. The long-term relationship between the guest and the host-country scholar needs to be enhanced by the development of long-term U.S.-overseas institutional relationships and of mechanisms that promote a sustained exchange of scholarship. The professional quality and commitment of the guest researcher or lecturer will be the determining factor of the success of an individual experience and of the idea of mutual understanding through educational exchange.

Ann B. Radwan received her Ph.D. in South Asian studies from the University of Pennsylvania in 1976. Between 1982 and 1984, she was a consultant with the Fulbright Program for the Near East and South Asia at the U.S. Information Agency, Washington, D.C. Currently she is the executive director, Binational Fulbright Commission, Cairo, Egypt. Her experience with the Fulbright program includes a student grant to India in 1962 and pre- and postdoctoral research grants to the Netherlands, India, Egypt, and Pakistan in 1970 and again in 1980-81.

I T is necessary to understand a bit about the academic environment of the Middle East before entering on a discussion of how the foreign scholar functions within that environment. Universities in the Middle East are public institutions the missions of which are to further the social and political objectives of the nation. These objectives include an equalization of opportunity for all classes of the society and the training of the successor generation. These missions must be pursued with grossly inadequate levels of funding, inadequate library facilities, and a crushing burden generated by the numbers of students entitled, by national policy, to university admission. The age structure of the population will guarantee that the pressure to maximize enrollments will continue indefinitely. In addition, the salaries of the professors are so low that they must supplement their incomes by private tuitions, the sale of lecture notes, and the acceptance of dual appointments.

These factors have a deleterious effect on the quality of education, the vigor of the institutions, and the attitudes of the professors. For example, a faculty of education at one of the smaller regional universities in Egypt has 10,000 enrolled students, while seating is available for fewer than half that number. The professors at a faculty of medicine at the premier Egyptian university fight a constant battle to limit the incoming class to 700 students. A typical associate professor's salary is approximately £E190 per month, roughly equivalent to the monthly wage of an experienced driver.

The truly amazing aspect of this system is the continuing ability of the professors to produce world-class research in all academic specializations including the sciences. With less than state-of-the-art laboratories, the scientists are able to publish and create a place for themselves in the international scientific community. The ability of the scholar to continue to perform, to do research under these conditions, is an indication of the extraordinary quality of the scholars and their commitment to the profession. What seems to be the case, contrary to Euclidian theory, is that the institutional whole is less than the sum of its scholarly parts.

American scholars are accustomed to high levels of supportive institutional infrastructure and noninterference in their research and teaching. Area specialists engaged in research requiring limited institutional support will be able to proceed in relatively expeditious fashion. However, those research scholars in the sciences whose work requires them to rely heavily on the institutional infrastructure will find themselves confronted by delays and the absence of the required facilities. The foreign lecturers will experience all of the frustrations of their host-country colleagues, uncertainty about the teaching schedule, classes ranging from 150 to 300 students, the absence of textbooks, and generally the lack of administrative support. They will also experience the noticeable enthusiasm of the students for individualized attention, a rare experience for many. It must be said that this lack of a direct relationship between professor and student is not due to the indifference of the host country's professors. It is, rather, a function of the very heavy teaching loads, the overwhelming number of students per class, and, in the Egyptian case, the demands placed on the professors by dual appointments at universities separated by hundreds of kilometers. What foreign researchers and lecturers find more impressive than these problems is the flourishing of the highest-quality scholarship in spite of the problems.

In all but the Gulf states and Saudi Arabia, the research and lecturing activities of foreign scholars are supported by funds generated from outside the region. These funds may be grants from public and/or private foundations or universities. In most cases, the American scholar seeking to do research or to lecture has not been specifically invited by any host-country institutions. The initial impetus comes not from the host institution or from host-country colleagues but from the individual Americans who wish to pursue a given activity in a country chosen by them. Similarly, the review and selection process for grants usually occurs outside the purview of the host governments or institutions. The Fulbright program grants, whether administered by the United States Information Agency or the U.S. Department of Education, offer an opportunity for the host country's input at the conclusion of the qualitative review. The more usual case, however, is for the final decisions to be made entirely without benefit of review by any entity in the recipient country.

The granting of permissions and the agreement by a university to receive a visiting lecturer is dependent on the perceived value of the specific activity and of academic and cultural exchanges generally, as they relate to mutual understanding, with the hoped-for side effects of greater mutual appreciation for the countries and cultures represented in the exchanges. All of these benefits are difficult, if not impossible, to quantify. Thus the positive response of host government and institutions requires a high level of belief in the efficacy of such activities.

Increasingly, the host-country governments and scholars are asking questions about what would be the tangible benefits for them if the activity in question were to take place. In the developing world, the priorities are in academic specializations commonly labeled developmental, such as applied science, health science, engineering, and agriculture. It is at this point that the priorities of the scholar seeking entry into a given country and the priorities of the governments and universities that are responsible for granting permissions and faculties begin to diverge.

Many of the Americans who regularly come to the area for research are area specialists, with discipline specializations concentrated in the social sciences and humanities. Their interests and research have added immeasureably to the body of knowledge available to the West through their publications and teaching. While it is essential for Americans to be aware of, let us say, the philosophical bases for Islam, is it of equal importance to the host government or to the host academic community that Americans acquire this type of knowledge? Generally, the answer is no.

Previously, in such specializations as archaeology, the host government was positively predisposed to granting permissions for foreign scholars, as there was a dearth of trained in-country specialists, limited money to be spent on such activities, and a strong desire to know one's own history. Nationalism acted as a fillip to the latter. Over the past two or three decades, however, the countries of the region have developed their own coterie of highly trained specialists in all fields, thereby decreasing the need for outside experts. The only continuing deficiency is money and perhaps that is a rather precarious base for guaranteeing long-term foreign access to research materials.

In my judgment, the rules of the game are changing. Scholars and bureaucrats of the host country have learned at least one lesson from their American colleagues: decisions regarding such activities and/or permissions should be based on a cost-benefit analysis. The cost factor is most often not money but rather potential social and political ramifications of the investigation into a given topic. While the benefits are intangible, the costs are often seen as all too tangible.

"OH, WHAT TANGLED WEBS WE WEAVE . . ."

Obtaining a grant is often the easiest part of doing research or of teaching in the Middle East and South Asia. At that moment there begins a minuet through the minefields of governmental approvals, non-objections certificates, research clearances, entry or residence visas, and permissions to use a specific collection or to visit a particular site. Each step in this dance bears the possibility of catastrophe: a nondecision can be as damaging as a "no" decision. Having been personally involved in this process for years, first as a grantee waiting for clearances and currently as an administrator, I find that there seems to be no more accurate way of knowing the answer to the question "What are the bases for X government's decisions?" than reading coffee grounds in saucers.

Recently the sources of funds for certain kinds of research have been a favorite subject of discussion among American scholars. For example, at a meeting of scholar-administrators held concurrently with the Middle East Studies Association in 1984, the topic of the funding of research by the Defense Intelligence Agency was raised. Quickly the comments began to focus on the appropriateness of the U.S. government's funding of research. After much righteous and not-so-righteous discourse, the assembled were asked whether or not this concern with accepting U.S. government funding included such programs as the Fulbright program, which is substantially funded by the U.S. government. The immediate response was an exclamatory "of course not." What was instructive about this episode was not the absolution of the Fulbright program, but the ease with which all of the research funded entirely or partially by the U.S. government can be tarred by the brush meant only for certain agencies within the U.S. government. If American academics can so easily lump all U.S. government funding together, why should it be expected that host-government agencies that grant research permissions or clearances be fully conversant with the unique agendas of any particular funding entity within the complex structure of the American system?

The imprecision of the debate within the American scholarly community is reflected and amplified in the host country. The result is that the specific character of the funding source and its real connotations are lost to all but the most careful observer. The debate about appropriateness of funding sources is an important aspect of American academic life. How important is this to the process of conducting research in the Middle East or South Asia? How do the funding sources or previous associations of an American scholar, with, let us say, the Defense Intelligence Agency, affect the decision to grant the necessary permissions? Seemingly, the decisions are based on the content of the current research project, the content of previously published material by the scholar, and the previous activities of the grantee in the host country. This is not to imply that funding emanating from such an obvious source as the Central Intelligence Agency would not be a factor in the host government's decision. Although the funding source might be used as one reason for non-approval, the decision is probably linked to other factors that carry more weight.

As the content and quality of the research proposal usually constitute the basis of the funding decision, it is the content that is most often the determining factor in the granting of the required permission by the host government. If the basis for the development of a research proposal is the reflection of a scholarly interest—a wanting to know—the review will focus on whether or not the host entity wants the information known and whether or not the scholarly investigation will cut too close to national sensitivities. American scholars know this, either by direct experience or by the experience of others. As a consequence there is often a tendency to become involved in second guessing, an attempt to choose the phrases that will not alarm those granting permissions. This path is a modest and acceptable technique, somewhere between diplomacy and obfuscation. Another route is to propose a benign research topic for the purpose of obtaining entry while the real research interests are totally different from those stated. This latter choice often causes the scholar's visa to be terminated and may have negative ramifications for those scholars following in the wake. At least, it casts a shadow of doubt and, at worst, it may generate an atmosphere of suspicion that affects even the innocent.

Veracity is the essential element. If the grant is awarded on the bases of the stated topic and the accompanying meth-odology, it seems a natural part of the contractual relationship, between the grantee and granter, that the actual activity be an approximation of the proposed activity. Mid-course corrections of topic and method should and do occur. These are not matters of concern. However, a shift from a proposal focusing on, for example, seventeenth-century markets to an active investigation of contemporary fundamentalist movements is a new direction, not a refinement of the plan based on the field experience. This type of action is usually a result of the inability, on the part of the person seeking permission, to judge accurately what will or will not be approved. As the individual scholar and the facilitating institution in the country are usually not told why permission was not granted, one is prone to engage in speculative exercises without the benefit of data.

Aside from the official hurdles, the American researcher has other barriers to overcome. One may be the attitude of the host country's academic community. In India, Pakistan, and Egypt, and doubtlessly elsewhere, there is a mounting concern that American researchers collect data and material available in the host country and depart with their photocopies and three-by-five cards without an opportunity for the host-country academic community to benefit from the research. The absence of any effective mechanism for facilitating this flow of completed research back to the host-country academic community is not the fault of the individual scholar.

The organizations and institutions that have been created to facilitate the exchange of scholars have not developed effective mechanisms to facilitate the exchange of scholarship. There is much talk of dialogue, but little has been done to make the voices audible to the other party. This interchange of ideas is one purpose of the Fulbright program. The technique of moving bodies around the world has been perfected, but we have not done as well with thoughts. Solutions are fraught with difficulties. Among the first is the lack of dollar funds for non-U.S. scholars or universities to purchase the resulting publications and the lack of money to establish comprehensive data banks. This impecuniousness is real enough, but it is exacerbated by the lack of concerted interest in the problem by the U.S. scholarly community, which could act as an effective lobby for the establishment of means to begin to solve this problem.

Perhaps the definition of "research access" in the Middle East and South Asia should be broadened to include access to the research findings by the host country's academic community and not only access for U.S. scholars to the data located within the region.

WOMEN AND RESEARCH IN THE MIDDLE EAST AND SOUTH ASIA

A few days prior to beginning this exercise, I was asked why there are so many American women studying and doing research in the Middle East. The questioner had visited Damascus and observed that a noticeable majority of the U.S. Fulbright student or senior grantees were women and that many of them were making every effort to extend their stay in Syria. The syndrome is not, in my opinion, unique or even rare. Prior to even a cursory discussion of the topic it is worthwhile to make a distinction between the professional experiences of women studying, lecturing, or doing research in the region and their social or personal experiences.

Middle Eastern and South Asian women have attained positions within their academic communities not as tokens but as integral parts of these elite groups. Women professors are not considered so noteworthy as to induce comment or unique treatment, at least not negative unique treatment. In the region under discussion, scholars and professors continue to be highly respected. Often this pedestal requires conformity to what a particular culture expects from this special category of persons. These expectations are rather like a nineteenth-century vision: the gentleman or lady scholar who is far removed from the overtly competitive, gloves-off milieu from which most American scholars spring. This background plus the urgency to complete specified research goals during a relatively short time leads to a situation where there is a noticeable impatience with host-country inefficiencies, with delays and obstacles that are not deliberately placed in the path of foreign researchers, men or women, but confront all scholars engaged in such activities.

Women, if anything, have an advantage over their male colleagues. Women who are preparing to do research that may be considered politically sensitive are often given permission when a male would be refused. Why? That nineteenth-century vision, which sees female scholars as ladies, does not allow the authorities to see these lady scholars as agents for intelligence gathering or as individuals wishing to foment political disturbances.

This perception, while facilitating access, has its less than supportive aspect on the emotional level for the American female scholar. It has often been my experience that while an informant is providing the information requested, there will be direct questions as to why

I am bothering myself with all this work, why I would be separated from my husband, home, and family for doing a job of lesser importance like research. Other questions that refer to husband's permission or comments about choosing profession over family matters all seem out of place at best and degrading at worst to the scholar who has trained herself to view her activities in a very different way. The visceral reaction to these comments is often negative and creates concern that one is not taken seriously as a scholar. The personal attitudes of the host country's bureaucrat or informant are only important if they affect the ability of the scholar to perform. The number of American women scholars who are regularly and repeatedly engaged in research in the region seems to indicate that such personal comments do not interfere with women's professional activities.

The situation for an American scholar whose surname demonstrates a personal cultural connection to the region is somewhat more difficult than for her Anglo-Saxon sister. The assertiveness that is acceptable for a foreigner is less so for someone who has this implicit cultural connection. If, in cultural terms, the ladies who have certain surnames should know better, in professional terms they are often afforded an opportunity to know more about that which is the subject of their research. This is especially true for studies of social phenomena and for all subjects directly or indirectly involving women.

The success or failure of the foreign woman scholar to achieve the purposes of her research is primarily dependent on her commitment to the project, her level of professionalism, and her determination to overcome the bureaucratic hurdles. These elements are common for all scholars working in the area and are not special requirements or obstacles designed only for women.

THE LECTURER EXPERIENCE

The Fulbright program is one of the few available for Americans wishing to lecture abroad. Lecturer grantees are not area specialists, although some may have had personal or professional overseas experience. Often the American professor who applies for a lecturing grant is seeking a cultural experience rather than pursuing an activity primarily related to his or her career trajectory, for it is well known that the inscription carved above the passageway to promotion and tenure is "research and publish." It has been my observation that generally the academic credentials of the lecturer applicant are somewhat below those of the research applicant. The net effect of this tendency is that the lecturer cadre may not represent or exemplify the dynamic that gives shape and momentum to the American academic community.

The lecturer often does bring one of the most unique aspects of the American educational system into the overseas environment, namely, a genuine commitment to the transmission of information to the students, coupled with a determination that they learn how to develop and express their own thoughts. Within the region, the primary, secondary, preparatory, and baccalaureate educational systems do not foster the development of critical analysis or independent thought. The information the teacher provides, the book contains, and the examiners will expect are the parameters of the learning process.

The American lecturer deposited in this context will find the students' habit of unquestioning acceptance of professors' utterances difficult to overcome or to adjust to. It often takes an academic year for the visiting professor to find a way to relate to the students as coequal partners in the learning process without falling from that pedestal upon which the system has placed him or her. One could counter this statement by insisting that it would not matter if the visiting professor were pedestalless. I believe that it is important in the regional context to bend, but not to break, the sometimes barnacle-covered traditions. The respect and cooperation of colleagues at the host institution is necessary for a successful academic and cultural experience. Many of the professors at the host-country university have received advanced degrees from institutions in Europe or the United States. They are aware of the positive aspects of these systems as they themselves have been, in their evaluation, direct beneficiaries. They are also aware of the differences between those systems and the one in which they function. The foreign lecturer and the host-country colleagues are therefore in somewhat similar positions as

they attempt to bring elements of one academic tradition into an often incompatible system. The foreign lecturer has an opportunity to act as a catalyst for change within a department or college.

One noteworthy benefit that often occurs from the lecturers' experience is the development of long-term institutional relationships. These partnerships of U.S. and overseas universities are not only the outgrowth of an individual experience, but are the logical extension of the traditional Fulbright program.

The Americans who choose to do research or to lecture in the Middle East and South Asia are expecting a special professional and/or personal experience. Their expectations are usually fulfilled. The success of all academic exchanges rests neither on the funds available nor on the administrative structures but rather on the individuals who are the participants in these exchanges. The history of academic exchanges between the United States and the region certifies that somehow those with "the right stuff" have been the ones selected.

ANNALS, *AAPSS,* **491,** May 1987

Education with a World Perspective—
A Necessity for America's Political
and Economic Defense

By BARBARA W. NEWELL

ABSTRACT: American businesses and the military are forming a new alliance with education for they are experiencing critical deficiencies in international expertise. As a result, they are calling for strengthening the international perspective of American education. Proposals to meet these needs should incorporate changes in the entire education system, build on the multicultural, multiracial characteristics of American society, take advantage of the vast expansion of the international information base made possible by computers, and incorporate an international extension service for American business.

Barbara W. Newell was U.S. ambassador and permanent delegate to the United Nations Educational, Scientific, and Cultural Organization from 1979 to 1981 and chancellor of the State University System of Florida. She is currently visiting senior lecturer at Harvard University and Regents Professor at Florida State University.

T HE time for a global perspective is now.

In a recent survey, 20 percent of American students could not even find the United States on a world map.[1]

In 1960, the United States was the world's largest exporter of manufactured goods. Today, the United States has been surpassed by Germany and Japan and our share of the world market has shrunk from 25 percent to 10 percent.[2]

A Japanese businessman in Paris, when asked what language he thought most useful for international trade, is reported to have responded in flawless French, "Sir, the most useful international language in world trade is not necessarily English, but rather it is the language of your client."[3] Yet one American high school in five has no foreign language instruction—modern or ancient—for its students.[4]

The result is that there were sales problems in Latin America when General Motors named its car Nova—meaning in Spanish "it won't go."[5]

The result is that Schweppes Tonic was advertised in Italy as "bathroom water."[6]

NEW ALLIES FOR
EDUCATIONAL CHANGE

Business and military leaders in the name of national self-interest are joining academics and internationalists in advocating expansion of research and instruction in the area of international affairs and languages. This new alliance can change the national education agenda. It also raises questions of free inquiry and academic priorities. This article aims to set out the issues raised by the new alliance.

Those with long memories have reason to wonder whether there is a new alliance. When in 1965 the International Education Act was passed,[7] there were high expectations, but funds to match these expectations did not follow. A decade later President Carter's Commission on Foreign Language and International Studies again attempted to rouse American attention to international concerns.[8] They found foreign language instruction in a shambles. Yet eight years after this finding America remains the only country in the world where one may graduate from college without even one year of foreign language study.[9] The commission also found Americans falling behind in education for international understanding—a polite euphemism for geographic and cultural illiteracy and curricular isolationism.

But I believe 1987 is different from 1965 and 1979. The economic climate and geopolitical posture of the country have changed. American business and the military are experiencing critical deficiences in international expertise. In this climate of concern two study commissions have been initiated by the Reagan

1. "America's Crisis in International Competence: Our Nation's Failure to Educate Students for the Future: A Compilation of Facts and Observations" (Manuscript, American Institute for Foreign Study and the National Council on Foreign Language and International Studies, n.d.).

2. Ibid.

3. Ibid.

4. Ibid.

5. Joseph Lurie, "America's Globally Blind, Deaf and Dumb," *Foreign Language Annals*, 15(6): 418 (1982).

6. Ibid.

7. International Education Act, Pub. L. 89-698-8, Stat. 1066 (29 Oct. 1965).

8. *Strength through Wisdom: A Critique of U.S. Capability: A Report to the President from the President's Commission on Foreign Language and International Studies*, 1979.

9. Lurie, "America's Globally Blind, Deaf and Dumb," p. 420.

administration. Both panels call for immediate action to correct the void in international education.

The first study resulted from a request by President Reagan to the Business and Higher Education Forum to explore ways to make American business more competitive. The movers and shakers of the business community recommended that the United States expand program and curricular requirements in the fields of foreign language, culture, and sociopolitical institutions.[10]

The U.S. Department of Defense initiated the second study by contracting with the Association of American Universities to prepare a report on the research and instructional needs of Americans in the area of international affairs and language. This report calls for the establishment of a foundation for international studies set up, like the National Science Foundation, as a federal agency.[11]

The military and the business community have different reasons for their concern, a different history of involvement with international academic programs, and different needs.

The Defense Department has long been a supporter of area studies and language programs and has been a beneficiary of these programs. Today, the needs for international expertise are greater than ever as new areas of the world are declared critical to our national defense. It is urgent that we know more about our newly recognized neighbors.

Academic programs capable of meeting these needs are retrenching at the very time the demand is increasing for more experts on more countries who are more and better trained. Inflation has cut in half federal support for the Fulbright exchange and for area studies programs, and federal dollars for university research budgets have been reduced even more.[12] The number of fellowships for foreign languages and international area studies that are federally financed dropped from a peak of 2557 in 1969 to 829 in 1978.[13] The Ford Foundation, which spent $27 million annually between 1960 and 1967 toward training and research in international affairs and foreign studies, dropped its annual support by the end of 1980 to $3-$4 million.[14]

State and university budgets have not taken up the slack. In fact, during recent years inflation and academic retrenchment characterize most university budgets. At such times interdisciplinary programs, which have a weak political base in the conservative world of academe, lose ground. Programs for esoteric languages with small enrollments have become harder to support.

The urgency of the business community is the product of a fundamental change in the dependency of the American economy on world trade. Roughly 25 percent of the United States' gross national product is derived from foreign trade, and the proportion is growing.[15] Almost one-third of U.S. corporate profits are generated by international business activities.[16] Over one-third of U.S.

10. Business and Higher Education Forum, *America's Competitive Challenge as Need for a National Response: A Report to the President of the United States* (Washington, DC, 1983).

11. Robert L. Jacobson, "Foundation for International Studies Proposed in Report to Defense Dept.," *Chronicle of Higher Education*, p. 1. (Oct. 1986).

12. Commission on International Education, *What We Don't Know Can Hurt Us* (Washington, DC: American Council on Education, 1984), p. 9.

13. Ibid.

14. Ibid.

15. Ibid., p. 6.

16. Ibid.

agricultural land produces food for export.[17]

As Lester Thurow summarized the American condition:

America is now in a world where transportation costs are unimportant and everything that can be traded is traded or soon will be traded, including many things normally considered untradable, such as buildings. . . . Firms that do not fight to capture foreign markets will find that they have to spend all their time defending their home markets. . . .

The reality of a world market is here, a reality which most Americans won't like, for no one likes to go from a position of secure isolated economic superiority to one of insecure competitive equality. Like it or not, however, Americans must cope with the situation that prevails.[18]

Illustrative of how international trade affects the skill requirements of the American work force is a survey by the Florida Consortium on Multilingual Multicultural Education of 320 Florida firms engaged in foreign trade.[19] Of 200 firms that responded:

—73 percent need employees able to speak a foreign language;

—66 percent need employees able to read a foreign language;

—54 percent need employees able to write in a foreign language;

—in a foreign country only 22 percent of business is conducted in English;

—24 percent train or retrain their employees in a foreign language;

—63 percent indicated that a knowledge of a foreign language is essential to conduct business abroad;

—76 percent indicated that a knowledge of a foreign country's business practices and customs is essential to conduct business abroad; and

—76 percent indicated that they foresaw a greater involvement by their companies with companies or individuals from other countries.

Multinational corporations loom ever larger in all aspects of the American economy. We are told the Ford of our future will have a Japanese transmission and a Brazilian motor and will be assembled in Mexico. The future president of the Ford Motor Company may even be European. If American managers are to compete in this world they must match the international sophistication of their competitors.

Different languages, different consumer buying patterns, different cultures of business do affect the U.S. balance of payments. American industry urgently needs help in retooling for this new world market.

For many who have dedicated their professional lives to international concerns, this emerging commonality of interests with the military-industrial complex is distasteful. All parties—academic, business, and military—can agree on the need to enhance the international expertise of the community of scholars and to expand curricula to incorporate an international perspective. But when one gets to issues of the generation of new knowledge and the dissemination of international expertise to the community outside the halls of ivy, disputes arise. The cultures of the academic world and their new allies come into conflict.

Many academics worry that the lines

17. Ibid.

18. Lester C. Thurow, *The Zero-Sum Solution: Building a World Class American Economy* (New York: Simon & Schuster, 1985), p. 52.

19. Anne Campbell and Clemens L. Hallman, "Foreign Language and Cross Cultural Skills: A Survey of the Needs of Florida's International Business Community" (Manuscript, Consortium of Multilingual Multicultural Education, University of Florida, 1983).

will become blurred between study and research for human understanding, on the one hand, and study to enhance military intelligence or corporate profit, on the other. They worry about acceptability and entreé abroad of the American academic community. Researchers fear loss of control of their research product. Questions concerning academic purpose and the control of the university agenda are raised. Understandings were reached before; however, we must now think through the implications of new activities and incorporate the concerns of a new generation of scholars whose formative years were the sixties and the seventies, rather than the forties and fifties.

Having described the need, underscored the urgency, and identified the political players who have sufficient muscle to bring change, we may now ask, What proposals might be on the educational agenda? How should the new proposals differ from those that have been on the educational docket for the past two decades?

PROPOSITIONS

I should like to underscore four propositions.

First, we must enhance the global perspectives of the entire educational system, not just higher education. Curricular change should be designed from kindergarten through college and professional school. Teacher training is a necessary building block for the elementary and secondary curricular enhancement. The need for cooperation is particularly obvious in the area of language instruction. Early exposure to foreign languages with more intensive training over a longer period has been recommended by commissions and experts. Now we should put these recommendations into practice.

Similar joint planning for the inclusion of geography and materials on other cultures, including history, political science, and economics, at all levels of the curriculum needs to get under way.

Second, besides a systematic approach to incorporate an international perspective in the curriculum, we would do well to build our curricular change on the ethnic and racial pluralism of this country. The United States is as multicultural a country as exists on earth, yet we are apt to build our international programs forgetting the richness of our own heritage. Starting where students are is good pedagogy. To emphasize understanding and appreciation of our heritage to students strengthens our community. To learn to articulate and utilize our diversity in the international community is to strengthen our hand at both the political and economic bargaining table.

Third, to meet urgent business needs, the plans of the eighties must incorporate an expansion of the international service component of the university. Businesses needing assistance to develop their foreign trade should have easy access to academic expertise. In a phrase, what we need is an international extension service for American business.

Universities should develop continually updated lists of faculty who have language and/or other expertise regarding different countries of the world. These lists could be used by the agencies needing consultants and could form the base for the public service component of an institution.

An example of a developing international service activity by universities is to be found in the cooperative endeavor under way in Florida and Georgia.[20] In those states a computerized list is being

20. The project is being undertaken by the World Technology Center of Atlanta, GA.

compiled of all faculty within public and private universities and colleges according to interests and talents. It is hoped in the near future that a business exploring trade, for example, with the Ivory Coast can find who has expertise about that country in all areas from language to religion, from the economy to the political climate. In addition to providing businesses with consultants, state institutions are preparing to provide short courses as needed to train America's businesspeople going overseas and nationals from abroad who have been designated by American companies as part of their trading endeavor.

A second example of such an expanded service component is the technical assistance by business school faculty to firms that wish to explore or expand their international markets. Such support can be particularly effective for small high-tech enterprises and businesses dealing in information services.

A fourth dimension that must be appreciated as we work to enhance the international perspective of our educational community is the impact of computers on research and our knowledge base. Computers grant us the opportunity for an explosion of information about things international. This opportunity needs to be fostered and, if appropriately nurtured, can drastically alter the scholarly base of the education community. International data bases could soon be as readily available as information about the local setting. New questions may be explored because of this enhanced information base. Scholarly inquiry will follow these new data. International questions are bound to expand their place on the American research agenda and thus throughout university curricula.

Such predictions assume that care will be taken to preserve and make accessible international data series and that knowledge resulting from research will be shared. Free access and publication must remain a pillar of academic practice if exploration of international issues is to be encouraged. There are two practical arguments for this stance. First, tenure and promotion depend on publication. Young academics must not be denied recognition if we wish them to undertake international research. Second, if we restrict access and publication, we may not be able to maintain access to foreign sources.

If one takes the long perspective, American education has changed markedly in the past half century. Non-Western studies are found on most campuses. Visitors from abroad have joined the most remote academic communities. The trend is in the right direction, but the urgency for a world perspective has so accelerated that we can no longer afford to be satisfied by small, incremental change. As jobs expand for the bilingually competent and business recognizes and makes known its needs for more internationally sophisticated employees, the payoff for students and institutions will increase the pace of change. But waiting for the market is not sufficient. Human survival, as well as business competitiveness and defense capability, depends on the speed with which American educational institutions incorporate an international perspective.

Thanks to high tech, Americans were able to watch the negotiations for the Tehran hostages, yet many of our college students are unable to identify Iran on a map. The Chernobyl accident is destroying the economy of Lapland, yet curricula have yet to recognize how small and interdependent our satellite has become. The time for a global perspective is now.

Durable Academic Linkages
Overseas: A National Agenda

By RICHARD D. LAMBERT

ABSTRACT: As a nation we spend about $1 billion annually on a bewildering potpourri of international exchange and training programs. Some attention to the cross-sectional profile of exchanges resulting from the many individual programs is needed. The current mix of programs is unbalanced as to sponsor, clientele, countries covered, and purpose. Four functions of exchange and training programs are identified: (1) the export of American technology and skills; (2) familiarization with another society; (3) transnational sharing of science and technology; and (4) research about other countries. It is argued that our overwhelming emphasis on the first two purposes must be balanced by greater emphasis on the latter two. In particular, in the social sciences and the humanities the provision of opportunities to build an interacting network of scholars similar to those in the natural sciences is called for. There is also a need for an increase in the opportunities for international affairs specialists to conduct their research abroad.

Richard D. Lambert is editor of The Annals, *professor of sociology at the University of Pennsylvania, and the first director of the National Foreign Language Center at Johns Hopkins University. He was formerly president of the Association for Asian Studies and of the American Academy of Political and Social Science. His most recent books are* Beyond Growth: The Next Stage in Language and Area Studies; A National Agenda for International Studies; Points of Leverage: An Agenda for a National Foundation for International Studies; *and* The Transformation of an Indian Labor Market.

W HETHER we like it or not, and many do not, since World War II our society has become increasingly enmeshed in a web of international linkages. We obviously cannot deal with the increasing internationalization of our society by staying at home, nor do we. The decades since World War II have witnessed a remarkable American diaspora, sending our citizens in ever increasing numbers to each and every part of the world. Before World War II American travelers to, say, New Delhi or Osaka were few and the number of American residents there minuscule. Now it is difficult to stand for very long in the airport of even so remote a place as Leh, Ladakh, without meeting at least one other American—tourist, businessperson, government official, professor, student. Recent terrorist attacks on air travelers and eddies of anti-Americanism may stanch some of the flow for a while, but millions of Americans will continue to travel abroad.

There is little point in trying to limit or direct much of this outflow, but part of the movement of people, ideas, and skills is so essential to our national interest that special government and privately supported programs have been developed to sustain them. Basing our international linkages solely upon the somewhat random process of individual-initiated journeys would assure that some of the most important ones would not occur. It is not surprising, therefore, that a thicket of intersecting, but separately funded and administered, programs, both public and private, should have grown up to foster what are usually referred to as international exchange and training programs. Almost every federal government agency and many private foundations have their own. Together, they comprise a bewildering potpourri of nationally supported international exchange and training programs, amounting to somewhere near $1 billion annually. In 1984, federal programs for international exchange and training involved approximately 90,000 participants moving in and out of the United States and cost $742.1 million,[1] and this is without counting an approximately $100 million program conducted by the Department of Energy for taking physicists and other atomic scientists to and from the United States.

In addition to programs of the U.S. government that provide direct support for international exchanges, federal funds mix freely with private funds and even those of other governments to sponsor a number of other exchanges. For instance, the Institute of International Education, a private organization in New York, in 1984 administered 163 different transnational education and training programs sponsored by 120 governments, foundations, corporations, universities, binational agencies, and international agencies worldwide.[2] In the same year, the Social Science Research Council (SSRC) and the American Council of Learned Societies (ACLS) jointly expended federal funds—primarily on regranting authority from the National Endowment for the Humanities—and private foundation funds—primarily from the Ford, Hewlett, and MacArthur foundations—to send 67 predoctoral and 132 postdoctoral re-

1. For these and other data on governmentally supported international exchange and training programs as of 1984, see "Report on U.S. Government International Research and Training Programs, 1984," mimeographed (Washington, DC: United States Information Agency, 1985).

2. *Sponsored Projects, Nineteen Eighty-Four* (New York: Institute of International Education, 1984), p. 5.

search scholars to 66 countries. In 1984, the International Research and Exchanges Board (IREX), again mixing federal and private moneys, sent 25 American graduate students, 27 professors, and 31 language teachers to the Soviet Union, while 21 students, 25 professors, and 32 language teachers came here. Additionally, the United States sent 63 junior and senior scholars to the seven other East European countries with which IREX organizes exchanges, while 78 scholars came here. And there are many programs whose support is entirely private. Some foundations—for example, the Marshall Fund, the Scandinavian Foundation, the Luce Foundation—run their own programs. And individual multinational corporations sponsor educational exchange programs for their own employees' children as well as others; such corporations include, for example, Caltex, American Express, Banco de Bilbao, Chase Manhattan, Citibank, Ford Motor Company, RCA, and Levi Strauss. And there are hundreds of thousands of students and faculty members going to and from the United States who fund their own transnational educational experiences. Together, these comprise substantial sums of public and private moneys and involve large numbers of people.

The consequence of such a rich array of programs for international exchange and training is, in one respect, a tribute to our country's diversity, its mix of public and private support in meeting national needs. Seen cross-sectionally, however, it borders on chaos. For instance, the combination of U.S. government agencies sponsoring exchangees must seem bizarre to the cultural affairs officer sitting in an embassy overseas who has to deal separately with each program. For example, in India for

1984, programs bringing Indians to the United States included two different programs of the Agency for International Development (AID), two different programs of the Department of Agriculture, one of Commerce, three of Interior, two of Transportation, six in Health and Human Services, two in the National Science Foundation (NSF), and seven programs in the United States Information Agency (USIA). There were 17 different U.S. government programs taking Americans to India. Similarly, for Japan, there were 25 different agency programs taking Japanese to the United States and 27 taking Americans to Japan.[3] And if we add the privately funded programs, the complexity increases even more. Each of these programs doubtless has its own rationale and mandate, but surely some overall planning articulating the various programs would not be out of order. Is a mirror image of the American governmental structure the way to organize our exchanges with these countries?

Similar questions could be asked about the overall geographic profile of our exchanges. If we were to start from scratch, would the distribution of international exchange and training programs among the different countries be what we have now? Leaving aside the Department of Defense training programs as a special case, would we by design put some one-fourth of all of our exchange and training resources in just six countries: the United Kingdom, Germany, Egypt, India, Japan, and the Philippines? Would almost a third of the Americans we send abroad under official auspices go to Western Europe and Canada and

3. For country profiles, see *"U.S. Government International Research and Training Programs,"* app. A.

only half as many to Latin America and the Caribbean?

And, given the likely change in the nature of technology flows in the world of the future, should we spend so overwhelming a proportion of our national resources on training people from other countries—42,252 foreigners—compared with the need to send Americans abroad? In 1984, in contrast, only 14,736 Americans were sent abroad. Would we put quite so much stress on training and the export of American technology, compared with a strategy for importing or exchanging technology and ideas with other nations?[4] Would military training—of 16,980 foreigners—supported by the Defense Department loom quite so large in our strategy, or AID with 10,143, or the Peace Corps with 5,661? Together these programs alone reach almost twice as many foreign nationals as the total number of Americans served. Reflecting, as it does, the period of unrivaled American technological and intellectual supremacy, the period in which we believed that the answer to the world's problems lay in bringing all nations to a technological par with the United States, is this emphasis on technology export the one best suited for the decades to come? How, in these changed circumstances, do we develop an intellectual import policy to match our highly developed export policy?

These are the kinds of issues that we should address through the collection of the relevant data and through the conduct of the public dialogue needed to create an overall national strategy. Given our system of productive pluralism, no one would suggest that a single czar in charge of all exchanges be created, nor that they should be bent to a single purpose. It would be useful, however, if we were to take a more than occasional look at what the full range of transnational exchange and training programs is with respect to a particular country or set of countries, private as well as public. A start on this process is represented by the establishment within USIA of an Exchanges Policy and Coordination Unit, which maintains a computerized file of federal agency programs and issues an annual report summarizing and aggregating data pertaining to those programs. This unit was established as a result, in part, of a General Accounting Office report urging "meaningful coordination" of our international exchange and training programs.[5] There is no evidence, however, that policy decisions have been made on the basis of these data, nor do they include consideration of any of the diverse private programs that are also operating in this area.

The essential point, however, is not just to assemble another computerized data bank, no matter how rich, but to use the cross-sectional data currently available to consider what our overall national policy ought to be. For a while, it looked as though this would be done. In June 1982 USIA established an Advisory Panel on International Exchange. At the outset it seemed as if it would make a try at establishing an overall federal policy in this area. Its mandate was to determine "the purposes, magnitude, and format of international exchange programs in each of the following

4. For an interesting discussion of this issue with respect to our reopened scholarly relations with China, see David M. Lampton, Joyce Madancy, and Kristen W. Williams, *A Relationship Restored: Trends in U.S. China Educational Exchanges, 1978-1984* (Washington, DC: National Academy Press, 1986).

5. *Coordination of International Exchange and Training Programs* (Washington, DC: General Accounting Office, 1978).

sectors in the United States: the U.S. Government, the private non-profit sector, the private-for-profit sector, and higher education."[6] However, by the time the final report was written, the panel's recommendations were focused solely on the Fulbright program, leaving the others in the data bank.

What is needed, of course, is a periodic look at the overall dimensions of our transnational exchange and training programs. At the minimum we must create a grid of purposes, clients, countries, and programs so that the government's various programs can fit into an overall national strategy, privatizing and helping to marshal nongovernmental resources where appropriate, funding and administering those programs that are obviously the responsibility of the federal government, and helping to facilitate and coordinate the full range of national activities. By this we mean coordination and not central control. International exchanges are almost the prototype of the mixed economy in international studies; that is, some portion comprises governmental activities, and another portion, private. The sponsors are widely dispersed both within the government and in the private sector. International exchanges also involve delicate bilateral negotiations that must be conducted separately with many different foreign governments. The difficult task is to develop a coordinating and facilitating strategy that retains the best of the energy and inventiveness of the individual initiatives but allows the nation constantly to take the overview: measuring the effect of the many dispersed initiatives against an overall national agenda; calling attention to cross-purposes and overlap; consolidating or subdividing programs where that is useful; and calling attention to, and in some cases actively seeking to fill in, glaring gaps in our national coverage.

THE FUNCTIONS OF INTERNATIONAL EXCHANGE AND TRAINING

Questions concerning the mix of sponsors, countries, and domestic versus overseas investments are worthy of examination. Even more important, however, is a fresh look at the fundamental purposes of exchanges and a consideration of whether they fully serve the diverse national needs arising from the increasing internationalization of our society. In the most general terms, it would appear that our international exchange and training programs serve the following principal purposes.

First, they train nationals of other countries in a particular skill or, more generally, expose them to our educational, particularly our technical education, system. Performing this function, for instance, are such programs as the Department of Defense's International Military Education and Training Program and Foreign Military Sales Program; AID's Academic and Technical Training, the Food and Drug Administration's Foreign Visitor's Program, and the Center for Disease Control's Visiting Scientist Program; the Peace Corps; the Department of Agriculture's International Training Program; the Department of Interior's training programs through the National Park Service, the Fish and Wildlife Service, and the U.S. Geological Survey; the Department of Labor's Technical Assistance Programs; and in the Department of Transportation, the Federal Aviation Administration and the U.S.

6. "Minutes of the First Meeting of the Advisory Panel on International Educational Exchange," mimeographed (Washington, DC: United States Information Agency, 1982), p. 1. The final report was issued in Mar. 1986.

Coast Guard, which provide both classroom and on-the-job training for foreign nationals. To some extent, the Fulbright lecturers program fits within this category as well, as do what might be called the show-and-tell programs in which the various agencies—including, in addition to those mentioned, such organizations as the Census Bureau, the Library of Congress, the Small Business Administration, the Social Security Administration—introduce foreign nationals to the agency's activities.

In addition to the publicly supported programs, there are a wide variety of private programs dedicated to the provision of technical training for foreign nationals. For instance, this has been a principal interest of the Ford Foundation for many years, and the Rockefeller Foundation has just committed $300 million over the next five years to promote social and economic development in the Third World, building upon the 2000 or so scientists and technicians they have helped train over the years. There are a number of nongovernmental organizations that specialize in providing just such services. And of course, substantial university funds serve this purpose through the award of fellowships or teaching assistantships to foreign students.

Historically, our second major purpose in international exchanges and training has been the provision of a general exposure of foreigners to the United States and of Americans to other countries as part of our public diplomacy and as an investment in long-term familiarity with and, it is hoped, friendly attitudes toward the host country. This is the classic purpose of the USIA's short-term visitor program and Fulbright program, explaining that agency's traditional emphasis on first-time visits. It

motivates the recently inaugurated Youth Exchange Initiative, the East-West Center, most of the General Exchange Agreement with the Soviet Union, the programs of the Japan-U.S. Friendship Commission, and a large number of privately financed programs for high school and college students including many study-abroad programs that are financed jointly by institutions and individuals. It is to serve this purpose that the various cultural exchanges in the visual and performing arts are conducted.

The third purpose is facilitating the exchange on a more equal basis of technology and information than the technology-export function of the first set of programs provides for. Such interchanges, including transnational sharing of research facilities and collaborative research, are especially notable in the natural and health sciences. These include the Public Health visitor and guest-worker programs in which foreign scientists are invited to work in their various laboratories, such as those maintained by the National Institutes of Health, the Alcohol, Drug Abuse, and Mental Health Administration, the Food and Drug Administration, the various facilities of the Department of Energy, and the National Aeronautics and Space Agency. NSF's cooperative science program falls in this category. Its goal is precisely the provision of a two-way street between the United States and other countries in the promotion of international science. In addition, other governments, international organizations, and the major universities themselves contribute to this function of international exchange.

The fourth function, the least developed of them all, is the support of research about other countries and the overseas training of those who conduct that research. This includes the research scholar portion of the Fulbright programs, and Smithsonian, National Endowment for the Humanities (NEH), and NSF international research grant programs, plus research funds provided by private foundations either directly or through broker organizations such as IREX or the ACLS-SSRC.

These, then, allowing a little for overlap and for a few specialized programs that do not quite fit, comprise our de facto policy goals for international exchange and training programs. Within this overall set of purposes, however, there are some key national needs that are not now being adequately met, needs that any set of programs viewed in terms of the national interest would surely want to serve.

LANGUAGE STUDY ABROAD

Until very recently, there was little if anything in exchange and training programs that was dedicated to raising the level of foreign language competency of Americans. This statement is a little too sweeping in that there were occasionally foreign language prerequisites, explicit or implicit, in predoctoral-level overseas research grants, and sometimes individuals were allowed to spend some of their fellowship time studying a language. Higher Education Act Title VI fellowships can be and have been held at the advanced overseas language training programs. Any many study-abroad programs sponsored by universities and colleges are either overtly or thinly veiled foreign language learning programs.

What is meant by this statement is that we have not really looked at the relationship of overseas exposure to the acquisition and reinforcement of foreign language skills. And yet, if very many of our people who may have to use a

foreign language in the future are going to rise above the novice level in their skills, they must top off their domestic training with a disciplined course of training overseas. If they are going to keep those skills active or rejuvenate them after a period of disuse, then repeated spurts of exposure in the country where the language is spoken is absolutely essential. And while professionals who need to use a foreign language skill for professional purposes need such exposure, an even more urgent case can be made for foreign language teachers, who can infect generations of students with their unfinished or decaying competencies. The rhythm, purposes, and mode of selection of our current overseas fellowship programs are not, to put it gently, pointed in that direction. The Rockefeller Foundation has just introduced a competitive program to send secondary school teachers abroad for just this purpose. This pilot program needs to be watched and, if successful, extrapolated with a combination of state and federal funds. Similar programs need to be aimed at other groups with a need to know.

What is needed, of course, is not just the fellowships to send people abroad for language training, but the creation and sustenance of the institutions where that training can effectively be given. Although not limited to them, this need is especially pressing with respect to some of the less commonly taught languages and has led to the creation of inter-university consortia to provide post-second-year intensive training in six countries for students preparing to be language and area specialists. Oddly enough, the federal support given to these programs does not come from funds appropriated for this purpose, but out of Fulbright-Hays funds administered through the Department of Education that are designated for group projects abroad in general. This is a precarious source of funding and makes difficult the establishment of long-term planning attuned to the needs of overseas language training. Beyond that, using this source puts them into competition for funding with a host of other, unrelated applicants and, given the precariousness and limited amount of funding, makes their support uncertain. The overseas advanced language training centers need to have their own appropriation and at a level sufficient to carry out an expanded mission.

These programs are now limited by and large to students preparing to be area specialists. The need is much more general. As is the case in other aspects of foreign language training, the overwhelming allocation of government resources is confined to government personnel. The Department of State and the Department of Defense maintain extensive overseas language training programs for government employees. Some resources need to be invested in the private sector as well. Similar overseas language programs are needed for American businesspersons, for established academics, and for other professionals with a need to acquire high-level skills. Training in the United States is not enough, and just dumping them into jerry-built indigenous language training schools in many countries of the world is to guarantee continued incompetence. We need an overseas program aimed precisely at the need of raising the language competency of a substantial portion of the American public.

FOREIGN EXPERIENCE AND THE TRAINING OF INTERNATIONAL BUSINESSPERSONS

The second aspect of the national agenda that should be addressed by our national policy on exchanges is the training of future business specialists to help improve our international competitiveness. It is curious that this pressing national need has entered so little into the planning for future directions of exchange programs. Part of the reason for this is that our notion of the function of exchanges is still rooted in part in the notion of the United States as the principal creator of science, technology, and business systems. It is under this premise that such a large portion of our international exchange and training is aimed at one-way technological transfer, as indicated earlier. The tens of thousands of foreign visitors who come to learn under our technology-transfer exchange and training programs, plus the 350,000 foreign students who annually study at our major universities, indicate that we still have a major scientific and technological base that draws people from abroad. But in many areas our dominance, our near monopoly of technology and technical education is beginning to slip. The countries with substantial AID and Peace Corps programs are contracting more and more to a subset of the least developed countries in Africa, the Middle East, Southeast Asia, and Latin America and the Caribbean. In earlier days, international science was dominated by Americans. Now only about a third of world-class international science is carried out in the United States. The same is true in the health sciences.

Nowhere is this multicentric trend in the location of technological innovation clearer than in business training. Harvard, Stanford, and the Wharton School still attract large numbers of foreign students, but increasingly, other institutions, particularly in Europe, are drawing them as well. The training pathways of American students studying to be business leaders, particularly those planning to specialize in international business, need to be rethought. They must learn to live in a multicentric business world where both companies and educational institutions are worldwide. Some recognition of this fact may be seen in the decision by the American Society of Engineers to send several hundred American engineering students to Japan for exposure to training there. American business students need to be exposed to the different business perspectives in companies and training institutions in other countries. They need opportunities to study or intern abroad to give them a more global perspective on the conduct of American business. And what is good for students is also appropriate for the continuing educational experience of business leaders. Executive seminars that provide training to midcareer businesspersons now occasionally take place in a foreign setting. This practice needs to be much more general.

Needless to say, none of the federally supported exchange and training programs are aimed at the needs of students training to be business leaders or of those already engaged in business. To some extent, international exposure and training already occur within the large multinationals, but it is not generally available outside of them. A more collective national capacity to foster such international experience is clearly needed. And since the investment in international expertise of business students and executives will benefit individual companies as well as the nation as a whole, some of the costs of this kind of exchange should be borne by business. There are already precedents for this in the Office of Private Sector Programs and in the private sector contributions to the President's International Youth Exchange Initiative in USIA.

OVERSEAS TRAINING AND RESEARCH OF AREA SPECIALISTS

Opportunities for foreign study among students training to be academic specialists on other countries are currently funded through a variety of sources. They include a section of Fulbright-Hays that is administered by the Department of Education in conjunction with the Title VI program for just this purpose; dissertation-level grants, largely using NEH and Ford Foundation funds, retailed through the area-oriented SSRC-ACLS joint committees; a similar program through IREX; an indeterminate share of the USIA's general Fulbright program for American students wishing to study abroad; and fellowships, again largely with federal funds, awarded by overseas research service organizations like the American Institute of Indian Studies, which regrants NSF, NEH, and Smithsonian funds, largely in surplus currencies. This diversity of sources, each with its own guidelines and application procedures, makes the search for fellowship funds a complex and hazardous process. The rhythm of graduate training brings the student to the fieldwork stage of education in a particular year; the scramble to find the resources to conduct that fieldwork—without it the student has no chance of becoming a fully trained specialist—leaves both the timing and the outcome of that search in considerable doubt. The amount of funding available for work in particular world regions is dependent on program preferences that have little to do with the nation's need for trained specialists on that area. Moreover, funds for the foreign sojourn come almost entirely at the dissertation stage, when all of the course work has been completed. Equally fruitful for students would be opportunities to spend perhaps briefer periods of time earlier in their training both to advance their language skills to such a level that they can genuinely use them in their course work and to give their substantive courses on the area a sense of reality that only a visit to the country on which they are specializing can provide.

In short, the current system of providing grants allowing future language and area specialists to visit the countries on which they are specializing is capricious, inflexible, and poorly tailored to the needs of students. There is a provision in the newly reauthorized Higher Education Act Title VI for the incorporation of funds for foreign travel into the fellowship package of students chosen for longer-term support. If this second tier of fellowships is adequately supported, overseas training may be fitted more effectively into the overall training of specialists. There will still be a need, however, for open-competition fellowships for students who do not quite fit into the full longitudinal pattern—who came to an area specialization too late, who are in disciplines where the amount of time that can be devoted to area specialization is limited, who are trained at universities where there is no major language and area studies center for their region. The support and management of the overseas training of future language and area specialists is a finite task that should at a minimum be coordinated by and at a maximum fully carried out by a single organization, preferably one that is concerned with the support and management of the other aspects of language and area studies as well. It can allocate the individual grants through national organizations such as the SSRC-ACLS joint committees, IREX, and the American Institute of Indian Studies where peer review and selection can be most effectively carried out, but collective attention would be given to issues of distribution, numbers, and evaluation so that the process can best serve the national interest.

The need for overseas exposure for those training to become language and area specialists is equally great for established specialists. We mean by the term "established specialists" not just academics on the faculty of universities, but people with a high degree of competency on other countries. This would include people in public policy positions, journalists, educational administrators, and others who are fully using that competency professionally in various occupations throughout the society. For all such people, the obsolescence of a language and area competency can be very rapid indeed and normal sabbatical rhythms make the fraying of competencies almost inevitable.

It seems odd that we invest so heavily in the training of new specialists but do so little to sustain the competencies of the existing pool. The situation of sparse, uncoordinated, ill-fitting fellowship support that is available for students is even more striking for specialists. The only fellowships specifically aimed at their needs lie in the small program of 40 grants annually covering all countries for faculty research abroad under Fulbright-Hays as administered by the Department of Education, plus a few country-targeted programs administered by regranting organizations such as IREX and the American Institute of Indian Studies. The ACLS-SSRC joint committees have small amounts of money to disperse for marginal, supplemental research support for faculty, but not of the scale to make a major trip possible. Some scholars fit their proposals into the general faculty research category of the Fulbright-Hays program administered by USIA, but these proposals are relatively few—716 for the whole world in 1984; more than half of them—392 in 1984—are for Western Europe, where language and area studies tend not to be well represented; they have to cover the entire research community, not just area specialists; and often there is a preference for first-time visits rather than the repeated-visit pattern more characteristic of area specialists.

Also like students, established specialists have flexible needs not just tied to academic-year-long grants restricted to a specific research project. Even more than the students, they need flexible funds to be spent on short-term visits to sustain contacts with scholars in the host country, to rehone language skills, and, particularly in the social sciences, to keep up-to-date with current events. Very few funding programs allow for such necessary functions.

While programs serving academic specialists are sparse and unintegrated, there are none, or almost none, serving nonacademic specialists. Theoretically, a number of programs admit nonacademic participants, but in fact their orientations and screening procedures make nonacademic applicants very unlikely and those actually winning awards even less common. If a program is to serve nonacademics, it must do so deliberately.

OVERSEAS RESEARCH FOR THE DISCIPLINES AND PROFESSIONS

While the needs for overseas visits of area specialists are both pressing and obvious, there is a broader intrinsic need of American scholarship in general for overseas research opportunities. It is self-evident that American scholars as a whole would be severely hampered were they not to have the opportunity for overseas research. This fact is clearest when we consider those academic disciplines and specialities that exist, or largely exist, only because they take as their subject matter phenomena that do not occur, or only partially occur, within our national boundaries. Many scientific disciplines expand the knowledge base for which they are responsible in direct relation to their access to materials and sites not located in the United States: anthropology, archaeology, botany, entomology, geology, linguistics, natural products chemistry, primatology, and zoology, to name some obvious examples. Were specialists in these fields limited to the United States, the sciences for which they are responsible would be severely limited in scope and importance. To this list can be added many other specialties that describe themselves as comparative, as in comparative economics or comparative literature. Thus the leading rationale for overseas scholarship is that whole disciplines and specialties would disappear, or nearly so, in its absence.

Closely related to this category of internationally oriented disciplines are those that take as their research matter phenomena that have to do with relations between nations. Scholars in these disciplines would be adversely affected by a diminution of overseas research opportunities. A case in point is research on international economics—trade and tariffs, the international monetary system, the transnational flow of capital and labor. Others include the investigation of international law and politics, and, of course, international security. Then there are topics that spill across international boundaries. Human migration, infectious diseases, Islamic fundamentalism, and transnational science are all obvious examples.

In these instances, then, we discover other aspects of science that draw their subject matter not from a single culture or nation, but from the facts of intercultural and international life. To conduct research in these specialties requires opportunities to travel and study abroad.

There is a third category of disciplines that may not be cross-national or international in focus, but that advance, in part through sharing with colleagues abroad, disciplines that include such long-established fields as mathematics and physics and such newer specialties as computer science and cognitive science. A significant "international science structure" has been put into place since the end of World War II in order to realize the substantial advantages of scientific sharing and collegiality.[7] As we noted earlier in the case of business and technological development, scientific and scholarly research has become increasingly multicentric. If we do not permit our scientists and scholars to go where the action is, as a nation we will slip behind and become largely irrelevant to the cutting edge of knowledge.

Because the need for interaction between scientists in the physical and health sciences has been so obvious, elaborate structures, both governmental and private, have been erected to make that interaction possible. Some problems limiting the mobility of scientists remain: conflicting national tax policies, national restrictions on the issuance of work permits, making provision for dual-career families, and home-institution sabbatical and promotion policies.[8] But programs supporting American participation in international aspects of the natural and health sciences are substantial. They include such extensive programs as NSF's Cooperative Science Program, which in 1984 supported 1287 American scientists, and Projects Related to Biological Diversity Conservation and Natural Resource Management. In addition, there are numerous bilateral arrangements such as the Indo-U.S. Science and Technology Initiative. The National Institutes of Health administers a number of international fellowships through the Fogarty International Center that include grants to American scientists by foreign governments, including the governments of Great Britain, France, Sweden, Switzerland, Germany, the USSR, and Rumania. The Department of Energy spends about $100 million a year on international scientific exchanges involving nuclear and fossil energy, including the management of internationally owned scientific equipment. An elaborate program of scientific cooperation to which the United States contributes both funds and personnel is maintained by the North Atlantic Treaty Organization as well.

In addition to the government-funded international programs, in the physical and health sciences there is an extensive network of private and semi-public organizations that provide a durable scaffolding to international science. For instance, the national academies of science, including our own, have international divisions that mediate scientific contact across national boundaries. So do the various professional associations for the scientific disciplines. These organizations and their functions are so

7. For a discussion of the issues relating to the internationalization of science, see *International Mobility of Scientists and Engineers* (Washington, DC: National Research Council, 1981).

8. Ibid., pp. 5-6.

extensive that they are gathered together into an International Council of Scientific Unions, which provides a place for constant liaison across national boundaries.

In spite of the fact that the same transformation toward multicentric research that characterized the physical sciences after World War II is now taking place in the social sciences and humanities, such an apparatus for scientific communication and collaboration is very weak in the latter fields. To some extent, the limited amount of transnational activity in the social sciences and the humanities is a reflection of the nature of those disciplines themselves. Particularly in the social sciences scholars can quickly venture into areas with a high political content, and there is no rock base of agreed-on methods and theoretical style to surmount the particularities of national perspectives. But this makes the task more difficult, not less urgent. The current support systems for scholarly transnational interaction are weak and becoming weaker. NSF's collaborative science program, which devotes $25 million per year to the promotion of America's role in international science, spends a minuscule amount of that money on the social sciences even though those sciences fall within NSF's mandate. At the outset, Vannevar Bush, the founder of NSF, was opposed to the inclusion of the social sciences in NSF, and they fit uncomfortably there to this day. In the promotion of international social science, they play almost no role. NEH has a strong bias in favor of activities that take place within the United States; finding NEH funding for Americans to host a humanistic conference somewhere outside the United States is an uphill battle.

Some of the efforts to bridge social science internationally resided in weak organizations such as the International Social Science Council, which tried to play the role of the International Council of Scientific Unions for the social sciences. Other segmental organizations such as the International Institute for Applied Systems Analysis in Vienna that attempt to bridge scholarship between the countries in the East and West are very weakly rooted. Moreover, these, plus a number of humanistically oriented transnational organizations, were heavily dependent for funding on the United Nations Educational, Scientific, and Cultural Organization (UNESCO). The twin processes of the diversion of UNESCO to the development needs of the Third World and the withdrawal of the United States from funding that organization made our participation in even these weak efforts minimal.

In addition to these organizational weaknesses in the development of international social science and the humanities, in country after country the efforts of individual American scholars to conduct social science and humanistic research in their territory is becoming more and more circumscribed. As it was put in the report of a conference on the topic held on 18-19 November 1985:

U.S. scholars long had the freedom to pursue their research interests in regions of the world that were either colonies of Western nations or economically and politically subservient to the West. However, since World War II, the situation has changed dramatically. Many of the new nations which have emerged in the past 40 years do not allow foreign scholars unrestricted access to visit and pursue their studies. The post-war emergence of the Soviet Union and the United States as antagonistic superpowers has complicated the issue further. Among the other barriers that have been erected worldwide are the withholding of visas, close scrutiny of proposed projects, and the negotiation of reciprocal flows of scholars and scholarship.[9]

The extent and reasons for this increasingly crippling state of affairs differ from country to country as do the steps necessary to work in the new environment. Essentially, there is no problem with respect to the countries of Western Europe and Japan. In the case of the Soviet Union and other politically adverse countries, strict reciprocity across the range of exchanges in detailed bilateral agreements is necessary. In others, the problem is the limited size and competencies of local scholarly elites, and until the social science and humanistic scholarly community grows stronger, relationships with American scholars will continue to be difficult. Sometimes the problem is the increasing expansion of the state into control of international research access, accompanied by increasingly dense bureaucratization and the multiplication of veto groups. The long-term answer is the careful building of durable scholarly networks that nourish the development of transnational norms of scholarship that can withstand the creeping trend toward constraint.

This role of promoter of international social science and humanities, a role imperfectly carried out and now dropped by UNESCO, is one that must be played. Whoever does so must be able to speak as coordinator of the full range of exchange and training programs funded by the U.S. government, linking programs together rather than watching the eddies of international politics divert them one by one.

The participation of Americans in international social science and the humanities is a delicate and complex task. It is now the responsibility of no central body. There are, however, organizations in existence focusing on particular countries. IREX, for instance, manages these matters with respect to the Soviet-bloc countries. There are a series of broker organizations—the American Academy in Rome, the American Institute of Yemeni Studies, the American Institute of Indian Studies, the American Institute of Iranian Studies, the American Institute of Pakistan Studies, the American Research Center in Egypt—that now serve as mediators between the American and foreign social science and humanities scholarly community. Although they are organized into a formal Council of Scholarly Research Abroad under the aegis of the Smithsonian Institution, the resources available for their important task are very, very small. Some of the ACLS-SSRC joint committees appoint foreign scholars to their membership, providing foreign input into the planning and peer-review process. These and similar activities can be part of a multifaceted strategy trying to build durable linkages across national boundaries in the social sciences and the humanities. The cost of continuing with the present system is increasing parochialism and isolation.

9. "Report on the Research Access Conference, November 18-19, 1985," mimeographed (Washington, DC: Smithsonian Institution, 1986).

ANNALS, *AAPSS,* **491**, May 1987

A Symposium: What Future Directions for Academic Exchange?

By PAUL SEABURY,
A. KENNETH PYE,
MARK BLITZ, and
JAMES H. BILLINGTON

ABSTRACT: Forty years leaves nothing unchanged, and certainly not the Fulbright program. How have its objectives changed, how should they change? Four informed observers and former or present participants in Fulbright and other exchange programs here present their views. Paul Seabury argues for a more sharply focused Fulbright program in an age when it is only a drop in a sea of exchanges, and urges that that focus should serve national interests. James H. Billington suggests that Fulbright or part of it be upgraded to focus on "brighter students or future leaders." Mark Blitz points out that the strong support the program now receives from the administration and in Congress is based not so much on the desire to "enhance academic opportunities or . . . 'mutual understanding'" but rather on the hope of improving prospects for democratic development, a central purpose of our foreign policy. A. Kenneth Pye emphasizes the traditional objective of mutual understanding, and the importance of avoiding politicization and respecting the independent role of the binational commissions; he presents a variety of proposals for improvement in the program.

Paul Seabury, professor of political science at the University of California, Berkeley, served on the Board of Foreign Scholarships from 1967 to 1971.

A. Kenneth Pye is Samuel Fox Mordecai Professor of Law at Duke University and chairman of the Council for International Exchange of Scholars.

Mark Blitz is associate director for educational and cultural affairs of the United States Information Agency.

James H. Billington, the chair of the Board of Foreign Scholarships from 1971 to 1973, is currently director of the Woodrow Wilson International Center for Scholars.

PAUL SEABURY: KNOWLEDGE AND THE NATIONAL INTEREST

I had the honor of serving on the Fulbright board in the late 1960s and the early 1970s. This was a time of very tense relations between academia and Washington, as well as a grim time in American colleges. For me, if for these reasons alone, the meetings of the Board of Foreign Scholarships were a time of rest and recreation from the savage conflicts that by then had become almost normal at Berkeley. Tucked away in a quiet boardroom in the State Department, we presided over a civilized, high-quality program of student and faculty exchanges designed to strengthen international understanding. Our deliberations were virtually uncontaminated by the bitter fights over foreign policy that then were swirling around us in Washington and elsewhere.

For a while, at the top end of the Johnson administration, our superior, the assistant secretary for educational and cultural affairs, was a friendly judge from New York. In his sessions with us, he would proudly pass among us packets of recent photographs of his very large extended family and deliver a standard homily on the importance of international understanding. There were a few White House or State Department interventions in our work—aside from perennial bad news about threatened budget cuts. There was the Vietnam war, but the Board of Foreign Scholarships was into pure foreign policy, building bridges of friendship—"minds without borders," as the saying goes. We were the mentors and the monitors of excellent American students, scholars, and teachers and their foreign counterparts from Europe, Asia, Africa—from all over! We were janissaries at the portals of learning-for-the-future.

I now recall one bit of cognitive dissonance that at the time only dimly registered in my mind. At one meeting, we received, at our request, a report from some agency or other that contained a puzzling little item. This was a hazarded estimate that that year there were more young Americans then studying theology in European schools, under private auspices, than all of our Fulbright exchange students in Europe. Theology! Here we were, making policies for a great, comprehensive program spanning all ranges and disciplines of knowledge, while theology—then hardly a mainstream subject—was outstripping us in numbers. The theology students were a bit like the undocumented aliens we speak of today, invisibly spreading across Europe with their own missions of learning and understanding. How odd. Around that time, *Time* magazine had just announced that God was dead!

Now if that was the case with those anonymous young Americans, what then were the proportions of all Fulbright-sponsored teachers and students—U.S. and foreign alike—to the total number of all students and teachers going to and fro between American and foreign centers of learning? For that matter, with no data at hand, I would bet that Fulbrighters number less than 1 percent of all student exchangees. There may be perhaps as many as 10,000 mainland Chinese students currently studying in the United States, with no federal program at all. These students pursue studies attuned to the educational priorities of their government.

Forty years ago, the Fulbright exchanges played an exemplary and pivotal role in international higher education. The war was over, isolationism was dead, the United States had suddenly become the global superpower, and

Americans were blinking out at a strange world. For that matter, what did the world know of us? The G.I. Bill of Rights then was revolutionizing higher education at home; the Fulbright program then symbolized a national commitment that young Americans and foreigners find out what their countries were like, by study and teaching. The program was a precursor of the Peace Corps idea and had strong bipartisan support. As an element of foreign relations, it had the added merit of being nice. And it proved to be a harbinger of a time—now, as a matter of fact—when overseas study would be a conventional feature of the curriculum of most American colleges and universities.

I mention the theology students of the 1970s simply to emphasize that the Fulbright program is now only a tiny element in international education and people-to-people diplomacy. To be sure, a Fulbright still has honorific implications similar to those of a Rhodes Scholarship, and the program by now has very distinguished alumni scattered across the nation. I am also sure that high standards are used to select American students and teachers on grounds of merit and promise.

I am sure many people want to keep the Fulbright program just the way it is. But I wonder. The world and America's place in it are very different today from 1946. Just for starters, since the program is actually an element in overall foreign policy, why not recognize it as such? A well-endowed educational arm of the national interest could, for instance, identify important fields of knowledge to see where serious national deficiencies exist bearing upon our future strength and vitality as a nation. Other governments do this routinely; why shouldn't we? Such a program—let us face it—

could positively contribute to the national interest. We are short of talent, for instance, in Japanese studies, while Japanese are swarming across our country. The strategic identification of foreign knowledge areas where we are deficient could, of course, be controversial but not impossible. So also could be a program more explicit in attracting foreign students to study here, not just to learn how nice America is, but, for instance, to study American political-cultural history seriously, in a systematic and rigorous way.

Skeptical pluralists may argue that such priorities would be impossible to find agreement on; hostile critics may see in them the cloven hoof of politics. They would threaten the traditions of apolitical purity, long the hallmark of these exchanges. Why not at least begin to talk about such matters? The original *raison d'être* of the Fulbright program—to enable young Americans and scholars to find out about the world and vice versa—seems to me to have lost its validity at a time when new challenges to American national interests call for new priorities in the realm where knowledge and national interest intersect.

A. KENNETH PYE: RECOMMENDATIONS FOR ADMINISTRATIVE CHANGE

Mutual understanding has been the ultimate goal of the Fulbright program since its inception, although thoughtful observers have long differed about what is meant by the concept and how best to achieve it.[1] Absence of consensus on such issues has not prevented the appreciation that reasonably precise objectives

1. Charles Frankel, *The Neglected Aspect of Foreign Affairs* (Washington, DC: Brookings Institution, 1966), pp. 80-98.

and priorities are desirable if the program is to continue to be successful and that such goals and means are more difficult to formulate in an international program where perspectives of others are important.

The independence of the Fulbright program from direct government control must continue to be emphasized. The program has operated traditionally as a constructive partnership between government and the academic community in which academia provides advice on policy and peer review for evaluation of candidates. The mission of the program is public diplomacy, but not in the same sense as direct initiatives of the Department of State, the U.S. Agency for International Development, or the United States Information Agency, including the Voice of America. Its legitimacy in the eyes of other countries and American academics depends in large measure upon the perception that it is not a direct instrument of American foreign policy.

Essential to such a status in many countries is the vitality of binational commissions in influencing priorities and policies. It is inconsistent with the program's purpose to expect a binational commission to conform to American policy dictates, and such an expectation is probably infeasible in those countries that provide significant funding. Likewise, a binational commission that behaves as an instrument of a foreign government, authorizing awards only in areas to which the foreign nation accords significance, is failing to appreciate that a primary strength of the program lies in collaboration when interests may not always coincide.

Fundamental to the vitality of the program is independent peer review for selection of Fulbright scholars going abroad. In selection of awardees, faculty serving on peer-review panels must continue to avoid considerations other than academic merit and suitability of candidates for the specific position being filled. The United States Information Agency and the Board of Foreign Scholarships should continue to avoid any appearance of disapproval of candidates on political grounds.

The nature of the program is obviously strongly affected by allocation of funds among different geographical areas. Difficulties may occur if funds are allocated primarily to achieve foreign policy objectives, particularly if the allocation does not reflect academic interests or existing pools of requisite expertise. Why some nations, such as Switzerland and Canada, are not part of the program deserves reexamination.

A significant percentage of present awards is limited to lecturers; many are restricted to American studies and teaching English as a foreign language. Much can be said for a greater concentration of the resources of the program on promotion of international scholarship. Awards to scholars who need to be abroad to conduct significant research, who are able to transmit disciplinary insights and research techniques to foreign colleagues and students, and who may serve as a catalyst for creation of long-term scholarly relationships yield significant direct benefits, in addition to improving the image of both the Fulbright program and American higher education. Such scholars should be expected to engage in some teaching, if nothing more than a single seminar, but the primary thrust of their work should be research. Moreover, research awards should be available for juniors. Experience as a Fulbrighter may have a lifelong impact upon a young scholar and shape the perspective with which he or she approaches a discipline and other cultures.

More open grants are needed rather than the more typical grants restricted to a narrow field. The pool of interested scholars will be larger in quantity and higher in quality if host countries do not exclude significant segments of the American professoriat by narrowly defining the expertise sought.

The nature of the existing program assures little continuity in contact over the years between an American Fulbrighter and faculty with whom he or she was associated abroad. Relatively minor modifications of the program would create a structure for such networking. Instead of visiting a country for nine consecutive months, professors might obligate themselves to spend a total of nine months on several occasions over several years, during which time they would initiate or continue a relationship with a professor in a host institution, ideally resulting in collaboration. The host-institution collaborator might receive a Fulbright to the United States to work with his or her American colleague once during the period. A junior Fulbright would permit a foreign graduate student to study in the United States under the American professor before returning home to complete his or her work and receive a degree.

Regional awards have proved extremely successful. Consideration should be given to thematic Fulbrights in which major international problems would become the focus, attracting scholars interested in cross-country study of problems such as environmental protection, immigration, refugees, population control, communicable diseases, and imbalance in trade.

Some former foreign Fulbrighters who have been away from the United States for a significant period should be brought back to American institutions at which they worked, if only for a refresher experience. Opportunities for renewing old acquaintances and bringing a foreign scholar up to date on aspects of a discipline in which Americans have made particularly significant strides could yield rich dividends.[2]

There is reason for concern that many of the best American academics may be less interested in applying for Fulbrights than was once the case. Changes in higher education, life-styles of the professoriat, the nature of awards available and their distribution, the image of the program, the lengthy process of application and review and the delay in receiving final approval, and especially the amount of the stipends have affected the size of the pool of qualified candidates and will continue to do so unless changes are made.

Many American universities have a high percentage of tenured faculty and will have few vacancies in the immediate future. Untenured junior faculty in research universities must not only publish or perish; they must do so during their first six years. Acceptance of a Fulbright that does not promise an opportunity for research that will produce a book during the requisite period is akin to playing Russian roulette.

Few of the ablest faculty in any rank are prepared to accept lectureships abroad, with the exception of distinguished senior lectureships, if research is infeasible. The objective of most is an opportunity to further research interests, not offer the equivalent of entry-level or intermediate-level courses.

More faculty wish to work in Western Europe than in other areas in the world. Despite a growing interest in the Third World and Eastern Europe, relatively few American academics possess the

2. Craufurd D. Goodwin and Michael Nacht, *Decline and Renewal* (New York: Institute of International Education, 1986), p. 71.

language qualifications and knowledge of cultures that are desirable in such environments. The result is a surplus of able people in Western Europe in some disciplines, and an inability to find as many able people as are needed in some other areas. The problem is aggravated by political turmoil and violence in some areas of the world that make such places less attractive.

The image of the Fulbright program must be improved. Unfavorable comparisons with the nature of grants and stipends in other programs have tarnished the aura of being a Fulbrighter. Confusion of the Fulbright program with other programs administered by the United States Information Agency, such as the linkage program, in which American academics are sent abroad without individual peer review, also tends to reduce the prestige of a Fulbright, as does confusion between junior lecturing awards and distinguished research awards, all of which are denominated "Fulbright."

The final straw for many is inadequate recognition of the significance of a Fulbright award by home universities. A concerted effort must be made to persuade universities that they benefit significantly from the opportunity afforded their faculty by Fulbright awards and that awards reflect recognition of some of their ablest people.

By far, the most serious problem is the amount of the stipends. Fulbright stipends simply do not approximate faculty salaries in most disciplines in most universities. The discrepancy is worse when other income sources are considered. Many faculty have grants that provide additional income for summer months. Others have significant consulting income. Some supplement their nine-month salary with summer session income. Faculty now receive

significant fringe benefits, many of which are nontaxable and many of which are unavailable to Fulbrighters. An estimated 80 percent of American faculty have working spouses who contribute to family income; rarely can suitable employment be found for both a husband and wife in the same university or same country. The new tax law may aggravate the problem.

Stipends must be raised to maintain the quality of the program. A reduction in the number of awards is an acceptable price for the higher stipends that are necessary to attract many of the most able.

The significance of the relatively small stipend is exacerbated by the length of stay required by the award in many countries. Many academics would accept the sacrifice of leaving a spouse and accepting a lower level of remuneration for a short period of time, but cannot do so for a complete academic year or even a semester. Adoption of serial grants, advocated earlier, would go far toward alleviating the problem.

An overall strategy including these or other proposals will enable the program to adjust to changes that have occurred during the last forty years and those that will occur in the future. There is no reason to enter the next century with a 1946-model program when it is possible to make minor modifications that will permit the Fulbright program to continue to be the flagship of exchange programs, as it has been during its first forty years.

MARK BLITZ: EXCHANGES AND FOREIGN POLICY

The United States has markedly increased its expenditures for academic and other exchanges over the past five years. The increase was initiated by

Congress but soon championed by the administration, whose budget requests now outrun congressional appropriations. Although substantial future increases are unlikely, a consensus apparently protects the current level.

The consensus, and, especially, the administration's share in it, is connected to foreign policy concerns. It was not primarily the wish to enhance academic opportunities or to increase vaguely defined mutual understanding that caused the recent growth. Rather, most observers now believe that exchanges can improve particular situations such as those in Central America and South Africa, and, more generally, can improve the prospects for democratic development. As Senator Dodd put it recently on the Senate floor:

The Senator from Rhode Island [Senator Pell] has accurately pointed out that there are virtually hundreds of people from one end of this globe to the next who are beneficiaries of this program and as a result have embraced and adopted much of the values and the principles of this country in no small measure because of the influence of the Fulbright Program.[3]

"They have," as Senator Simon remarked during the same debate, "a feeling of kinship not only toward the United States but to the whole process of a free democracy at work."[4] Senator Lugar expressed similar views in a speech at the University of Arkansas honoring the Fulbright program's fortieth anniversary.[5]

The wish to encourage representative democracy and its characteristic habits and institutions for others as well as for

3. U.S., Congress, *Congressional Record,* 99th Cong., 2d sess., 1 Oct. 1986, p. S. 14418.
4. Ibid., p. S. 14486.
5. Senator Lugar spoke at the University of Arkansas, Fayetteville, AR, Sept. 1986.

ourselves runs throughout American history. The principles upon which our republic is based are not national characteristics, but natural laws. Indeed, advancing democracy and preserving our national security are now the two central purposes of our foreign policy.

These two purposes do not bring forth identical actions in every circumstance. Ultimately, however, the spread of representative democracy should not detract from our security even if it would not simply guarantee it. This judgment, though normally unexpressed and taken for granted, is worth pointing out because it is shared by both moderate liberal internationalism and moderate principled conservatism. As such it anchors our bipartisan foreign policy.

Exchanges consist of the academic years abroad standard in the Fulbright program, as well as shorter visits to and from the United States by academics and other professionals. Taken together, exchanges enhance national security by creating opportunities for foreign citizens to understand us directly. One may debate the effect of such understanding on any given individual, or the effect of understanding when what is understood is a country other than our own. But for the United States, to understand us results on the whole in respect and sympathy.

Understanding, respect, and sympathy together form a sensible context in which we can articulate our intentions and actions. To the degree that our national security depends on persuading foreign citizens and winning their consent, therefore, exchanges serve national security. Healthy public opinion engenders trust in our immediate actions and supports the self-defense of our allies and other friends. In fact, exchanges that increase others' understanding of us are all the more important because they concentrate on future and present leaders.

A sensible context of public opinion is crucial also as a decisive element of liberal democratic development. Exchanges serve democratic development by allowing others to grasp enough of the substance and interplay of representative democratic institutions so that they can imitate them, if they choose, while adjusting for their own circumstances. Exchanges obviously are not the only way in which foreign citizens can understand democracy. But they are an excellent way to give others some experience of how our institutions work. It is especially important that journalists, lawyers, soldiers, and entrepreneurs as well as academics learn how professionals and their institutions conduct themselves in a free country. This is more significant, indeed, than learning this or that technique. Such broader, or constitutional, understanding is facilitated enormously by seeing our country, or hearing directly from our citizens, in thoughtful, balanced programs. A country is developing democratically when its citizens come to understand the operation and coordination of all institutions and sectors of life in terms of the principles of representative democracy on which the government itself is based. By advancing this more subtle comprehension, exchanges help change merely paper democracies to functioning democratic communities and help preserve already functioning democracies, our own included, in their better habits.

Exchanges benefit individuals as individuals, and they allow us always to keep in mind activities and perspectives—the search for truth, the experience of beauty and reverence—that transcend any concrete political community.

Still and all, most of us cannot be permitted, or permit ourselves, the luxury of a purely private life. And the goals that transcend politics are for most of us inseparable from the existence of a decent political community. It is therefore fortunate that exchanges serve foreign policy; not, as some might have it, a source of shame or regret. The special status of exchanges as somehow beyond politics does not arise from their being apolitical. It derives, rather, from the ability of successful exchanges to serve the bipartisan purpose of a healthy foreign policy. As long as we Americans remain proud of our way of life, therefore, exchanges will have a place in our foreign affairs.

JAMES H. BILLINGTON:
A SEARCH FOR LEADERS

American academic exchanges in general since World War II—with the Fulbright program as the centerpiece—almost certainly constitute the largest higher-educational exchange in human history. Despite the large number of people who write history in the United States—many of whom are Fulbrighters—the history of this enterprise has yet to be written. There is not even a systematic inventory of Fulbright alumni. The program has come to be taken for granted as if it were a minor part of the landscape rather than a significant part of postwar American history.

If a comprehensive history ever were written, it would probably show how the great immigration of earlier years was continued as a new immigration of ideas. The story would tell how a strong cadre of informed internationalists was spread throughout the United States, ending the monopoly that the Boston-Washington corridor had held on international interests in the interwar period. The most important part of such a history might well be an inventory of the impact that those with foreign study experience had in areas like international banking, law, and the professions as well as on the academic establishment. The Fulbright program had an even greater importance for journalists, politicians, and other men and women of affairs who came to America from abroad.

Even more important than the population explosion in the contemporary world has been the explosion of the educated population, the rising desire of more people everywhere to be exposed to the best thinking anywhere. It is an enormous asset to the United States that so much of the best thinking in so many fields takes place here. Higher education is one of the most valuable national assets of the United States as it relies increasingly on its wits rather than on its power to sustain its preeminent position in the world.

We need better to understand the influential position in the developing world of the small educated elite. For it is precisely these people, in whom the thirst for freedom and curiosity for learning are the greatest, who have most often and most vehemently questioned American objectives in the past.

Curiosity about America—even negative curiosity—could provide in the future the recruiting force for a fresh and more expertly targeted academic exchange. Americans studying abroad could be directed to mine much more deeply the rising in-country, in-language resources of countries to which they are going rather than to dabble lightly for a year, as has too often been the case in the past. From the other side, the hundreds of thousands who come to America to study should not simply use America for technological training, but should be exposed to broader American objectives and ideals.

The national academic exchange program under the Fulbright-Hays Act should eventually be given some dignified administrative base of its own outside the line departments of the U.S. government. This is not because either the cultural affairs section of the State Department or the United States Information Agency has exerted all that much political pressure on these programs, which have their own traditions and forms of self-regulation. It is rather because government bureaucracy inherently promotes inefficiency and mediocrity, which have been attenuated only by the heroic dedication of individuals within those structures. Some kind of British Council structure or independent agency is needed to enhance the stature and preserve the structure of these programs.

Some new flagship program should also be devised to set a higher standard for international exchanges and identify them with the aspirations and upward mobility of brighter students and future leaders throughout the world. Whether it is to be a totally new program or an overhauled junior Fulbright program for foreigners coming to America the flagship program could do worse than model itself on the Rhodes scholar program, which provided much of the original inspiration for the Fulbright program. Other leadership programs such as the Harvard summer school programs of the 1950s and the more imaginative recruiting programs of leading business schools today could help provide models for a new national program. Some thousand future leaders could be chosen from around the world on the basis of an open international competition with the benefit of interviews conducted jointly by Americans and in-country national leaders. An independent agency could place these carefully selected future leaders in different universities throughout the United States, and this process could engage local communities and universities throughout America much more fully in the Fulbright program than they have been in the past.

There would be all kinds of abrasions, and Americans would no doubt learn at the grass-roots level more about discontents in distant parts of the world than most Americans would like to hear. But the future foreign leaders would learn more about America than they get from our exported consumer culture. They would in turn give us a link with the emerging world of the twenty-first century. Crafting a program of this size and dimension would involve working creatively not just with new countries, but with new categories of institutions in older countries: polytechnic institutes, open universities, new academies and institutes, and new categories of people—women, workers, and others—in familiar countries who are being, in many ways, educated for the first time.

New exchanges with China may well play as important a role in determining the future orientation of leaders there as have much smaller, earlier programs with countries like Finland. I had a Fulbright there and have watched how the program has helped sustain the continuing westward orientation of that otherwise geographically eastern land. But the mere mention of a country the size of China illustrates the practical fact that an exchange program cannot be all things to all people. We need a flagship program that frankly looks for the leaders—and in the process helps to define a new leadership generation that will almost certainly be better inclined toward America and toward the values of freedom than it would be without such a program.

Book Department

INTERNATIONAL RELATIONS AND POLITICS

DEUTSCH, ROBERT. *The Food Revolution in the Soviet Union and Eastern Europe.* Pp. xix, 256. Boulder, CO: Westview Press, 1986. Paperbound, $25.00.

JONES, JAMES R., ed. *East-West Agricultural Trade.* Pp. xv, 256. Boulder, CO: Westview Press, 1986. $27.50.

PAARLBERG, ROBERT L. *Food Trade and Foreign Policy: India, the Soviet Union, and the United States.* Pp. 266. Ithaca, NY: Cornell University Press, 1985. $29.95. Paperbound, $12.95.

The first two books in this triad examine relationships between food and politics and between East and West. The third expands the analysis to all players in international food markets. The first two also display an emerging anti-Malthusian exuberance. They document the way that the human species, planning its destiny through bypassing markets or making little use of them, can meet its food problem. The possibility of more efficient and less costly options, in both material and social-welfare terms, is not considered.

The second and third studies share a focus on public policy, development patterns, and production aggregates. Both analyze the way trade is negotiated between structurally different markets, where constant changes in the rules of the game and in decision-making hierarchies make it impossible to apply uniform theory. Nevertheless, the several authors succeed in furnishing impressive analyses for perusal by specialists.

Robert Deutsch, with considerable skill, presents an abridged "history of agricultural and food economics" of the Soviet bloc. He treats the current food revolution as the very core of the modernization process, designed to end a policy of deferred gratification and accede to rising consumer demand. The latter, he argues, is linked increasingly by the Comecon leaders to political stability and the preservation of power. They are caught between liberalizing their economies in order to meet growing consumer demand, on the one hand, and resorting to repression, on the other. The background for this kind of analysis has been clearly laid out by Seweryn Bialer in his recent book, *The Soviet Paradox: External Expansion and Internal Decline.* Deutsch analyzes the record of Comecon members under two heads, "relative success stories" and "petrified economies," and then proceeds to an epilogue, "toward a socialist welfare society."

However, in terms of cause and effect, I have difficulty with Deutsch's contention that socialist revolutions have been instrumental in bringing forth the consumer revolution. Quite apart from political systems, mass consumption patterns are attributable worldwide to industrial revolutions. Today these technological changes have reached the remotest corners of the earth. In this process, and, one may add, with considerable lags, the Comecon countries have displayed the usual changes.

The volume on East-West trade contains eight chapters by 13 authors. It reports meticulous research based on a wide range of sources, dealing with various aspects of the way centrally planned economies conduct their foreign trade. Their Achilles' heel is the livestock products sector, specifically meat supply, analyzed in an input-output flow model by Young and Kramer. Its components include livestock, nutrients, feed supplies, and livestock off-take matrices; the model offers quantitative evaluation of the interaction between livestock and grain system. A static model like this, using fixed coefficients between feed input and livestock output, does not lend itself to evaluating changes in price relationships and in technology, especially when handicapped by poor data. The feed count model measures nutrient contributions in metric tons and other standard aggregates. This raises problems for comparative analysis because feed conversion ratios differ very widely between East and West, while there is insufficient documentation to permit incorporation of this variation into the model.

Robert Paarlberg's study addresses the important question, Has food become an important instrument of foreign policy? He suggests that the recent debate on food power rests on two assumptions: (1) nations now frequently do attempt to use food power; and (2) when they do, food-exporting nations enjoy a relative foreign policy advantage over food importers. Testing the validity of these assumptions with case studies of

India, the USSR, and the United States, Paarlberg maintains that in fact food trade has seldom been manipulated for foreign policy reasons, since nations assign higher priority to domestic food and farm policy objectives. It is not clear how this conclusion squares with the U.S. wheat embargo, the current policies of Ethiopia and Cambodia, or the arguments advanced by Deutsch.

PETER S. ELEK

Villanova University
Pennsylvania

FREI, DANIEL. *Perceived Images: U.S. and Soviet Assumptions and Perceptions in Disarmament.* Pp. xvii, 323. Totowa, NJ: Rowman & Allanheld, 1986. $26.50.

HERRMANN, RICHARD K. *Perceptions and Behavior in Soviet Foreign Policy.* Pp. xxi, 266. Pittsburgh, PA: University of Pittsburgh Press, 1985. $31.95.

A fundamental lack of understanding of the adversary's views about international affairs has plagued U.S.-Soviet relations since 1917. It helps to explain the current impasse on arms control and other important issues.

The books under review enhance our understanding of Soviet-American relations by addressing the perceptions of the superpowers toward each other. Daniel Frei's *Perceived Images* views both Soviet and American perceptions, while Richard K. Herrmann's *Perceptions and Behavior in Soviet Foreign Policy* examines only the USSR's perceptions of the United States.

Frei's volume purports to follow "an exclusively descriptive orientation" in viewing Soviet and American perceptions. Given this perspective, his contentions that Soviet perceptions possess a "coherent and systematic character" or that "all published statements on problems of national security reflect a unity of views and ultimately rest on key concepts adopted by the highest authorities [in the USSR]" surprise the reader. They are controversial, demanding of a proof that Frei does not provide.

Even though Frei tries to develop a conceptual framework, one is left with a series of mostly disconnected chapters: the Soviet view, the American view, the Western literature, and finally the consequences of the views for disarmament. They are interlaced with so much quotation that the reading becomes tedious. While the compilation of quotes may make a useful reference work and the comparison of perceptions in the last chapter may tantalize the reader, the book would have been much improved with a comparative effort throughout and the promulgation of a clear thesis.

Herrmann's work stands in contrast, for it consciously develops an argument about Soviet perceptions of the United States in an attempt to arrive at an image about the motivations of Soviet foreign policy. His purpose is "diagnostic" rather than prescriptive. He examines three theories about the motives for Soviet behavior, called communist expansionism—"that the Soviet Union is motivated by a determination to spread communism and dominate the world"; realpolitik expansionism—"that Moscow seeks to expand its influence by exploiting opportunities while protecting its security"; and realpolitik self-defense—"that the USSR is primarily committed to self-defense." After discussing the assumptions of each theory and evaluating them with respect to Soviet statements and behavior in three one-year periods—1967, 1972, and 1979—Herrmann concludes that the realpolitik defense theory is the most plausible for explaining Soviet motivations. In analyzing the assumptions of three prevailing schools of thought, Herrmann contributes importantly to the literature on Soviet foreign policy.

GEORGE E. HUDSON
Wittenberg University
Springfield
Ohio

GARTHOFF, RAYMOND L. *Detente and Confrontation: American Soviet Relations from Nixon to Reagan.* Pp. xviii, 1147. Washington, DC: Brookings Institution, 1985. $39.95. Paperbound, $16.95.

If the enormity of a book were to indicate the seriousness of a subject, then this volume indeed concerns an important topic. Though a virtual compendium of recent global events, this work unravels the pursuit of détente from its inception in the Nixon administration down to its collapse with Reagan's assumption of the presidency. The author of the book, Raymond L. Garthoff, is both an academic, currently associated with the Brookings Institution, and a practitioner of foreign relations, having served with the U.S. Department of State for many years, most recently as ambassador to Bulgaria. As a Soviet specialist, Garthoff brings a wealth of knowledge from his foreign service experience to bear on this insightful analysis. He also brings the unusual perspective of a career diplomat to examine a subject matter traditionally the preserve of academic scholars.

The focus of Garthoff's work is the Soviet-American interaction in the context of détente with an emphasis on impediments to the implementation of this new policy initiative formulated under President Nixon with expert guidance from Secretary of State Henry Kissinger. Relying essentially on primary sources of data, both memoirs of American policymakers and Soviet writings, Garthoff uses perceptual analysis as his conceptual framework in examining the behavior of the two antagonists during a period when both sides called for "relaxation of tensions." He does a commendable job in relating American and Soviet perceptions to their respective modes of behavior and taking into account values, national interests, and ideologies as explanatory variables. While he looks at the Soviet Union from his own cultural frame and interprets for the reader the expressions of Soviet perceptions and intentions, his analysis seems to be fair and reasonable.

Garthoff submits that the policy of détente, while well meaning and well intentioned, got bogged down from the start. The strategy for the pursuit of détente was ill conceived, confused, and badly executed. The major stumbling block was the U.S. Congress, where the late Senator Henry Jackson, a notorious cold warrior, together with some others, demanded unacceptable and humiliating concessions from the Soviet Union as a price for this policy. Nixon, moreover, did not build a base of public support for his policy initiative, since much of the work of deténte was conducted in secrecy. To make matters even worse, at a particularly sensitive juncture in American-Soviet negotiations, Nixon found himself involved in the Watergate imbroglio, thus rendering the presidency ineffective in dealing with the Soviets.

Garthoff shows that détente was meaningful only under the two Republican administrations, those of Nixon and Ford. Under Carter's presidency there was no clearly articulated strategy for an American approach to the Soviet Union. In fact, Carter blundered along, antagonizing the Kremlin leaders by raising irrelevant issues such as human rights, and cultivating relations with China in such a way as to make them appear designed against the USSR.

On the Republican side, however, as soon as Reagan became president he demolished any hopes for the resumption of détente. His orientation was one of confrontation and dealing with the Soviets from a position of strength. The demise of détente had become a reality the moment Reagan directed his attention to the Soviet Union.

Garthoff holds the United States largely responsible for the collapse of détente, although he is not unmindful of the Soviet activities that may have contributed to its destruction. As seen from the Soviet perspective, there were simply too many American initiatives, asserts Garthoff, that could not but have rendered détente meaningless. Garthoff finds Soviet concerns for the undermining of détente much more credible than those expressed by American officials.

The Garthoff volume is a carefully written, highly readable, well-documented and remarkable piece of scholarly work. It is a thorough, detailed, and balanced treatment of a controversial issue of contemporary significance. The painstaking and laborious task undertaken by Garthoff illuminates for the student of international relations the behavior of hegemonic actors as they interact with one another in their eternal search for power.

GHULAM M. HANIFF
St. Cloud State University
Minnesota

GIDDENS, ANTHONY. *A Contemporary Critique of Historical Materialism.* Vol 2, *The Nation-State and Violence.* Pp. vi, 399. Berkeley: University of California Press, 1985. No price.

For a number of years Anthony Giddens, professor of sociology at the University of Cambridge, has been working with extraordinary productivity in the area of the classic tradition of modern social theory—the writings of Marx, Weber, and Durkheim and their critics. This book is part of a major attempt at synthesis and reconstruction of that tradition, which has as its point of departure the Marxist analysis of the role of capitalism in determining the shape of modern society. The first volume is entitled *Power, Property and the State.* The two volumes are complementary, yet each can be read on its own. Certainly the second volume, reviewed here, has its own logical cohesion.

Nowhere is the inadequacy of Marxist analysis more obvious to readers of the late twentieth century than in the early treatment of the place of the nation-state. Marx saw it as something contingent and of secondary importance to the forces of capitalist production and the exercise of class power. Giddens is certainly correct in trying to provide a more complete explanation for the shape of modern society by emphasizing the central position of the nation-state and its social consequences. In this sense it is a clear rejection of any monocausal or reductionist explanation of modern society, and it is a telling critique of simplistic versions of Marxism.

Giddens is also correct in trying to give warfare and the implications of industrialized military mobilization a central place in modern social theory. What he has to say about war and notions such as those of the military-industrial complex or of an international order based on violence is not particularly new. What is interesting is the way that he relates the national and international culture of warfare and threat to the well-worn discussion of the role of capitalism, bureaucratization, and state sovereignty. In fact, there is very little in the book that has not been said clearly and loudly by earlier theorists. The value of Giddens is that the synthesis puts together well-tested ideas into a new map of relationships.

As with most of Giddens's work, the writing is clear and mercifully free of jargon. Yet the argument is very tight and requires careful reading. He breaks with a long tradition of discussion about the modern nation-state by refusing to treat it, as does Marx, as some kind of logical progression from earlier forms such as the medieval city-state or the political dimension of feudalism. He claims that the modern state can be clearly understood only as something different—in a context of capitalism, industrialization, and modern international relations—not as something evolving from earlier forms. He has enlightening things to say about the difference between frontiers and regulated borders and the implications of that difference. He makes a telling argument about the tension in modern nation-states arising from a strong tendency toward increased democratic participation at the same time as an equally strong tendency toward totalitarian surveillance by the state.

Despite the title of the book there is no extended treatment of violence as such; it is warfare that concerns Giddens overwhelmingly in this context. In giving the nation-state a central place in his reconstruction of the classic tradition he—in my opinion— underestimates forces both at the international and at the intranational level. His assessment of the political relationships between states in a context of international organization is accurate enough, but he is too readily dismissive of the economic power of transnational corporations and of the whole international marketplace in undermining national sovereignty. At a lower level, his perspective of each nation clearly defined by the spatial boundaries of national borders is very much the perspective of a resident in a unitary state rather than a federation. When some future author is reconstructing the classic tradition in the twenty-first century Giddens will be criticized for underestimating the cultural ties of regional and linguistic separatism in order to provide a tidy geographical unity to the nation-state. Yet, and this is a measure of the importance of the work, for such a future social theorist Giddens will certainly be a central figure in the classic tradition.

MICHAEL HOGAN

University of Sydney
New South Wales
Australia

GUNNELL, JOHN G. *Between Philosophy and Politics: The Alienation of Political Theory.* Pp. x, 240. Amherst: University of Massachusetts Press, 1986. $25.00. Paperbound, $12.95.

THOMPSON, KENNETH W. *Toynbee's Philosophy of World History and Politics.* Pp. 230. Baton Rouge: Louisiana State University Press, 1985. $27.50.

Kenneth Thompson, a political scientist who has focused upon questions of international relations, has long been fascinated by Arnold Toynbee and his writings. In this volume, *Toynbee's Philosophy of World History and Politics,* he outlines and then analyzes Toynbeean perspectives on major questions in contemporary international relations. His approach throughout is quite straightforward. He first provides a large-scale introduction to the Toynbee corpus, outlining the British scholar's basic theories of metahistory—here defined as history writ large—as the search for overarching schemas in historical development that transcend era or even specific culture or civilization. He then goes on to examine Toynbee's views on questions of international relations and war, on issues related to peace and international order, on the workings of diplomacy and the nature of international politics, and on the prospects of the West within the world arena. He concludes his study with a critical appraisal of these aspects of Toynbeean thought.

While Thompson does find much to find fault with in his subject's works and demonstrates this by citing the works of those who have been critical of various elements in the Toynbee schema, he writes primarily as an admirer. He finds that the Toynbeean message, vast and romantic as it is, has much to say to our times. In my opinion Thompson has given us a thoughtful, gracefully written, and rather leisurely exposition of the key ideas of one major twentieth-century intellectual.

In *Between Philosophy and Politics* John G. Gunnell deals with an entire subdiscipline within political science, that of political theory. Gunnell begins by presenting a history of the development of modern political theory. In doing so he introduces his readers to the major thinkers in the field and to the key concepts they were responsible for. Here he also defines his basic thesis—that modern political theory has become an end in itself and that it has become increasingly removed from the realities of the politics it is supposed to be analyzing. In the chapters that follow he analyzes this body of theory from a number of different perspectives. In a clear prose he presents the heart of his deconstructionist critique: that the theorists in political science were so enamored of the intellectual frameworks developed by scientists that they attempted to borrow the underlying positivist

philosophy whole cloth, a philosophy ill suited to the needs of political thinking, and that in the process they were caught in a set of traps from which they have yet to free themselves. Brick by brick he builds his argument that political theory is now alienated from the very subject it is attempting to have us understand; in the attempt to be mainstream and scientific it has created its own intellectual universe, one unrelated to the one we all share. This volume, then, is a stinging and insightful deconstructionist critique of a major field of modern social science.

These studies seem, at first glance, to have little in common. A deeper analysis will show that they are indeed related, for each concerns itself with broad sets of ideas and theoretical perspectives. Each book, one gentle and kind, the other deeply analytical and sharply critical, is valuable in its own way for its author's very willingness to explore wide-ranging intellectual environments and for making these environments—these meta-theoretical universes—comprehensible to a larger audience.

MURRAY A. RUBINSTEIN

Baruch College
New York City

MARTEL, WILLIAM C. and PAUL L. SAVAGE. *Strategic Nuclear War: What the Superpowers Target and Why.* Pp. xx, 249. Westport, CT: Greenwood Press, 1986. $35.00.

HOLLAND, LAUREN H. and ROBERT A. HOOVER. *The MX Decision: A New Direction in U.S. Weapons Procurement Policy?* Pp. xiv, 289. Boulder, CO: Westview Press, 1985. Paperbound, $22.50.

Decisions on the building and targeting of strategic weapons have become more political, hence less purely military, in recent years—and these two volumes reflect the consequent debate.

Martel, of Rand, and Savage, of St. Anselm's College, contend that the disintegration of nuclear policy and the resultant instability in deterrence are attributable to the inability of the United States to coordinate advances in weaponry with the evolution of policy, as well as to the rapid development of Soviet counterforce capabilities (p. 176).

Their contention rests on two premises: first, that targeting Soviet military forces—counterforce strategy—is preferable to holding cities under the gun—countervalue strategy; second, that the American public mistakenly identifies counterforce targeting with planning for a first strike instead of a retaliatory capability. The United States, they suggest, is thus mired in the outdated targeting strategy of mutual assured destruction, which does not deter a Soviet regime focused on military options. In short, their judgment is that the balancing of counterforce with counterforce is the most stable deterrence system.

Their most controversial argument, reached after nearly 200 pages of painstaking analysis of the available information on force capabilities and on changes in the Single Integrated Operational Plan, is likely to be this: "A counterforce first strike is an illusory option given that even under the most favorable of circumstances it would strain the American arsenal to its operational limit." The Soviet first-strike capability is presumably even more limited, so that retaliation is inevitable—and deterrence still possible. Martel and Savage therefore go on to make far-reaching recommendations to enhance stability by disavowing a first strike, aiming only at strategic military targets, eliminating ground-based intercontinental ballistic missiles and making do with only submarine and bomber forces, and so forth. The chief obstacle to a strategy of balanced counterforces, in their view, is the disorder in American policymaking; the chief danger, drifting toward a situation in which even a counterforce balance is impossible.

Holland, of Utah University, and Hoover, of Utah State, see the MX debate as a potential departure in procurement policy because it involves political, even public, challenges to the military establishment. To be sure, some of the conditioning factors in the MX decision—the localized impact on constituents of important members of Congress, the arguable flaws in strategy and technology involved, the reformist temper of the 1970s—may simply have divided the executive branch and made the "bureaucratic model" of procurement decision-making temporarily vulnerable. But other factors—the growing scale of weapons projects, the dissolving strategic consensus, the equipping of Congress for a larger role in military policy in the wake of the Vietnam war, even "the increasing democratization of the federal administrative process" via mandated public hearings—lead them to conclude that "it is not inconceivable to imagine these forces operating in future weapon procurement decisions, although not perhaps to the degree of intensity as that for MX."

Despite its grammatical errors and its arguing via propositions as political scientists are prone to do, *The MX Decision* manages to convince. Changed circumstances surround procurement decisions because of a heretofore unheard-of linkage among strategic, diplomatic, and domestic factors. NATO and Utah officials, not to mention congressional and executive-branch doubting Thomases, now often refuse to consider weapons in isolation from arms control and environmental issues. Decisions once made by the triple alliance of the Pentagon, the defense committees in Congress, and the arms manufacturers now take place in an expanded "arena of conflict."

Jointly, these books raise two vital questions, one military and the other political. Militarily, does the Strategic Defense Initiative set a new scene by leading toward the counterforce balance envisioned by Martel and Savage? It seems likely that Martel and Savage would see space-based weapons as less vulnerable and less domestically controversial acquisitions akin to submarine and bomber forces. From such weapons, which do not rest in any constituent's backyard, a counterforce balance supported by a domestic consensus could, they might argue, be brought into being—provided that the notion that counterforce and first strike are synonymous can be overcome. Holland and Hoover would probably argue that, politically, the expense of the Star Wars scheme, its debatable effectiveness, and the West Europeans' fear of abandonment by a Strategic Defense Initiative-protected United States will inevitably make it more controversial than the MX, particularly in view of the first-strike potential that space-based weapons might at least provide by increasing the capacity of either strategic arsenal. The crux, alluded to at the end of *The MX Decision*, is therefore whether to trust to participatory or expert judgments in such matters—an issue symbolized by the fact that, detailed though they are, these works are not based on classified information.

THOMAS J. KNIGHT

West Virginia University
Morgantown

ROSECRANCE, RICHARD. *The Rise of the Trading State: Commerce and Conquest in the Modern World.* Pp. xiii, 268. New York: Basic Books, 1986. $19.95.

Richard Rosecrance's extremely lucid study of major trends in international politics provides a welcome antidote to those gloomy commentaries that see the modern world as doomed to constant conflict and inevitable nuclear war. Rosecrance is critical of those analysts who reduce international political life to a Hobbesian world of war of all against all and who focus exclusively on states' territorial ambitions and military conflicts. Rosecrance maintains that two completely different ways of organizing international relations have developed with particular force since the end of World War II. One system is the "territorial system" composed of "states that view power in terms of land mass; the more territory the more power." These states seek self-sufficiency and self-reliance from the rest of the world. This system is presided over by the USSR and the United States "to some extent." The alternative system is the "oceanic or trading system . . . based on states which recognize that self sufficiency is an illusion" and seek free trade with other states as the key to their welfare. This system is dominated by Japan and the European states headed by the Federal Republic of Germany.

Rosecrance examines modern international politics in terms of the relative significance of these two alternative systems for various states and leaderships. He argues with considerable force and verve that those political leaders who have turned increasingly away from the territorial system have brought immense prosperity to their states and that all national leaders are faced with increasing pressures from both the international environment and their own domestic economies to broaden their participation in the trading system. Rosecrance is both optimistic about the capacity of leaders to choose between these two systems and realistic about the continued appeals and importance of the territorial system for political leaders in the United States, the USSR, and the former colonies.

Rosecrance's emphasis on the two competing systems as the major determinants of state behavior does have its pitfalls. His tendency to reduce leaders' motives to "territorial expansion" often blurs the diversity of their ideological and political objectives and gives insufficient attention to their short-range perceptions of threat and opportunity in various areas as the basis of action. Far more important, however, Rosecrance's study helps to restore a sense of hope to the study of international politics by insisting that leaders can change their basic orientations on the basis of rational cost-benefit analysis.

JONATHAN HARRIS

University of Pittsburgh
Pennsylvania

ROTUNDA, RONALD D. *The Politics of Language: Liberalism as Word and Sym-*

bol. Pp. xii, 136. Iowa City: University of Iowa Press, 1986. $14.95.

Rotunda argues that the label "liberal" was introduced into English politics as late as 1830. In the United States, though used occasionally before, it became an important political symbol only with Roosevelt's New Deal. After some struggle between Democrats and Republicans as to who represented true liberalism, the matter was finally settled in FDR's favor. First reluctantly, then more and more willingly, his opponents accepted the conservative label.

So far, so good. What troubles me about this book is that I am not sure what it is trying to be. A history of liberalism? Surely not. John Locke's name is not even mentioned in the text. A political history? A good part of the narrative suggests that, but according to the title the emphasis is supposed to be on language, on "liberalism as word and symbol." On this score I find the work wanting.

Rotunda's problem is that "liberalism" seems to be a fitting label for Roosevelt's New Deal policy, indeed. He himself admits, "If we could imagine Roosevelt in England, we would more easily appreciate how similar his philosophy was to that of the British Liberals." Granted, laissez-faire advocates and New Dealers both had a legitimate claim to calling themselves liberal, because they represented the two major branches of the same tree of liberalism. Incidentally, on the European continent the Liberals do indeed stand for laissez-faire. In the United States of the 1930s, however, welfare-state liberalism was simply more relevant than rugged individualism and the survival of the fittest. With FDR occupying the "bully pulpit," he was, of course, also in the superior position to claim the prize. When his opponents started identifying liberals as people being "liberal in spending the taxpayer's money," they had basically surrendered the label.

In the end Rotunda asks why the term "liberal" has lost its appeal to the label "conservative." He adopts the standard answer that "liberalism has become a victim

of its own success." If the ups and downs of the language symbol "liberalism" are merely a reflection of the underlying substantive policies, though, we hardly need some linguistic theory to explain that.

Some of the details of this book make for interesting reading, but overall Rotunda's essay, which is sandwiched between an introduction by Daniel Schorr and a remotely related afterword by M. H. Hoeflich, seems to be ill-conceived.

KARL H. KAHRS

California State University
Fullerton

AFRICA, ASIA, AND LATIN AMERICA

ADAM, HERIBERT and KOGILA MOODLEY. *South Africa without Apartheid: Dismantling Racial Domination*. Pp. xviii, 315. Berkeley: University of California Press, 1986. $18.95.

This volume is cut from the same cloth as Heribert Adam's earlier and much celebrated *Modernizing Racial Domination* (University of California Press, 1971). It is not a study based on a particular research project, but a work of mature scholarship. It discusses ideas, insights, comparisons with other societies, strong opinions, and a series of policy recommendations.

It is hard to sum up such a rich and provocative book. Adam and Moodley reject Marxist and neo-Marxist analysis, although they see South Africa becoming increasingly a class-based society. Adam and Moodley are not sympathetic to a violent strategy. They are self-declared realists, liberal and reformist.

The claim that heightening present misery provides a shortcut to revolution is not only empirically false but also morally despicable when made by those who will not themselves be victims. The derision with which many left-wing academics greet liberal attempts at realistic mediation and reformist improvements only demonstrates their own political paralysis (p. 76).

In brief, Adam and Moodley see the regime trying to make a transition from an overtly ethnic state based largely on coercion to a superficially multiethnic polity based on class alliances and social conditioning. The government attempts to incorporate the politically unincorporated urban blacks economically with consumer substitutes and in that way co-opt a black bourgeoisie. They liken it to the perspective of Huxley's *Brave New World*, which hinges on conditioning, rather than to Orwell's *1984*, which is based on intimidation.

Yet Adam and Moodley argue that the pseudo-reform process cannot succeed for many reasons, not the least of which are the divisions in the white polity and the particular structure of the black community. The very people such "technocratic reform" tries to co-opt are increasingly alienated from their would-be patrons.

Adam and Moodley's "realistic optimism" is based on an awareness that in South Africa "economic interdependence in a resource-rich country gives all groups a stake in accommodation," mutual appreciation of Afrikaner and African nationalisms, the mediatory possibilities in common Christian values and Western consumerism that transcend color rigidities, and a regime that has already committed itself to modifying its control mechanisms. But government's current policies are forcing the African National Congress to bomb its way to the negotiating table. If that occurs, the African National Congress that sits down to decide the fate of South Africa may be considerably different from the nonracial, democratic, mildly socialist, and extremely multifarious body that it is today.

This book asks the important questions, provides clear but invariably debatable solutions, and gives cause for hope. No doubt it will be pounced upon by the Left, the Right, and by many liberals who do not share such facile analysis and prescriptions. But it will serve to focus discussion, and it will be widely read and will become a reference point for future policy proposals.

KENNETH W. GRUNDY
Case Western Reserve University
Cleveland
Ohio

BRASS, PAUL R. *Caste, Faction & Party in Indian Politics.* Vol. 1, *Faction & Party.* Delhi: Chanakya, 1983. $28.50.

Paul Brass has brought together a collection of his essays and articles on Indian factions and political parties written over a twenty-year period. All but the last piece were previously published between 1964 and 1984. Though not so identified, the unifying theme of all three parts appears to be instability as a product of factional struggles as well as an opportunistic and personalized style of politics that marks both leaders and followers of political parties, Congressmen and non-Congressmen, independents and "political entrepreneurs"—a rather flattering term applied to defectors from political parties.

Chapter 1, published in 1977, traces cabinet instability to the weakness of party organization and inadequate institutionalization—as manifested in the opportunism of individual politicians and the lack of party discipline. Comparing Indian state politics to European politics—a rather dubious undertaking given the disparate levels involved—Brass finds that the very features that in India are destabilizing would be salutary in Europe, whose politics are plagued by too much ideology and too rigid a commitment to principle.

The second chapter, reproducing a 1969 article, attempts to explain why an inverse relationship between institutionalization, which Brass finds declining along with the Congress organization, and political participation, which he finds increasing, does not violate standard political modernization theory, which assumes a direct relationship between these two trends. Without explaining this discrepancy—or the connection between political weakness and deinstitutionalization—he attributes the Congress decline to factionalism and weak leadership primarily.

The theme of factionalism and leadership conflict is further developed in the two chapters comprising part 2, which span more than a decade. Chapter 4, written in 1964, traces two important developments that explain why factional conflicts have come to be organized around personal and affective/instrumental ties rather than socioeconomic and ideological ties: (1) the elimination of ideological issues from political debate with the defeat of Hindu revivalists and socialists; and (2) the transfer of power from older, authoritative, and more ideologically inclined leaders to young virtuoso politicians. These new leaders, though highly skilled in the opportunistic pursuit of power, were neither respected figures nor skilled arbiters. Deprived of such traditional attributes and faculties for reconciling conflict and having shunned modern democratic mechanisms of conflict resolution, political parties became increasingly susceptible to splits. These were especially pronounced in the Socialist movement, as noted in chapter 5. Being very narrowly based it suffered all the more from typical Indian political flaws, including weak organization and parochial leaders.

The three chapters of part 3, published between 1968 and 1984, address the theme of central power vis-à-vis state and local governments and parties. Chapter 6, written in 1984, finds a substantial increase in New Delhi's power at the expense of the state governments and of the Congress Party at the national, state, and district levels. But there has been at the same time an increase in the power of local—nonpolitical—leaders and power structures, such as district councils, cooperatives, and local police.

The paradox here—one of many that are not adequately explained—is that, despite the center's tremendous power to make and break state governments and leaders, the system is "not really centralized," but "highly pluralized, decentralized, and fragmented." The emergence of these local power centers only partly explains this paradox, for it is difficult to imagine that the "linkages of dependency" render the "giant" of New Delhi a perennial hostage to the local "Lilliputians" on issues of national import.

Though written a decade and a half earlier, the following chapter anticipates the declining fortunes of the Congress Party in due course. Focusing on the largest and politically most crucial state of Uttar Pradesh, Brass returns to the theme of factionalism, which, together with the militancy of the opposition parties in Parliament, frustrate government's efforts to enact needed social and economic programs.

Here we have the main ingredients of the electoral debacle suffered by Congress, which Brass failed to predict in the pre-1967 portion of this elections piece. The postscript analyzes these elements of defeat, elaborating also on the magnitude of their effect on the Congress's political fortunes. Immobilized by internal factionalism and the obstructionism of the opposition parties, the drift in policy generated enough hostility against the Congress government to lead to its defeat and ultimately its replacement by a coalition government representing a broad spectrum of opposition parties.

This marked the rise of agrarian interests and issues in the politics of Uttar Pradesh and indeed of the nation as a whole, as Brass tells us in the last essay. Led by Charan Singh, a new party—the Bharatiya Kranti Dal, later the Bharatiya Lok Dal—became the voice of the "peasantry," by which Brass means the middle-status landed castes excluded from power and patronage by the ruling Congress in favor of the rich upper-caste peasants and the rural poor. When Charan Singh defected from the Congress in early 1967, he took with him this crucial component of Congress's power base, pitting the middle and upper ranks of the landowning castes against each other and depriving the ruling Congress in New Delhi of an assured electoral power base in the Uttar

Pradesh. Indeed, no central government could henceforth enjoy stability without the support of this important state. In this fashion, the very integrity of the federal system was undermined.

As we have come to expect from Paul Brass, he offers us a number of penetrating insights in this first book of a two-volume work on "caste, faction & party in Indian politics." Some can be found in his article on the historical origins of opportunistic politics—chapter 4—while chapter 5 offers us an illuminating discussion of the disintegration of the Indian Socialist movement.

The major problem I had with this otherwise challenging work was that the thematic organization was undertaken at the expense of chronological or historical clarity and coherence. While the introduction tries to pull together some of the many and varied threads of this rich and elaborate canvas, it falls short of the mark. Part of the problem is that some of the writing tends toward opacity, making concepts and arguments appear more complex than they are.

A concluding chapter was essential to clarify some of the contradictions introduced by the passage of time and to tie together the observations and conclusions reached over a twenty-year period. How is it, for example, that the factors preventing splits in Congress up to 1964—as argued in chapter 4—failed to do so in 1969 and thereafter? Then, too, some articles—written to address issues peculiar to their time—relied on then-current theoretical assumptions that in the meantime have been modified—for example, on political modernization. Some theoretical updating would have been helpful.

In all, however, this book is a work from which the specialist can benefit in that it brings together the observations and insights made over an extended period of time by one of the more penetrating analysts of the Indian political scene.

MARY C. CARRAS
Rutgers University
Camden
New Jersey

BROWN, DAVID G. *Partnership with China: Sino-Foreign Ventures in Historical Perspective.* Pp. ix, 175. Boulder, CO: Westview Press, 1986. $17.50.

CROLL, ELISABETH, DELIA DAVIN, and PENNY KANE, eds. *China's One-Child Family Policy.* Pp. xvi, 237. New York: St. Martin's Press, 1985. No price.

PIAZZA, ALAN. *Food Consumption and Nutritional Status in the PRC.* Pp. xiii, 256. Boulder, CO: Westview Press, 1986. $25.00.

Brown's book roughly divides into a historical survey of joint business ventures between Chinese and foreigners up to Mao's death in 1976, and a treatment of new laws and institutions created since reforms began in 1977. Most of the materials in the first part of the book, while familiar enough, are well summarized, including the dramatic change after 1842, when the character of trade with China altered from foreigners' paying tribute for trading privileges to the forced opening of the treaty ports where Chinese compradors joined with foreign businesses in a variety of joint ventures. The gradual demise of joint ventures after 1920 during the recurrent civil wars, the Japanese occupation, and the establishment of the People's Republic of China (PRC) in 1949 are also discussed.

The historical perspective provided in chapters 1 and 2 makes recent policies of the PRC discussed in chapter 3 the more dramatic. While China has clearly sought cooperation with foreign firms since 1977 primarily to modernize its economy and to gain technological knowledge and expertise, this might have been accomplished with fewer parallels with nineteenth-century experience. But the leaders of the PRC were not content simply to purchase foreign goods and to copy the technology; rather they sought active joint production with private foreign firms. An initial experiment with special economic zones (SEZs) widely scattered in China, a number being located in the interior with poor transport facilities, did not produce a large influx of foreign firms. This led to an emphasis on SEZs in 14 coastal cities where, not unlike the treaty ports, foreign firms—including overseas Chinese firms—could operate under laws different from those in the rest of the PRC. Of course, foreigners forced the treaty ports on China, while the PRC has itself established the SEZs. But as Brown makes clear, critics of the present leadership can find plenty to criticize about the SEZs—material and cultural corruption, for example—including historical parallels.

Brown in his conclusion leans to the view that the recent expansion of Chinese joint ventures reflects the continuity of Chinese experience, while the autarkic periods under Mao were exceptions. This is a useful book for anyone interested in the role of China in the international economy.

While economic reforms have created much discussion within and outside of China, the one-child family policy initiated in 1979 is equally or more controversial. While a population can maintain its size with two children per family, the PRC leadership felt that given the age distribution in China, which would have put the period of constant population off at least 40 years, with another half billion population growth, more drastic policies needed to be formulated. As in many of the social programs in China, the one-child family policy required local population groups, like communes, to establish norms for deciding which families could have a child each year and to try to discourage—including by means of encouraging abortions—others from having children. Many positive incentives, in the areas of housing, health, and education, were provided to families with only one child, while systems of penalties were imposed for exceeding the norm. Thus far, there have been major successes for the program in the larger cities, especially Shanghai, and much less success, and reaction against the policy, in rural areas.

The collection of essays edited by Croll, Davin, and Kane provides a wide-ranging treatment of this remarkable program. Croll provides a very clear introduction to popula-

tion attitudes and norms in China both before and after 1949, as well as a concluding chapter on how the program appears to be operating in Beijing. The remaining essays take up the implementation of the policies in rural and urban areas, provincial differences in fertility, the relation of one-child policies to old-age security, fertility experience in Singapore, and birth control organization in China. Each essay has a useful bibliography, and there is an index. The volume provides a very good introduction and analysis of one of the great social experiments of this era.

During the past 20 years, it has become common to use some measure of stature, like height or weight per height, given age, as a measure of nutritional well-being of a population. It appears that some populations can have different adult heights with comparable levels of nutrition; when the same population is observed over time, if average height per age increases, then nutritional status can be taken as improved. In his book, Piazza has been able to utilize surveys from as early as 1950 up to 1982 on heights by age of Chinese to make inferences about nutritional status. The major problem with the surveys is that they usually deal with school children, and those present and attending school are likely to be somewhat better fed than those who are not, which may be fairly important for differences between regions and between rural and urban areas.

Piazza's finding overall is that there has been a substantial increase of height by age for China between 1950 and the 1980s. This is consistent with data on the availability of food, and so it is not terribly surprising. The result is very robust, however, which is comforting in itself and also makes his results by region particularly interesting. What Piazza finds is that those populous provinces along the coast that had usually been associated with undernourishment had experienced substantial improvements since the 1950s and were usually near or above the national average. The provinces that remained below the national average were Gansu in the northwest, Hunan and Guangdon in the south, and Yunnan and Sichuan in the southwest. This is also consistent with the general view that China has made only limited progress in reducing regional differences in agricultural production, despite a number of investment and resource transfers to some of the poorer provinces. In addition to providing basic data on heights, weights, and age for China, Piazza also surveys Chinese data on nutritional intake, agricultural growth, and related issues. Like the other two books, this is a very solid account of an important subject, providing materials for the general reader and a good bibliography for those wishing to pursue the subject further.

ALAN HESTON

University of Pennsylvania
Philadelphia

DAVIS, NATHANIEL. *The Last Two Years of Salvador Allende*. Pp. xv, 480. Ithaca, NY: Cornell University Press, 1985. $24.95.

Nathaniel Davis was President Nixon's ambassador to Chile from 1971 through the bloody military coup of 11 September 1973 that overthrew the duly elected constitutional government of President Salvador Allende. The film *Missing* portrays him as involved in promoting that coup, and I want to say immediately that he has convinced me that he was not thus involved.

Davis aims to answer two main questions: "First, what political and economic developments in Chile produced the 1973 coup? Second, what was the U.S. role in this sequence of events and their culmination?" His answers rest almost entirely on the public record already available, plus the knowledge he gleaned in two years as our ambassador in Chile and the findings of his own questioning since then of high U.S. officials with intimate knowledge of our government's role in these events.

Davis is correct to suggest that "Allende's tragedy had indigenous roots" and that it was not merely an "external force" or "foreign agent"—that is, the United States—that "caused Allende's fall." The horrific military coup and its aftermath were the culmination of internal class struggle over the destiny of the nation; Chile's own arrogant and proud landowning and capitalist families not only successfully mobilized the mass support of small business and other middle-class elements against Allende's working-class-based government, but also did their part in promoting the coup. They sought that end, as Senator Francisco Bulnes said shortly after the coup, to "de-toxify Chile of the venom that was spread by Marxism. . . . All this takes years and could not have occurred in a democratic regime."

Much of Davis's book consists of a meticulous and plausible but, in my view, unconvincing rebuttal of the charge that U.S. covert action played a direct role in the coup that overthrew Allende. Unfortunately, Davis is so absorbed in trying to rebut that charge that he all but ignores, and entirely fails to assess, the dreadful impact of the pervasive intervention of the United States in Chile's internal affairs. Covert U.S. action exacerbated dissension and created economic turmoil and political chaos, without which the hitherto staunchly constitutionalist military could not have been induced to end Chilean democracy.

"We preached to the military the need to ignore the constitution and to overthrow a popularly elected government. . . . we did everything in our power to destroy the economy of Chile," as Morton Halperin, Kissinger's own former assistant and former deputy assistant secretary of defense, said in 1975. "And then we were told by the administration that we were not responsible for the coup because the day before the coup the generals who carried it out did not come to us and say, 'should we carry out the coup?'"

The last sentence applies precisely to Davis's own variant of that official story. His legalistic method of reasoning and his failure to find that proverbial smoking gun end up obscuring the U.S. government's share in the historic responsibility for bringing to power the unprecedented garrison state in Chile.

But Davis's specific brief for the defense of the United States against the charge of direct involvement in the coup is unconvincing. He was, in one sense, obviously assiduous in seeking evidence of such involvement. Over many years he has talked to many persons in the intelligence community and elsewhere in our government who he thought might have close knowledge of Central Intelligence Agency (CIA) or other clandestine U.S. operations in Chile. They all denied that the United States had a hand in the actual coup, and he believed them. Of course, as he acknowledges, his predecessor as ambassador, Edward Korry, was lied to precisely by such—and some of the same—people. Korry suspected that Nixon and Kissinger had the CIA working to promote a coup behind his back, but his five years of "independent questioning... failed to uncover," as he testified, "an iota of proof." Yet Davis has a strange faith that to him such officials would not lie.

I say "faith" because he himself supplies a number of instances—and lame excuses for them—in which he was willfully deceived or at best uninformed about CIA covert activities in Chile. Davis also points out emphatically that Kissinger misled Senate investigators in "executive-session testimony" on 17 September 1973 when he denied having intimate information on the coup planning; Kissinger also falsely claims in his memoirs that neither he nor Davis knew of a "specific plan," "time frame," or "date" for the coup. On the contrary, Davis reports that the first words Kissinger said to him when they met in Washington three days before the coup were: "So there's going to be a coup in Chile!"

But, Davis lets slip that he could have warned Allende by providing him with "detailed information about the plotters," but considered such an act a "betrayal"; he also acknowledges that the United States could have tried "to forestall the coup [by going]... to the plotters and [telling] them in the strongest terms of our opposition to their plotting, threatening dire consequences in their relations with the U.S. should they persist." If Washington had authorized it, he could have done this "in the formative stages of the plotting, perhaps in July or early August." But of course no one would have dared asked for such authorization from the very men whose "firm and continuing policy" was, as CIA director of clandestine operations Thomas Karamessines testified about his "marching orders" from Nixon and Kissinger, "that Allende be overthrown by a coup."

Illustrative of how Davis argues his case that the United States did not promote or assist the actual coup is his consideration of the so-called Brazilian connection. He says that he has "no real doubt"—as former ambassador to Chile Edward Korry also claims—that Brazilian businessmen gave "a lot" of money to Chile's rightist opposition, including the terrorist organization Fatherland and Liberty, and Brazil's military regime provided the actual technical and psychological support for the 1973 coup in Chile. He also notes that the Brazilians who plotted the overthrow of populist President João Goulart in 1964 were the same people who aided and advised the Chilean Right's coup against Allende. The question, then, is whether the Brazilians were acting as CIA agents. Davis accepts the "categorical assurances" given him by former CIA director William Colby and by David Atlee Phillips, who headed CIA clandestine operations in Latin America at the time of the coup, "that the CIA did not use Brazilians or Brazil to conduct programs in Chile." He also says that "presumably," if the "40 committee," which was supposed to consider and approve all clandestine operations, had authorized covert assistance to the anti-Allende insurgency, channeled through Brazil, then the Senate Select Committee would have found "traces" of it.

But Davis passes over in silence the question of how much credence the word of even such honorable men as William Colby should be given. In June 1975, Colby and Phillips, knowing that Korry was about to debate *New York Times* reporter Sy Hersh about the U.S. role in the coup, met with Korry personally but never gave him an inkling that the CIA had tried to organize a military coup in Chile while he was ambassador or that the CIA had been under Nixon and Kissinger's orders to lie to him. Davis also fails to explain why he "presumes" that if Brazilian "cutouts" or intermediaries were used as CIA agents in Chile, then "traces" of this should have been found in the 40 committee's records. He knows, after all, that in the fall of 1970, Nixon and Kissinger not only ordered CIA director Richard Helms to keep Korry in the dark about the CIA's coup activities, but also to hide those activities from the secretaries of state and defense and, most important, even from the 40 committee headed by Kissinger. Davis also must know that most major covert action proposals never came before the 40 committee for discussion or approval. CIA statistics show that only about a fourth of all covert action projects were considered by the 40 committee—and even being considered often meant in practice no more than clearance by a telephone call.

Davis fails to mention—aside from the close resemblance between the pattern of preparation for these coups in Brazil and Chile, as well as their actual execution, and aside from the involvement of the same Brazilians in both of them—that the CIA had helped the Brazilian military and civilian conspirators to oust Goulart. He knows, too, that Phillips, who assured him that the CIA had not used Brazilians in promoting or assisting the coup in Chile, also served in Brazil in 1970 and was there in 1971-72, where Phillips "presumably" must have had close and continuing contacts among the same Brazilians who were involved in destroying the constitutional democracies of both countries. Finally, as Davis tells us, Kissinger, by then secretary of state, wanted to give money to the independent truckers and others involved in the disruption and paralysis of Chilean commerce in August 1973, which was a prelude to the coup; but when Davis and Jack Kubisch, assistant

secretary of state, strongly opposed doing so, Kissinger's proposal somehow merely "drifted off into the bureaucratic haze."

Now, Kissinger's dissimulation and lying even to the highest government officials who were supposed to be in charge of such things are matter of record. After all, before he and Nixon ordered the CIA to promote a coup in Chile, they also had ordered General Burton Wheeler to hide Operation Menu in Cambodia—which meant falsifying Air Force records of the 3630 B-52 bombing raids of that neutral country over some 14 months—even from the secretary of the Air Force, the chief of staff of the Air Force, and the U.S. intelligence arm in Saigon.

Is it the gullibility of the cynical that leads one to conclude that present and former U.S. officials have misled Davis about the actual involvement of the CIA in the coup—perhaps precisely because Davis had ordered his embassy staff, including the CIA station chief, that "no one was to involve himself in coup plotting?" Or is it that even the evidence in his own book, upon close examination, points toward direct U.S. complicity in that coup and the death of democracy in Chile?

MAURICE ZEITLIN
University of California
Los Angeles

DE MESQUITA, BRUCE BUENO, DAVID NEWMAN, and ALVIN RABUSHKA. *Forecasting Political Events: The Future of Hong Kong.* Pp. x, 198. New Haven, CT: Yale University Press, 1986. $22.00.

The power and value of scientific prediction permeate modern society. Their distribution among scientific endeavors is quite uneven, as social scientists are keenly aware. The successes in economics, psychology, and other areas are limited. Continuous efforts to expand social scientific theories with predictive potency deserve resources and serious attention. The book reviewed here is a substantial effort at political theory and prediction worthy of careful consideration.

The work, built upon earlier efforts by de Mesquita, deals with the

scope and durability of China's future policies toward Hong Kong through the application of a formal interest group theory of politics that explains the process by which policy decisions are made and predicts specifically the resolution of the concrete issues that comprise the agenda for collective choice (p. viii).

There are three sets of analyses and predictions: structure and contents of the Sino-British agreement on Hong Kong, completed by de Mesquita, Newman, and Rabushka before the 1984 final accord; changes from 1985 to 1997; and changes after 1997. The model provides a rigorous method of investigating politics that analyzes what policy choices are reached, identifies what political realignments may result from a forecasted policy decision and the implications of these new alignments, and evaluates the significance of alternative assumptions. De Mesquita and his colleagues claim parsimony, power, and flexibility for a method that includes Lakatos criteria, mathematical equations, econometric-like formulations, expert factual inputs—all emulating microeconomic propositions. Certainly, whatever the ultimate verdict, systematic checklisting itself can lead to more powerful results.

The predictions and supporting analysis for the Sino-British accord were on target except for the issue dealing with property lease renewals, where they were slightly off. For 1985 to 1997 and after, predictions are that, because of internal Chinese policies, some commitments of the 1984 agreement will not be realized. For example, personal freedoms, the economy, and new land leases will be regulated in line with the Chinese economy.

Two issues concern us: the predictions or analysis about Hong Kong's fate after 1997 and the efficacy of the "expected utility decision model." The predictions on Hong Kong are based on assumptions about the Chinese economy remaining much as it is now—and on other unidentified assumptions

that may loom large. They may or may not be borne out, and a positive outcome, in itself, will not be validation. Only consistent predictive success will. Though supportive of efforts in this direction, I must voice skepticism on longer-term political predictability given our present knowledge. The relative salience of variables included or excluded and the often swiftly changing reality that undergirds important assumptions describe inadequately a hazardous endeavor.

CHARLES HOFFMANN
University of California
Berkeley

DOMES, JURGEN. *P'eng Te-huai: The Man and the Image.* Pp. xii, 164. Stanford, CA: Stanford University Press, 1985. $25.00.

Several factors have conspired to limit our knowledge of the leading actors in recent Chinese history. One is a general cultural reluctance on the part of Chinese political figures to reveal in public the details of personal and family life that are so important to the daily press in the West. Another factor has to do with the management style of the Chinese Communist Party. Once a comrade entered the Party, his or her personal life was replaced by a party life that emphasized the importance of the movement at the expense of the individual. A third factor concealing Chinese leaders from our view is the cult of Mao Tse-tung. Since Mao's death in 1976, the arrest of his closest associates, and the official reevaluation of the great leader's career, there has been a concerted effort to restore some balance to the Party's early history.

One of the revolutionary heroes restored to a place of honor after Mao's death is P'eng Te-huai. P'eng was a senior military figure who commanded the Chinese volunteer forces in Korea and then went on, in 1954, to become the highest military commander of the People's Liberation Army. A courageous and loyal soldier, P'eng was a better organizer than tactician. He had no credentials as a theorist and was not a member of the innermost political leadership. What made him most famous was his criticism of the folly of Mao's Great Leap Forward. P'eng spoke out at the Lushan conference in the summer of 1959. His defense of the plight of the peasantry made him a hero among the common people but an enemy in the eyes of Mao Tse-tung. During the Cultural Revolution P'eng's honesty was rewarded with imprisonment and death.

In this slim volume, Jurgen Domes, a leading German scholar of recent Chinese affairs, demonstrates his mastery of the craft of gleaning and organizing information about the inner workings of the Chinese political system. While artfully reconstructing the story of P'eng's life, Domes also manages to raise significant theoretical issues in each chapter.

EDWARD L. FARMER
University of Minnesota
Minneapolis

JACOBS, NORMAN. *The Korean Road to Modernization and Development.* Pp. x, 355. Chicago: University of Illinois Press, 1985. $24.95.

The Korean road, according to this well-organized and provocative study, turns out to be patrimonial. That is, in contrast to a feudal society, such as Japan's, which is based on warriors who owe allegiance to a lord, a patrimonial society is based on a civil bureaucracy that is supported not by the produce of fiefs, but by stipends, which Norman Jacobs terms "prebends," gained through taxation and doled out by the central authority. Thus Korea differs from Japan far more than from China, where the model originated.

By developing this theme, Jacobs comes to the conclusion that today Korea is modern-izing, but hardly developing. That is, Korea is adjusting to the modern world while holding onto a traditional system that is basically authoritarian and cannot allow interests and forces from below to arise and participate in the decision-making process. If such forces as the farmers and workers did articulate their interests and struggle for the realization, then development—political and economic—would take place and institutional change occur.

As Jacobs makes his case, it is clear he is a sociologist, treading in the footsteps of Max Weber in the selection and organization of his material. The chapters concern: (1) concepts and theories; (2) authority from the center to the localities; (3) political authority and the populace; (4) the squeezed agricultural economy; (5) the favored urban commercial and industrial economy; (6) the occupations—not classes—from the bureaucracy to the industrialists; (7) social stratification; (8) kinship and descent; (9) the role of traditional religions; (10) contemporary religions; (11) how Korea has reacted to modernization; and (12) why Korea did not enter the stage of developmental modernization.

That South Korea is hardly a modern democracy is generally conceded, but in this book exactly what it is is beautifully described in its array of strengths and weaknesses. This is not just a factual description but an astonishingly judgmental one. The reader is told what processes are effective and what are not, what the degree and role of corruption is in this or that ministry or economic sector. But it is hard to check specific statements because footnotes do not document each evaluation; rather, each footnote comes at the end of the discussion of a subject and lists all the sources, primary and secondary, that have presumably been consulted. These are not only in English but also in Korean and Japanese, Jacobs having learned Japanese during World War II. The volume of cited materials is impressive. Smoother reading would have resulted from reducing some of the jargon such as the endless repetition of the word "patrimonial" itself.

This study is a reevaluation of explanations of what are generally assumed to be successes and failures of the Korean economy. Jacobs does not see its successes as the result of its choice of a capitalist planning strategy, but rather he considers that its planning strategy is what it is because of its patrimonial character. While not dealing with North Korea as such, Jacobs's supposition is that its economy or society is a socialist version of basically the same patrimonial tradition. This implies a new and different classification of developing economies.

Whether one accepts the conceptual scheme of the book or not, the reader will find it crammed full of startling insights and fascinating detail from economy to religion, though not so much specifically on politics. This is therefore an important supplement to books that focus on the political arena, and it is highly recommended to sociologists, historians, and all who are interested not only in Korea but also in basic questions of development.

GEORGE OAKLEY TOTTEN III

University of Southern California
Los Angeles

University of Stockholm
Sweden

KIRKBY, R.J.R. *Urbanization in China: Town and Country in a Developing Economy 1949-2000 A.D.* Pp. xiii, 289.New York: Columbia University Press, 1985. $35.00.

COPPER, JOHN, FRANZ MICHAEL, and YUAN-LI WU. *Human Rights in Post-Mao China.* Pp. xii, 117. Boulder, CO: Westview Press, 1985. Paperbound, $15.00.

The two books under review here deal with widely different aspects of China, but at their core is a common problem, namely, how best to think about Chinese society in a comparative context. For Kirkby the context is a worldwide phenomenon of urbanization; for Copper and his colleagues, it is the universal question of human rights. In both books we see close to one-fourth of the human race grappling with problems that plague humanity in general, and from both we learn something about the hazards and benefits of such broad comparative analysis.

Copper, Michael, and Wu have written an impassioned book, marked by a deep concern to protect and enhance human rights everywhere, but especially in China. Indeed, the book builds to a conclusion that calls for greater international attention to human rights and for a U.S. foreign policy that includes a major human rights component. But the heart of the book is an evaluation of human rights trends in China from 1977 to 1984. The standards of judgment held by Copper and his coauthors are firm and absolute. They measure post-Mao China first by "the Western tradition" of human rights, and second, by a Chinese "humanist tradition that grew through several millenia of history." They insist that communism is a totally alien and "antagonistic" system that was "superimposed" on China in the chaos of World War II and an ensuing civil war. They regard the prewar years under the Guomindang (Kuomintang) and Jiang Jieshi (Chiang Kai-shek) as years of nation building that "harmonized" modernization with "Chinese cultural tradition"; by contrast, they see post-1949 China as totalitarian "barbarism," Mao as a Stalinist who was an even harsher dictator than Stalin, and the period 1977-84 as only marginally different from 1949-76. Their basic point is that Communist systems are rooted in a doctrine that is intrinsically incompatible with freedom of thought and are therefore incapable of protecting human rights; Copper, Michael, and Wu are able, of course, to cite a dismal litany of human rights violations in China. For the future, they offer a hope that "the true Chinese heritage" will reassert itself, and they call upon others, especially the United States, to encourage this process.

The thesis summarized here raises many questions, most of which derive from the authors' preference for unmixed judgments.

I am dissatisfied with their simplified characterizations of Western and Chinese traditions and especially with their ludicrously one-sided profile of the Guomindang regime. For evaluations of human rights in post-1949 China, I refer readers to James D. Seymour's writings, notably *The Fifth Modernization*—incorrectly cited in the book under review here—and *China Rights Annals*. Seymour is no less passionate about human rights, but he is equally alert to violations of them everywhere; he is subtler in his historical analysis, and he takes more seriously the interplay of different political forces in China and their changing relations over time.

Where Kirkby's book intersects with the foregoing is at the point where China's internal dynamics intersect with the outside world. Before the twentieth century, tensions and struggles had existed for centuries in China between forces of control and conformity on the one hand, and people's desires for a wider range of thought and action on the other. These tensions and struggles, waged in overwhelmingly Chinese terms for more than two millenia, acquired in the twentieth century an additional dimension of Western concepts that created an explosive mix. Somewhat similarly, a process of urbanization can be traced back to the second millenium B.C. in China, but it underwent numerous transformations, notably from about A.D. 750 to 1250. By the nineteenth century it was an enormously complex home-grown hydra to which a foreign treaty-port dimension was then added, followed by widening industrialization and then by an accelerating industrial revolution with all its implications for modern urbanization.

Kirkby, previously unknown to me but described as honorary lecturer in the Department of Town and Regional Planning at the University of Sheffield, lived in China from 1975 to 1980 and made several shorter visits there. His knowledge of the literature of Chinese urbanization is limited, and his book has its gaps and weaknesses, but he makes a heroic effort to unravel some of the major mysteries of the subject—beginning

with the far-from-simple questions of what exactly a city is in China and what Chinese urban data really tell us. He comes remarkably close to answering these better than anyone else has. In addition, he manages to combine an essentially Western social science framework of analysis with an appreciation of China's peculiarities, a healthy skepticism, an astute eye even for contradictory detail, and a willingness to reexamine his own and others' assumptions. His China thus turns out to be a society in enormous flux, full of anomalies, and far from the monolith portrayed by Copper and his coauthors. Specialists will find much to dissent from in Kirkby, but they will have to read him.

MICHAEL GASSTER

Rutgers University
New Brunswick
New Jersey

NISHIHARA, MASASHI. *East Asian Security and the Trilateral Countries*. Pp. xi, 111. New York: New York University Press, 1986. $25.00.

This book was first written as a report to the Trilateral Commission. Masashi Nishihara, a professor at Japan's National Defence Academy, and his advisers, editor John Roper of the Royal Institute of International Affairs and Professor Donald Zagoria of Hunter College, interviewed 89 experts on three continents to compile it.

The result is a lucid and brisk survey of the current balance of power and potential security threats in the region, and of various military, political, and economic interests of the principal Trilateral countries—comprised of Western Europe, North America, and Japan—in East Asia. Topics touched upon include the geostrategic and economic importance of the region, the changing roles of China and the Soviet Union, the potential for Pacific Basin cooperation, and problems that may arise in Korea, Indochina, the Philippines, and the South China Sea. Statistical tables provide data on selected Tri-lateral-East Asia transactions.

As an introduction or reference the book has potential usefulness. But its disparate topics are treated rather too briefly, with no documentation and little depth, to satisfy a reader with much familiarity with contemporary Asia. Scope and succinctness have taken precedence over depth, focus, and subtlety, a trade-off acceptable in a report but less so in a book published by a university press.

Trilateral countries range from Japan to Spain, from Canada to Greece, from the United States to Austria. Nishihara assumes, implies, and asserts they have common interests in East Asia—itself a diverse area—but does not make a substantial case, only a series of observations about bilateral interests. He concedes that "not all trilateral countries need to be involved in all major issues and certainly not in the same way . . . discrepancies should be accepted if they are within a common trilateral frame of reference."

Another book elaborating that "common trilateral frame of reference" vis-à-vis East Asia would be welcomed. Until then Asian-country specialists may remain skeptical that the Trilateral and East Asian countries collectively have much in common besides the Trilateral Commission and the Nishihara report.

STEVE HOADLEY

University of Auckland
New Zealand

STEPHENS, EVELYNE HUBER and JOHN D. STEPHENS. *Democratic Socialism in Jamaica: The Political Movement and Social Transformation in Dependent Capitalism.* Pp. xx, 423. Princeton, NJ: Princeton University Press, 1986. $55.00. Paperbound, $14.50.

Stephens and Stephens take Jamaica as an example of a number of states in the Third World that are dependent capitalist societies with democratic politics and relatively mobilized populations. The entire study is conceived within "the class struggle frame of reference."

Stephens and Stephens assume that "dependent development" is incapable of improving societies such as Jamaica. They note, for example, that while Jamaica from 1960 to 1972 experienced rapid economic growth, both income inequity and unemployment increased substantially. Further, they argue that the Seaga government during its first three and a half years in office, 1980-83, and despite enormous material and moral support from the Reagan administration and prominent U.S. capitalists, failed to produce even the minimum expected of free market/private-sector-oriented development: sustained growth and alleviation of the balance-of-payments problems.

The core of the study is an examination of the Michael Manley administration, 1972-80, as an attempt at "democratic socialist development"—as distinct from Latin American-style "populism," "state capitalism," "non-capitalism," and "European social democracy." This democratic socialist path is characterized by five goals or major policies. In brief, they are reduction of economic dependence; state-sector-led development in the context of a mixed economy; increased social, cultural, and political equality; deepening political democracy; and a struggle for international economic reorganization. Stephens and Stephens then argue that this path has three strategic requirements: a broad class alliance; a working accommodation with sections of the bourgeoisie that are not part of the basic alliance; and the construction of a political movement centered on an ideological, pragmatic, mass-based party buttressed by unions and other popular organizations. This last is the socialists' organizational counter to the bourgeois control of property in the struggle for hegemony in society.

The Manley administration fell short of its goals and was rejected overwhelmingly at the polls in 1980. The present work includes a detailed examination of, first, the extent to which Manley did achieve the goals of democratic socialist development and, second, the reasons for the shortfalls. Within the latter context, Stephens and Stephens consider five analytically distinct sources of problems: general difficulties of socialist transformation; difficulties caused by general features of dependent capitalism; factors associated with Jamaica's position in the world economy and geopolitical space; specific features of Jamaica's historical legacy and political and economic situation in the early 1970s; and mistakes made by the leadership of the People's National Party while in office.

This is a profoundly researched, finely argued and nuanced study. As Stephens and Stephens intend, it is far more than a detailed study of a particular Jamaican administration, or even a demonstration of the utility of class analysis as a key to understanding political events. It is an argument for the possibility of a socially just and politically democratic development path for countries such as Jamaica, and it posits a set of lessons for democratic socialists who would seek to pursue a model other than dependent capitalism or "scientific socialism." For me, at least, the question remains, Which U.S. government would tolerate the success of such an alternative, especially within its mare nostrum?

DONALD HINDLEY

Brandeis University
Waltham
Massachusetts

UNSCHULD, PAUL U. *Medicine in China: A History of Pharmaceutics*. Pp. xii, 367. Berkeley: University of California Press, 1986. $65.00.

American and European scholars who are unaware of the wealth and diversity of textual sources in the history of Chinese medicine will find this book and its two companion volumes—forthcoming from the same publisher—to be a revelation. In this lavishly illustrated and carefully organized work, Paul Unschuld traces four major traditions of Chinese scholarly writing on pharmaceutics: the main materia medica tradition, dating from the Han period (206 B.C. to A.D. 220) to the Sung (ended in the twelfth century); the neo-Confucian Chin-Yüan tradition (twelfth to fourteenth centuries); the eclectic tradition (sixteenth century and later); and the conservative tradition of Han studies (seventeenth century and later). Major texts affiliated with each of these categories, as well as works on dietetics, individual drugs, and pharmaceutical technology, are listed and considered in their relationship to previous and subsequent texts. Numerous excerpts are translated.

In any consideration of a body of literature of the size and complexity of that relating to medicine in traditional China, certain principles of selection must be employed. Unschuld's preferences are not entirely explicit in this volume, but they are not difficult to detect. He distinguishes Taoist concerns with the prolongation of life from the curative concerns of the main tradition, and while he acknowledges Taoist influence at various points in the literature on materia medica, he confines his attention to procedures for curing illness. By imposing this more contemporary definition of what comprises medicine or pharmacy on earlier eras of Chinese practice, he separates demonological and alchemical practices from medical practices as if such a separation had always been important. This procedure will not disturb historians of science and medicine who are, like Unschuld, searching for the origins and precursors of modern knowledge, but it might be seen as a problem by historians and sociologists of China.

In a related ethnocentric gesture, Unschuld is particularly concerned to argue that the pharmaceutical literature of China never comprised a pharmacopoeia in the sense of a state-sanctioned drug code. After an early consideration of this distinction, in which he cites the first true pharmacopoeia as that of Valerius Cordus of Nuremberg (1546), Unschuld demonstrates that the Chinese literature tended to accumulate the observations—sometimes contradictory—of many generations of scholars rather than to evaluate and standardize them critically. Judging from his closing chapter, in fact, standardization appears for Unschuld to be the sole culmination toward which pharmaceutical work ought to aspire. When he turns to the twentieth century, a period that has seen a massive and complicated expansion of interest in and research on traditional Chinese medicine, especially in the People's Republic of China, Unschuld focuses his attention on Chinese drug codes translated from Western models. These offical drug codes are almost exclusively concerned with the pharmaceutics of Western medicine and consequently display almost no continuity with the rich textual materials explored in the foregoing sections of this history. Readers whose interest is partly in contemporary Chinese medicine will be disappointed.

JUDITH FARQUHAR
University of North Carolina
Chapel Hill

EUROPE

BERMEO, NANCY G. *The Revolution within the Revolution: Workers' Control in Rural Portugal.* Pp. 263. Princeton, NJ: Princeton University Press, 1986. $28.50.

OPELLO, WALTER C., Jr. *Portugal's Political Development: A Comparative Approach.* Pp. xii, 235. Boulder, CO: Westview Press, 1985. Paperbound, $21.00.

On 1 January 1986 Portugal and Spain officially joined the European Community, thereby increasing global interest in their political profiles. Fortuitously, two recent publications by American academicians augment awareness and understanding of Portugal's problems and prospects. Opello's is much more enlightening to the average reader, because its preparation was based specifically

upon his premise that American social scientists know too little about Portuguese society and politics. As he is of Portuguese descent, his efforts appear at least partially motivated to remedy the present situation, in which specialists in European history and geopolitics definitely have neglected his Lusitanian ancestral homeland more than any other West European country.

One of the Westview Special Studies in West European Politics and Society, this classic country political analysis covers key themes: the origin of Portugal as an independent nation-state; causes and consequences of Portugal's persistent revolutions; political parties and their performances; regional voting behavior; attitudes toward politicians by the electorate, and so forth. Opello's main thesis is that much of Portugal's political history and development can be interpreted as a struggle to create new political institutions to deal with its varied social and economic problems. Successfully he shows that such struggles have much more in common with similar developments in other political units of Western Europe than in Latin American countries.

In sharp contrast to the broad focus of Opello's book, Bermeo's study—begun as a doctoral dissertation—analyzes theoretical issues of interest to an academic audience extending beyond Portugal and beyond that group of scholars interested in Portugal per se. Significantly, it is based upon fieldwork done from 1977 to 1980—a few years after the April 1974 bloodless revolution that in 36 hours terminated a corporate dictatorship that had dominated Portugal for nearly half a century. In an analysis of one early result of that revolution, Bermeo specifically focuses upon workers' control of forcefully seized estates in the Alentejo, an extensive area of southern Portugal traditionally dominated by *latifundia*.

In less than one year, more than 23 percent of Portugal's farmland changed from operations under private ownership into 500 cooperatives farmed and managed collectively. This study illustrates how landless farm workers came to control the land, how its control changed their lives, and how their new enterprises affected and were affected by post-1975 political developments. Today only a minority survive—one consequence of ideological differences between the Communist Party and the Socialists who came to power in 1977. Ominously Bermeo concludes by predicting that in southern Portugal "the experience of workers' controls leaves a legacy that justifies future hostility to the post-1974 order."

RICHARD J. HOUK
DePaul University
Chicago
Illinois

BOTTING, DOUGLAS. *From the Ruins of the Reich: Germany 1945-1949.* Pp. ix, 340. New York: Crown, 1985. $17.95.

This book reads like a Hollywood script that will seem incredible to anybody who was not there—and to many combat soldiers who were there, but did not remain for the occupation. With an engaging style, Botting describes the battle for Berlin and the German surrender, and then he proceeds to what followed.

Germany was a surrealist tableau of disasters, a land of ruins peopled by ghosts, without government, order or purpose, without industry, communications or the proper means of existence. It was a nation that had forfeited its nationhood, and had sunk to a level unknown in the western world for a hundred years (p. 123).

In the British zone by the end of the year [the food ration] was in some instances down to 400 calories a day—half the figure for Belsen concentration camp under Nazi rule (p. 142).

The repatriation of Soviet prisoners by the British, American, and other western countries was one of the most repugnant episodes to arise out of World War Two. . . . Several nations were thus involved to a greater or lesser extent in forcibly handing Soviet subjects over to the untender mercies of the NKVD . . . and the Gulag (pp. 156-57).

The Russian prisoners after the war suffered a comparable fate in comparable numbers to [that of] the Jews during the war (p. 170).

The occupation of Germany by the Western Powers was like a new Raj—colonial, exploitative, but in part paternalistic and well-intentioned. Like most colonial rule it suffered from indecisive, out-of-touch direction from the home government (p. 193).

The New York Times reported that on average one American family displaced eight German families and that in the Grünewald district of Berlin one thousand German civilians were made homeless when the Americans requisitioned 125 houses for dependents (p. 215).

Many [Germans] had greeted [the Americans and British] as liberators rather than conquerors, welcoming the Americans with garlands and wine in Munich and speaking warmly of the "fair play" of the "English gentlemen" who had captured Hamburg. Those who had not supported Hitler looked forward to a new era of freedom and democracy, even under Occupation. But their hopes were not fulfilled and disillusionment often led to anger. . . . Armed robbery, looting, and car theft were rife. . . . The Congress in Washington was told: "The German troops occupying France had a better record in their personal contact with the population than the American troops occupying Germany." A special study of . . . Marburg in Hesse showed that though many inhabitants had been well disposed to the Americans when they arrived, most had totally ceased to cooperate with them by the end of 1945 (p. 221).

In general it could be said that the Allies made a good job of demilitarizing the former Reich by plundering and exploiting what was of use to them and destroying what was not. The same dual approach could be seen in their handling of the denazification program, which must rank as the greatest of all the Allies' failures during the Occupation (pp. 260-61).

On January 1, 1947, the British and Americans merged their zones for economic purposes into a single unified zone called Bizonia and handed over much of the administrative responsibility for running it to the Germans. . . . Six months later the USA, Great Britain, France and other West European countries agreed to a plan to create a West German state which would enjoy a limited degree of sovereignty by 1949. A prerequisite for an independent nation was a revival of its economy. . . . On June 18 the new currency was announced to the world. The result was electrifying. West Germany's economic miracle began on that day (pp. 302-3).

The Soviet reaction to the currency reform was the blockade of Berlin. Botting applauds the surprising success of the American-British airlift, but he does not disclose his opinion of Robert Murphy's contention that the airlift—as opposed to a direct challenge to the Soviets on the ground—was a great mistake.

Often it seems to be the case that the people of a vanquished nation suffer more in the aftermath than in the war itself. For many Southerners the Reconstruction was more bitter than the Civil War that preceded; the German civilian population had suffered more in the year after the Armistice of 1918—including eight months when the blockade was continued—than during World War I. But far worse was the suffering in the wake of World War II. Botting notes in his preface, "This book does not celebrate VE Day in a conventional festive sense, for it knows all too well what was to follow the day after, and the day after that."

Botting offers an impressive bibliography and gives evidence of being thoroughly familiar with it. He lists sources for each chapter, but does not provide specific footnotes. These would have been especially helpful in a book that presents so many controversial points. Altogether the book is well organized and well written. This is an important work as a study of recent history and a commentary on human nature.

JAMES A. HUSTON

Lynchburg
Virginia

GREEN, THOMAS ANDREW. *Verdict According to Conscience: Perspectives on the English Criminal Trial Jury, 1200-1800*. Pp. xx, 409. Chicago: University of Chicago Press, 1985. $34.00.

As a long-praised bulwark of Anglo-American liberties, the English criminal trial jury has often been studied and commented upon by legal historians and lawyers. Soon after it came into existence early in the thirteenth century, Bracton commented upon its functions and place in common law in his *De Legibus et Consuetudinibus Regni Angliae*. Thereafter many distinguished legal minds studied this jury, among them Fortescue in the fifteenth century, Coke in the seventeenth century, Blackstone in the eighteenth century, and Maitland and Holdsworth in more recent times. There has been, moreover, an amazing amount of research published in monographs and articles. This book is, therefore, most welcome because it provides the only modern and scholarly history available on the criminal jury, with special attention to the practice of nullification, whereby the jury acquitted defendants who according to legal theory and on the basis of the facts known to jurors should have been convicted. Actually, this is a study of how the criminal jury became an institution of mitigation that commonly lessened the severity of charges against the defendants as well as the punishments.

When in the twelfth century the Angevin kings sharply increased the punishments for all felonies, making most of them capital, ordeal was still the form of criminal trial. This meant that no group of men had the responsibility of determining the guilt or innocence of a defendant. This was done by God. But after the Fourth Lateran Council of 1215 forbade clergy to participate in trials involving bloodshed, trial by ordeal had to be abandoned. It was replaced by the criminal trial jury, a method of trial that had its antecedents in the jury used for civil cases since the reign of Henry II (1154-89). Now faced with the fact that a guilty verdict could lead to death, criminal juries began to decide that various crimes did not warrant the death penalty or that a law-abiding individual should not be put to death for a homicide that was provoked by a variety of possibly defendable reasons. Because the criminal jury was a fact-finding body into the Tudor period and was usually familiar with the defendant, it is obvious why nullification was so often resorted to.

Although the Tudor and Stuart governments developed legal machinery whereby royal officials assumed the task of gathering evidence and of presenting it to criminal juries mostly ignorant of the facts and of the defendant, verdicts continued to be rendered in favor of obviously guilty defendants, a practice that the courts did not frown upon so long as those defendants of established ill repute and open guilt were found guilty. During the eighteenth century philosophical thought and reformist movements worked for the reform of the criminal law and of the penal system with the result that beginning in the nineteenth century Parliament enacted statutes reducing the punishments for various kinds of felonies. In addition, certain felonies were reduced to misdemeanors, which carried lighter penalities such as fines or short prison terms.

Packed with twenty years of research entailing familiarity with a vast corpus of legal literature on criminal justice as well as archival work with legal records such as court records and the Year Books, this book is a fine piece of legal scholarship that will be valuable not only to legal historians but to lawyers. The only blemish is that most of the chapters were originally articles and they do not always smoothly and logically mesh with each other.

BRYCE LYON

Brown University
Providence
Rhode Island

HAIGH, R. H., D. S. MORRIS, and A. R. PETERS. *German-Soviet Relations in the Weimar Era: Friendship from Necessity.* Pp. viii, 206. Totowa, NJ: Barnes & Noble, 1985. No price.

The preface indicates that this book represents part of a larger study on the "Nazi-

Soviet Aggression [*sic*] Pact" of 1939. Separated as it is from Haigh, Morris, and Peters's chief focus, it carries little introduction and makes limited effort at reaching conclusions. The main message is that Soviet-Weimar relations were influenced by the course of the individual relations of Germany and the USSR with the other powers. "The German-Soviet friendship was one of calculation rather than one of genuine affection; . . . compatibility of objectives and not a deep-rooted affinity provided the *raison d'être* of their association."

This traditional view is substantiated in chapters devoted to the armistice, the peace treaty, Rapallo, Locarno, and military collaboration. The discussion of the two nations' reaction to the recreation of Poland is well done. Haigh, Morris, and Peters believe the Allies' efforts to keep Germany and the USSR apart helped to bring them together. The failure of the Kapp putsch played a role, for it enhanced the influence of General Hans von Seeckt, who was willing to deal with the Bolsheviks. Rapallo was the unsurprising result of German efforts to reduce the impact of Versailles and Allied hegemony and of Soviet efforts to protect the revolution and escape economic strangulation. The key to the strengthening of the Soviet international position following 1927 was German neutrality during the period of crisis. Later, tensions between Soviet willingness to accept the European status quo, compared with German desire to revise it, became more evident as Soviet isolation reduced and Germany gained strength. Military links were weakened by the forced resignation of Seeckt in 1926, the desire of the German foreign ministry not to upset the West, and the accession to power of Hitler when German-Soviet military relations "were no longer capable of being viewed as indispensable to either party."

This is a good synthesis of recent writings on Soviet-Weimar relations. Quotations from other secondary accounts are numerous and at times carry the narrative. While some memoirs and documents are cited, the account does not rest on them. Citations to scholarly periodical literature are few and the bibliography is not exhaustive. Emphasis on the desires of nations—Germany or Britain, for instance—is such that the role of individuals in shaping policies sometimes is lost; this occurs despite such portrayals as that of Seeckt. Lengthy sentences require the reader's concentration. I would wish the publisher to choose a style that permits periods after initials and abbreviations.

J. E. HELMREICH

Allegheny College
Meadville
Pennsylvania

KAMINSKY, ARNOLD P. *The India Office, 1880-1910.* Pp. xv, 294. Westport, CT: Greenwood Press, 1986. $49.95.

The "jewel in the crown," as British India seems to be called these days, showed its special position in the constellation of British imperial possessions by having an administrative department of its own in London, separate from the Colonial Office. This was the India Office, constituted in 1858 when the East India Company was abolished and crown rule established in the subcontinent. This book examines the structure and procedures of this department over a period of thirty years, which corresponds to the tenure of Sir Arthur Godley as permanent undersecretary of state for India from 1883 to 1909—in British parlance the top civil servant in a ministry headed by a senior cabinet member called a secretary of state. His unusually long tenure in this position gave Godley an extraordinary degree of influence in the shaping of British policy toward India at a time when the Indian empire provided the economic and strategic underpinnings to Britain's role as a first-class power. Hence this book is at once a study of an administrator as well as of the department of state that he administered.

The effective administration of India from London required an efficiently organized and functioning India Office, and Kaminsky clearly shows how Godley achieved this in the first chapter, entitled "Policy Making and the Flow of Paper." Subsequent chapters examine the role of that peculiar body, the Council of India—a small group composed mainly of retired members of the Indian Civil Service appointed to advise the secretary of state—and the problems and sometimes tensions that developed in the India Office as a result of Indian affairs being conducted by a corporate entity, the Secretary of State for India in Council. The India Office also had to take account of the role of the British Parliament and cabinet in developing Indian policy. Above all, it had to work out a relationship with the government of India itself. These topics form the subject of chapters that show how Godley fended off parliamentary and even royal interference in the conduct of Indian affairs by the India Office and how the latter asserted its ultimate power as the decision maker when differences developed between London and Calcutta over such issues as the tariff to be levied on British cotton goods, opposed by British manufacturing interests but favored by officials in India; or the licensing and compulsory examination of prostitutes, which the government of India wanted in order to control the incidence of venereal disease among British soldiers but which did not sit well with moral pressure groups in late Victorian England. In all such cases, the India Office imposed its will. India was governed from London.

Kaminsky has written an extremely interesting book on a subject that could be extremely dry, and he has left no stone unturned in digging out all possible sources. Assuredly this book is the definitive study of the India Office for the period it covers. The 781 footnotes take up 46 of its 294 pages, there is a 20-page bibliography, and the appendixes occupy 55 pages. One appendix lists every member of every committee of the Council of India for each year between 1858 and 1905. Such attention to detail would surely have won Sir Arthur Godley's approval. Indeed, it is tempting to speculate that in another time and place, Arnold

Kaminsky—ultimately, Sir Arnold, of course— would have been an excellent permanent under-secretary of state for India himself! His work is a model of careful and balanced analysis and he succeeds in bringing to life the way in which the British managed their Indian empire in its heyday.

PETER HARNETTY

University of British Columbia

Vancouver

Canada

MARRUS, MICHAEL R. *The Unwanted: European Refugees in the Twentieth Century.* Pp. xiii, 414. New York: Oxford University Press, 1985. $24.95.

Michael R. Marrus, a professor of history at the University of Toronto, has written the first comprehensive study of twentieth-century European refugees. Marrus's central focus is the impact of refugee movements on relations between the European states. His work looks at who the refugees were, why they became refugees, and what happened to them. He also examines the various agencies that worked to provide relief and facilitate resettlement of the refugees—private groups such as the Red Cross and international bodies such as the League of Nations and the United Nations. The focus of this study, however, is the response of European governments to refugee movements and to other European governments' policies and practices toward refugees.

Marrus shows that refugees became a massive problem in the twentieth century as the result of three changes in the character of refugee movements. First, the number of displaced people became overwhelmingly large—4 million between 1918 and 1938, 60 million during World War II, and about 14 million during the immediate postwar era. Smaller but still considerable numbers of refugees remained a problem into the 1960s. Second, the refugees of the modern era were stateless persons without destinations. The

modern refugee was removed very dramatically and completely from civil society, lacking elementary rights that had come everywhere in Europe to be defined by national governments. Third, the refugees of the twentieth century often remained refugees for a very long time—sometimes passing the status to a second generation. The sheer numbers of the displaced and the restrictive policies of national governments both worked to preclude any easy redefinition of nationality for the stateless.

Marrus first treats the hugh Jewish exodus from Eastern Europe during the last two decades of the nineteenth century and the first one of the twentieth century. He then examines the unmixing of peoples in the Balkans before World War II as Turkey's decline and the emerging nationalism of Serbs, Bulgars, Armenians, and others led to the flight or expulsion of minorities on all sides. The displacements of World War I, of the Peace Settlement, and of the Russian Revolution, all massive in comparison to what had gone before, are also examined. It was in response to these refugees that national governments began to sponsor and support international efforts to address refugee problems. The first international refugee commission, headed by Fridtjof Nansen, the Norwegian explorer, was created to deal with the problem of Russian refugees, but it evolved into a high commission of the League of Nations addressing the problem of all the stateless. Nansen's office assisted many and developed and secured national recognition of procedures for certifying refugees and guaranteeing them certain rights and protections. Depression and the rise of fascism, however, dramatically worsened the refugee situation during the 1930s. By 1938 there was already a refugee crisis, which exploded with the coming of war and took until the 1960s to resolve fully. Thereafter, refugees became mainly a problem of the Third World, where decolonization and rising nationalism replicated many of the pressures Europe had faced in 1900.

Marrus's book depicts some heroic failures to resolve the refugee problem by Nansen and by many other individuals of goodwill. But the usual responses to refugees by the governments and peoples of Europe were indifference and hostility. The accomplishments of the post-World War II era were considerable. Medical and sanitary sciences kept refugees alive, and national governments and the United Nations got them repatriated or resettled—often very quickly. It is well to bear in mind, however, that refugee movements ceased to be a major problem of European politics not because of humanitarian endeavors or enlightened national policies, but because Hitler liquidated the vast majority of European Jews and the Soviet Union blocked the flight of Eastern Europeans to the West. Marrus shows very convincingly that the most appropriate symbols for the resolution of Europe's twentieth century refugee crisis are the swastika and the Berlin Wall.

THOMAS M. HILL

Grandview
Missouri

PATCH, WILLIAM L., Jr. *Christian Trade Unions in the Weimar Republic, 1918-1933: The Failure of "Corporate Pluralism."* Pp. xix, 259. New Haven, CT: Yale University Press, 1985. $22.50.

SPIRES, DAVID N. *Image and Reality: The Making of the German Officer, 1921-1933.* Pp. xvi, 260. Westport, CT: Greenwood Press, 1984. $29.95.

The two works under review here are products of American Ph.D. theses. Both works undeniably make a contribution to scholarship and deserve their place on the library and specialist's bookshelf. Finally, both illustrate the continuing fascination of scholars, well versed in the literature, with the institutions of the ill-fated Weimar republic. Beyond this, their similarity ceases.

William L. Patch, Jr., a graduate of Yale University, has written a sensitive and intelligent study of the Christian trade unions of the Weimar republic. He delves into the philosophical mentality of the union movement, explores their historical sense of the ills of industrial society, and discusses the Christian trade unions' program for "corporate pluralism" as it evolved in the 1920s. The Christian unions could never mobilize mass support and remained a relatively minor, if energetic, group in German politics. Yet in the broadest sense, their fortunes illustrate a recognizable pattern in the fate of the Weimar republic itself—namely, the draining away of popular support from the democratic structure of Weimar under the hammer blows of economic crises and radical discontent. The Christian trade unions embraced the Weimar structure and died with it. As Patch relates in his introduction, "corporate pluralism" was not an inspiring cause worth defending on the barricades. Yet at least the Christian trade unions knew how to distinguish a flawed society from an evil one. That knowledge, as Patch posits, was based on an outlook that recognized the "corrosive effect of class egotism." Armed with this humble weapon, the Christian trade unions went on to prove themselves among the most active opponents of Hitler.

The same could hardly be said for the institution that is the subject of David Spires's study, the Weimar army. Spires, a serving officer in the United States Air Force, has written a thoroughly professional, if narrowly documented, book about the Weimar officer corps. The "image and reality" of his title hints at the central thesis of his work, namely, that the standard accounts of the Weimar army have focused on its political impact or on its peripheral activities in secret rearmament, thereby distorting the true story of the Reichswehr's successes and failures in the military sphere. As there were, of course, no wars that tested the Weimar army's mettle, Spires offers a history from "within," by which he means an account of the evolution of that army's officer corps from postwar disarray to the turbulent eve of the Nazi takeover.

Two useful contributions are made by this book. One is the emphasis that Spires places on the contradictory missions that the Reichswehr had to face and somehow harmonize. These missions included both the creation of a cadre force of trained officers as the vanguard of a mass army of the future, when the restrictions of the Versailles treaty could be safely ignored, and the more immediate deployment of a combat-ready army able to make the best job of the Weimar republic's military deficiencies. According to Spires, the pursuit of these contradictory aims remained an elusive feature of the work of every Reichswehr chief from Seeckt to Schleicher. The result was an army the officers of which were highly talented professionals, enjoying to a degree "careers open to talent" as the early Napoleon would have understood it, but narrow in their military thinking, and prone to conformity and a careerist mentality. The second contribution made by Spires proceeds from this finding. Of the various Reischswehr commanders, he gives credit to Wilhelm Heye as the one general who managed, even temporarily, to match the army to its given tasks. Spires rightly emphasizes Heye as the "forgotten general" of the Reichswehr, a point also made by Wilhelm Deist in his recent work. More study of this officer might well be rewarding.

Whether Spires is correct in suggesting that the historical "image" of the Weimar army has been distorted is arguable. Certainly his broader findings do not bear out this revisionistic sally. The mixture of professionalism and political conformity found by Spires in the army's makeup is scarcely new, but Spires has served to remind us that these characteristics were bred in the 1920s and were not simply a nostalgic inheritance from the Wilhelmine past. It is worth noting that the strength of both Spires's study and the more subtle work of Patch rests in the ability of these authors to root their chosen institutions in the contemporary and troubled age of the twenties.

WESLEY K. WARK
University of Calgary
Alberta
Canada

PRAGER, JEFFREY. *Building Democracy in Ireland: Political Order and Cultural Integration in a Newly Independent Nation.* Pp. xi, 259. New York: Cambridge University Press, 1986. $34.50.

MUNCK, RONNIE. *Ireland: Nation, State, and Class Struggle.* Pp. xiii, 185. Boulder, CO: Westview Press, 1985. Paperbound, $18.50.

These studies of modern Irish politics highlight the impossibility of any easy resolution of the Irish problem. In studying the emerging system of political order in the Irish Free State, Jeffrey Prager argues that without "cultural integration" no political stability would have been achieved. Ronnie Munck surveys modern Irish history and claims that no resolution of the Irish problem is possible until a united working class establishes a republic embracing north and south.

Prager's is a finely argued essay in political sociology. He is interested in the larger question of the difficulty in establishing democratic stability in nations recently emerging from colonial status. Following the lead of Clifford Geertz, he insists that such societies must reconstitute their "traditional culture" in a new form. This normative base must be built into their design for democratic stability.

To demonstrate his thesis, Prager turns to the history of the Irish Free State (1922-32). Initially William Cosgrave's presidency established the institutional framework for order. This, however, would have been to no avail, had not Eamon de Valéra's Fianna Fáil Party drawn the mass of the Irish to the new state based on the integration of earlier cultural symbols and the values of traditional Ireland. The near perfect synthesis was thus achieved for southern Ireland as Cosgrave's Irish Enlightenment tradition merged with de Valéra's Celtic Romantic tradition.

Prager's controlled use of complex historical phenomena to arrive at certain conclusions can be disconcerting. Nonetheless, his book adds substance to the view that a nation's normative cultural base cannot be ignored in evaluating its potential for political stability.

If Prager stands aloof from the passion of Irish politics, Munck is a partisan. This, however, does not detract from the usefulness of his Marxist analysis. He maintains that the source of the present Irish conflict is found in "the complex interaction between British imperialism, the Irish nation *and* the social classes that make up both nations."

Munck's best chapters deal with the trade union movement. In the north he finds a "Protestant labor aristocracy" benefiting from its links to British imperialism and thus ignoring the national cause. In the south, the unions have focused on narrow economic issues, bypassing the drive for a united Ireland. He argues that neither socialist nor republican can succeed without the other. They must join forces to create a united Ireland.

Munck's book is a proper corrective for those who would blithely overlook the economic factor in Ireland's turmoil. However, his angry Marxism sweeps aside equally important political and cultural problems, and he fails to persuade that more violence stands as a viable solution to Ireland's woes.

EDMUND S. WEHRLE

University of Connecticut
Storrs

ROBERTSON, DAVID. *Class and the British Electorate*. Pp. xi, 250. New York: Basil Blackwell, 1984. $34.95.

Once paramount, the role of class in British politics is now widely questioned. Many argue that class no longer meaningfully organizes votes or motivates social conflict. Provocatively, David Robertson's methodologically sophisticated study argues that class is still important, though less obviously so because its character is more complex than ever before. This should reassure Conservative and Labour partisans and worry Alliance backers.

A companion volume to Sarlvik and Crewe's *Decade of Dealignment* (Cambridge, 1983), Robertson uses the same 1979 British Election Study data to examine the effects of social background on electoral behavior and to advance a new model of class voting. To the notion that class distinctions correspond to occupational categories, Robertson adds life-style interests in order to enrich his conception of the voter as a rational, self-interested actor. More significant in Britain than elsewhere, class's importance has declined since 1966 because the decay of class consciousness has led to workers deserting the Labour Party. Conservatives have benefited by the trend toward economic individualism.

That voters are self-interested applies to the analysis of various structural factors. Age and sex are shown to reduce to individual interests. The occupational structure, especially the nonmanual-manual division, clearly distinguishes voting patterns. Moreover, higher levels of income and consumption encourage voters' self-interested behavior, though trade union membership transforms economic interests into Labour support. There has also been a decline in the passing of Labour voting from one generation to the next. Finally, subjective class identifications, ideological and communitarian, have been replaced by more instrumental attitudes, indicating a breakdown in the traditional relationship between class and individual interests.

To show how this apparent decline of class is consistent with its continued importance, Robertson develops a more complex notion of class, centering on three classes—upper, intermediate, lower—and three partisan groupings—Conservative, neutral, Labour. Of these nine possible class-party groups, four electoral subgroups become crucial when related to ideological attitudes about economic radicalism and social liberalism. Significantly, the two ideological dimensions interact differently for party and class: party reinforces economic interests, but higher class status corresponds to social liberalism. Given that policy attitudes matter more than social factors like class and party, what appears as volatility in the electorate actually reflects a calculus of self-interest based on new, more complex class-partisan-ideological groupings.

Contrary to its aim, this model of voting actually confirms the decline of class, not its continued importance. The new clusterings, like the structural factors, reveal increased economic individualism. To redefine class in terms of the pursuit of a multiplicity of self-interests simply makes the concept meaningless. Despite the inventiveness of Robertson's analysis, his argument about the importance of class in British politics remains unconvincing.

JOEL D. WOLFE
University of Cincinnati
Ohio

SCHAIN, MARTIN A. *French Communism and Local Power: Urban Politics and Political Change.* Pp. 147. New York: St. Martin's Press, 1985. $25.00.

Scholarly concerns with communism in France usually deal with the national party (PCF) and its relationship to the central government in Paris. Linked with this perspective has been an understanding of the PCF as the party of dissatisfied, deprived, and alienated French citizens. Correspondingly, explanations of its electoral fortunes have run more often along economic, sociological, and psychological lines than political ones. To enlarge and correct this understanding, Martin Schain examines the "generally neglected" although "most enduring experience" of Communists in power at the level of local government.

Schain, an associate professor of politics at New York University, focuses on the fact that since 1925 Communist mayors have successfully run a network of French municipalities whose size they managed to maintain or increase, even during the Fifth Republic, until 1983. How this was done, and what impact it has made on French politics, are the central questions of this study. Schain argues that within the constraints of the central state and their financial dependency

on it, local governments have developed considerable political latitude. And in view of their handicap in Paris, Communist local officials have done especially well. Their success appears to have been the result of "a different pattern of governing, a different pattern of generating support within the [larger political] system, and a different way of building local electoral support."

The last point is clearly the most salient in Schain's study. Analyses of voting patterns at the local level indicate that until 1983 support for Communists increased most when the party aspired to or shared power in the national government—an obvious contradiction of the old opposition-protest-vote model. Moreover, this support has come in areas well beyond the traditional "red-belt" communes: "By 1981, 42 percent of the seventy-two larger towns with Communist mayors were in the provinces, and only 14 percent had a majority working-class population." Of the discernible reasons for this development, Schain emphasizes what others—Crozier and Thoenig—have also observed, that communes headed by Communist mayors are among "the best run and best-equipped in France." Schain finds the essential explanation of this perception in the policy differences that distinguish Communist-run municipalities from those governed by other political parties. Although he offers little comparative data, he locates these differences in the spending priorities of Communist local officials for school programs and school services for children, as well as for public housing, health, sports, and cultural services. Clearly, public policies of this kind may be understood as nonideological responses to the shifting social environment of a modern industrial society whose implications go beyond voter appeal.

Schain's rather slender volume raises a number of other interesting issues that make it well worth reading. Among its shortcomings are the terminological obfuscation of communes, towns, and cities; the absence of a bibliography, which appears to reflect the current state of research; and the occasional violence done to the English language, as in the example of Socialist mayors to "all innovated new programs."

J. H. HOFFMAN
Creighton University
Omaha
Nebraska

SOUCY, ROBERT. *French Fascism: The First Wave, 1924-1933*. Pp. xix, 276. New Haven, CT: Yale University Press, 1986. $25.00.

In his classic work *The Right Wing in France*, René Rémond argued that the militant, nationalist, antiparliamentary groups that formed in France in the early 1920s were not authentically fascist. He prefers to see them as heirs of Bonapartism, Caesarism, authoritarianism indigenous to the history of the Right in France. Robert Soucy, an established scholar of fascist inclinations in France, totally rejects this interpretation. He proposes that associations such as the Jeunesses patriotes, founded in 1924, and above all the Faisceau, established in 1925, were indisputably fascist movements. He considers that their hatred of the democratic institutions of the Third Republic, support of capitalism and corporatism, will to violence, desire to seize power in a coup d'etat, and recruitment from the middle classes, veterans, Catholics, and the young constituted an endemic French fascism.

Soucy maintains that the support these movements received requires a serious consideration of the possibility that they might have violently come to power. Although these movements were a failed prospect by 1927, they nevertheless serve as evidence for Soucy of fundamental and continuing fascist tendencies throughout the remaining life of France's Third Republic. To support this argument, original and effective use is made of the only recently available reports of the police to the ministers of the interior. Paradoxically, there is no analysis of how the various governments in this time understood and assessed these very concrete reports.

The most valuable chapters are those Soucy devotes to the Faisceau and to Georges Valois, its founder and leader. Valois's particular defense of the family and religion, admiration for Mussolini's Italy, and confidence in the use of violence, corporatism, and hierarchy do indeed make it hard to distinguish his intentions from those of Italian fascists. Yet Soucy undermines his analysis of the collective mentality supporting this French ideology when he explains the collapse of the Faisceau in 1927. He suggests that the economic stress experienced by France in the years 1924 to 1926 was insufficient to jeopardize middle-class security, which was reassured when Raymond Poincaré became prime minister in July 1926. This is also the position of Eugen Weber, the historian of *Action française*. But Soucy's adoption of this explanation subverts his analysis of the psychological basis of an ideology resting on the premises of masculine superiority, integral Catholicism, the prescriptive rights of *patrons*, irrational nationalism, lust for violence, detestation of open societies, and unlimited capacity for hatred. Can a collective identity dependent upon these bonds between authoritarian personalities be surrendered in a brief moment of modest economic expectations?

Soucy's history is certain to create a valuable debate. Participants in this discussion will be disappointed by his curt dismissal of the need for a taxonomy of fascism. They will wonder why on this critical subject he does not cite in his text or bibliography Stanley G. Payne's *Fascism: Comparison and Definition* (1980). Discussants will also miss any references to Jean-Louis Loubet del Bayle's important *Les non-conformistes des années 30* (1969).

EDWARD T. GARGAN
University of Wisconsin
Madison

WILLIS, DAVID K. *Klass: How the Russians Really Live*. Pp. 355. New York: St. Martin's Press, 1985. $15.95.

A major U.S. newspaper that has international coverage will always send a top-notch reporter to live in Moscow, and the *Christian Science Monitor* sent David Willis between August 1978 and January 1981. Almost as surely, the reporter, upon return to the United States, will synthesize the experience of living in Moscow and write it up for armchair travelers. *Klass: How the Russians Really Live* follows this illustrious tradition, which was earlier established by Hedrick Smith, Robert Kaiser, Elizabeth Pond, and others. It also fits that tradition in giving us a discerning, well-written analysis of Soviet society today.

Having lived in Moscow, I can empathize with a reporter's need to mull over the experience of living there, to separate out what was simply foreign from what was alien, and to write it down. I can also appreciate the difficulty of pulling together the various perceptions into a common theme. David Willis has chosen class—in Russian, *klass*—the delineation of social, political, and economic boundaries in a socialist system that espouses egalitarian goals.

The idea of class in a socialist society is in itself unexceptionable, for any modern society of any ideology will differentiate social rewards and penalties to express and achieve its goals. Willis emphasizes two major differences in the Soviet Union. First, he indicates, money does not matter as much to Russians as to us, for many important privileges that accrue to a high class require status, not money. In the vernacular, "rank talks louder than rubles." To travel abroad, for example, requires more status than money.

A second difference between class there and here is that our middle class, which we take for granted, is well established and strong, but their middle class, which Willis calls "the rising class," is a relatively late arrival that still seeks its ultimate strength. Willis documents persuasively the stress that this burgeoning group places on the system of privilege. In particular, the privileges that the upper class receives costlessly from its status are the privileges that the middle class increasingly receives from the second economy. This second economy—not wholly illegal, but not quite legal either—is a true

market economy in that prices move easily and so do buyers and sellers, but it is indissolubly linked to the socialist economy, which controls its supplies.

While *Klass* has exceptional, assiduous documentation of the many aspects of Soviet class, it also is written with great wit and even some affection for the Moscow environment. One example is where Willis humorously explains that Soviet class might be measured by the kind of liver allocated to each class: the upper class eats calves' liver; the middle class, beef liver; the lower class, pork; and for the classless, no liver at all. It is these homespun examples that above all recommend this book to any reader with any interest in class, socialist society, Moscow, or the Russians.

ELIZABETH CLAYTON
University of Missouri
St. Louis

UNITED STATES

BLOCKER, JACK S., Jr. *"Give to the Winds Thy Fears": The Women's Temperance Crusade, 1873-1874.* Pp. xix, 280. Westport, CT: Greenwood Press, 1985. $35.00.

The tens of thousands of American women who prayed, marched, and picketed in the Women's Temperance Crusade of 1873-74 constituted "the largest women's movement up to that time in the United States." In Jack S. Blocker, Jr., they have a sympathetic chronicler. Employing both traditional sources—newspapers, memoirs, manuscripts—and quantitative analysis, Blocker explains the origin, scope, membership, motives, and results of the Crusade.

Sparked by a male temperance lecturer in Fredonia, New York, the Crusade quickly spread—through newspaper reports and personal contacts—to 911 communities in 31 states and the District of Columbia. Ohio proved the most fertile ground for the Crusade, the South the stoniest. Although most Crusaders were well-to-do "native-born whites of native parentage," the wives and daughters of leading citizens, their attempts to close down local saloons and liquor dealers were prompted neither by a desire for social control over the lower classes nor by an ethnocentric concern about imbibing immigrants. Instead, Blocker argues, they feared the impact of strong drink on their own families.

Rapid expansion of the liquor business in the late 1860s and early 1870s everywhere except the South, coupled with lax enforcement of existing liquor laws, alarmed these women. They knew they had no real protection or redress against the profligacy or physical abuse of a drunken husband, let alone the heartbreak of a dissolute son. Thus vulnerable at home, they entered the public sphere with a campaign of moral suasion and peaceful coercion. Unlike their contemporaries in the suffrage movement, the Crusaders had no faith in the law as a tool for social reform; they hoped to change the hearts and minds of saloon keepers and liquor sellers.

The Crusaders were most effective in small towns, where many proprietors succumbed at least temporarily to their pressure and pleas. In the cities the liquor interests prevailed, though the Crusade had the ironic effect of arousing renewed interest in the legal regulation of alcohol. Ultimately, the failures were more important than the successes, for the next major temperance organization, the Women's Christian Temperance Union, founded in the waning months of the Crusade, adopted different strategy, tactics, and goals.

Blocker makes a strong case for the Crusade as "a distinctive product of the age of the village." Yet he raises questions that are relevant to any mass social protest movement. He clearly hopes other historians will follow his analytical and quantitative lead, and well they might. If Blocker's statistics occasionally underline the obvious, they also add clarity and precision. If his numerous

tables and his explanatory models sometimes overpower the narrative, his use of Washington Court House, Ohio, as a case study preserves the human element. In the end, Blocker manages to convey both the magnitude and the intensity of this "true grass roots movement."

CAM WALKER

College of William and Mary
Williamsburg
Virginia

FRASER, WALTER J., Jr., R. FRANK SAUNDERS, Jr., and JON L. WAKELYN, eds. *The Web of Southern Social Relations: Women, Family, and Education.* Pp. 257. Athens: University of Georgia Press, 1985. $25.00.

From a symposium on the South held at Georgia Southern College in April 1984, here are 13 essays, examples of the "new history," hoping to show how new insights can be derived on crucial topics. They "are meant to provoke questions for all students of southern society, especially those who want to know more about ordinary lives." An introduction summarizes this well. In this review, an overall impression of each essay is provided.

In "The Experience of Status of Women in the Chesapeake, 1750-1775," by Lorena S. Walsh, we find that, as the colony matured, the well-being of women improved even as they acquired a subordinate role in marriage. "Caught in the Web of the Big House: Women and Slavery," by Catherine Clinton, finds women both black and white victimized by the system, thus unable to recognize themselves as "sisters under the skin." Theda Perdue, in "Southern Indians and the Cult of True Womanhood," shows that Indian women lost independent status when their tribes became assimilated to the ways of so-called civilization. "My Children, Gentlemen, Are My Own: Poor Women, the Urban Elite, and the Bonds of Obligation in Antebellum

Charleston," by Barbara L. Bellows, assesses attempts of public charities to influence poor women of the city. In "The Perrys of Greenville: A Nineteenth-Century Marriage," Carol K. Bleser evaluates letters of Elizabeth Perry to her husband, Benjamin, and shows that, more than the conventional helpmate, she was a talented woman of wit and intelligence in a marriage of give and take. "The Not-So-Cloistered Academy: Elite Women's Education and Family Feeling in the Old South," by Steven M. Stowe, found less transition from one sheltered existence to another than a rough dialectic of feminine worldliness. In "Antebellum College Life and the Relations between Fathers and Sons," Jon L. Wakelyn asks, As microcosm of Southern life in general, to what extent did college life reflect the paternalistic planter father model or a more open middle-class nineteenth-century father-son relationship? "Higher Education in the South since the Civil War: Historiographical Issues and Trends," by Thomas G. Dyer, emphasizes that becoming increasingly aware of dynamics of social and economic modernization, scholars cannot ignore this important topic. "Black Schooling During Reconstruction," by Bertram Wyatt-Brown, argues that combination of new history and reflection on experience in modern Africa can help answer the question of why black Americans have failed so often to reach their educational potential. "Women and the Progressive Impulse in Southern Education," by Joseph F. Kett, explores similarities and differences between Northern and Southern experiences in this matter. "Colored Ladies Also Contributed: Black Women's Activities from Benevolence to Social Welfare, 1866-1896," by Kathleen C. Berkeley, helps answer the question of how black populations managed to cope in the emancipated South. "The Effects of the Civil War and Reconstruction on the Coming of Age of Southern Males, Edgefield County, South Carolina," by Orville Vernon Burton, finds a pattern whereby blacks succeeded in winning positions in a new opportunity structure while whites, traumatized by war and reconstruction, lacked

adequate motivation. In "Folks like Us: The Southern Poor White Family, 1865-1935," J. Wayne Flynt gives a poignant picture, finding on balance poor whites more resembling hardworking middle-class families than the hard-drinking stereotype of conventional wisdom.

PERRY H. HOWARD
Louisiana State University
Baton Rouge

GLAD, BETTY. *Key Pittman: The Tragedy of a Senate Insider.* Pp. xviii, 388. New York: Columbia University Press, 1986. $45.00.

Key Pittman, Democrat from Nevada, was a prominent U.S. senator in the first half of the twentieth century. From 1933 until his death in 1940 he chaired the Senate Foreign Relations Committee. During this period he also became an alcoholic. Thus the drunkenness of the Senate's chief spokesman in international affairs complicated the difficult political environment in which the Roosevelt administration was led to participation in World War II.

This monograph gives full treatment to Pittman's early career and to his personal life, but Glad, a political scientist at the University of Illinois, has wisely chosen to focus on the period of the 1930s.

Glad draws on two bodies of literature to examine Pittman's activities in the thirties. On the one hand, she looks toward the psychoanalytic work of Heinz Kohut. On the other, she employs studies of political role-playing. She concludes that there was a congruence between Pittman's personality and his role performance. Pittman was a man of "narcissistic vulnerabilities" unable to "prioritize values." The senator's "role enactments" and "role expectations" meshed when he worked in a structured situation; when the situation was fluid, as it was in the late thirties, his vulnerabilities became pronounced and impaired his "role performance."

The weakness of the book is that Glad's narrative abilities and insights into human character are rather limited, and the behavioral science theories insufficiently spelled out. Consequently, it cannot be ascertained if the conceptualizations add anything to the evidence that is presented. Nonetheless, there may be something to her analysis.

Pittman's private life did not give him satisfaction in the 1930s, and throughout that time he was also shut out of Roosevelt's circle. But as Roosevelt made his way to war, he offered the Senate—and Pittman—little direction in foreign policy. The senator was not a man of great competence, and as the job became too much for him, his drinking increased. Further interpretive research must be carried out to learn if these facts can be illuminated by Glad's use of political science and personality theory.

BRUCE KUKLICK
University of Pennsylvania
Philadelphia

HALLIN, DANIEL C. *The "Uncensored War": The Media and Vietnam.* Pp. viii, 285. New York: Oxford University Press, 1986. $22.50.

"The further we get from the war," historian George Herring recently commented on reviewing a number of works about Vietnam, "the less inclined we seem to be to grapple with the major issues raised by Vietnam." Fortunately, Daniel C. Hallin's fine book, *The "Uncensored War,"* is an exception to Herring's perception. Indeed, a brief review of this study cannot do justice to its rich historical content, complexity of analysis, or the quality of its discussion of media news and the Vietnam war. Although Hallin offers a case analysis of how newspaper and television journalists responded to the Vietnam conflict and the extent to which they shaped public debate on that controversial war, it is more than that. Some of its most interesting themes focus on the broader implications of the media-Vietnam relationship—the nature of professional journalism, the link between journalistic and political establishments, and the manner in which ideology often determines what news is and is not conveyed to the general public.

Assessing the national media's reporting on the tortuous history of Vietnam is a monumental task. As Hallin notes, the "problem is not simply one of volume, although the output of even a single news organization over the years of American involvement is immense. It is also a problem of diversity." Although he never confronts the full implications of these difficulties, Hallin's method of analysis and his conclusions suggest that a diversified public reading and viewing experience may have less significance than one might assume.

The "Uncensored War" is divided into two parts. The first covers the years from 1961 through 1965, when the basic assumptions of America's escalating "commitment" in Vietnam were firmly established. Relying primarily on the *New York Times*, Hallin maintains that despite tensions between the Kennedy and Johnson administrations and some journalists, the *Times* and other news agencies offered the public a sympathetic view of U.S. engagement in Vietnam. In the second part, covering the years from 1965 to 1973, Hallin analyzes the response of national network television to shifting American policies and to the turmoil produced by the war at home. Even though network accounts became more pessimistic about the war following Tet and Lyndon Johnson's declaration not to seek reelection in 1968, Hallin argues that television continued to show the war in terms supportive of American interests and hostile to those we were fighting against.

Thus Hallin disputes the notion that negative media coverage of Vietnam helped turn the American public against U.S. efforts. Although newspaper and television journalists operated differently, both tended throughout the Vietnam years to report the war from a perspective largely consistent with official American policy. It was only after the obvious contradictions in those policies became apparent to some within the government and dissent became more widespread at home that the media showed the war in a more critical light. Adherence to its own "uncensored" definition of "objective" journalism and acceptance of American cold war ideology limited the media's ability to explore in depth the deeper significance of Vietnam for the American public. It was this inability—rather than its adversarial reporting of the war—that ironically led to the simplistic, still widespread belief that Vietnam could have been "won" if only the media had remained steadfast in its accounting of U.S. objectives in Southeast Asia.

Hallin's book needs to be read and pondered by all to be fully appreciated. It not only offers us a fresh perspective as to how Vietnam entered into American political and cultural consciousness, but it tells us much about why we continue today to view certain places in the world, such as Central America, in ways that fail to convey their complexity or indicate why U.S. policies in such areas lead so often to tragic consequences.

JOHN B. KIRBY

Denison University
Granville
Ohio

LANG, DANIEL G. *Foreign Policy in the Early Republic: The Law of Nations and the Balance of Power.* Pp. ix, 175. Baton Rouge: Louisiana State University Press, 1985. $20.00.

This study examines the influence of *The Law of Nations* by the Swiss diplomat Emmerich de Vattel on Alexander Hamilton, Thomas Jefferson, and James Madison in the foreign policy of the early American Republic. Vattel's ideas on the just war, the law of nations, and the balance of power are the subject of the first third of the book, with illustrations from both American and European history. Three chapters follow that discuss American foreign policy, one a summary of foreign policy in the 1780s and 1790s, a second on the "Hamiltonian Approach," and a third on the "Jeffersonian Approach."

Lang sets out to show that in events such as George Washington's Neutrality Proclamation there was "an identity of morality and policy" consistent with "the science of international law and politics of that day, for which the question of the just war was a primary moral and political concern." Hamilton's writings, "the best expression" of Federalist foreign policy, drew most heavily on Vattel. Hamilton relied on Vattel's criteria for the just war and the balance of power in the positions he took on the Nootka Sound crisis, the treaty obligations of the French Alliance, the Jay Treaty, and the quasi war with France in 1798-99. Supporting Britain against France, he saw France as "the unjust power" engaged on a course of universal empire, which Vattel taught was "just cause for war."

The influence of Vattel is less clear in Lang's discussion of the Jeffersonians. Jefferson and Madison "strove to go beyond" Vattel, he writes, and to change "the law of nations pertaining to trade and neutral rights [that] largely reflected British dominance of the seas." Jefferson did not regard the United States as part of the European system but used the principle of balance of power. The commercial measures of the embargo were "sanctioned" by Vattel, and Jeffersonians saw themselves as acting in Vattel's "just-war/limited-war" tradition. Difficulty of generalization here is evident as Lang summarizes that "Jeffersonians defined the American national interest more broadly than the Federalists" and sought to shape conditions beyond our shores, while in Jeffersonian constitutional doctrines, "only wars of self-defense were santioned."

This study provides a detailed account of the influence of the law of nations on Hamilton, Jefferson, and Madison as they confronted the great questions of national power, war, and peace that faced the new American

Republic in a world constantly threatened by the power of France and Great Britain.

RONALD E. SHAW

Miami University
Oxford
Ohio

LEONARD, THOMAS C. *The Power of the Press: The Birth of American Political Reporting*. Pp. 273. New York: Oxford University Press, 1986. $22.50.

STEELE, RICHARD W. *Propaganda in an Open Society: The Roosevelt Administration and the Media, 1933-1941*. Pp. x, 231. Westport, CT: Greenwood Press, 1985. $35.00.

These two books illustrate the evolution of the American press and its impact on our political process in the pre-television era.

Leonard's work provides a comprehensive history of the development of political reporting from the colonial period to the early twentieth century. Particular emphasis is placed on the popularization of the press in the nineteenth century, which led to increased interest in government and politics. The roles of Thomas Nast, the first great political cartoonist, and the muckrakers are well analyzed. As the press became more aggressive and popularly significant, Leonard concludes, it contributed to the decline in voter turnout: "Progressivism, and especially its journalism, undermined the ritual of political participation." In short, Leonard's analysis suggests that the reformer press—seeking to stimulate the public to greater interest and political participation in order to bring about good and honest government—actually contributed to the concept that politics is a dirty business and thus alienated the average voter. "Party loyalty itself was a virtue of the old politics that progressive journalism helped turn into a vice."

Steele's book contributes to communication analysis by presenting a detailed case study of the interaction of Franklin Roose-velt's administration with the media in the period 1933-41. The early sections of the book deal with the attempts by FDR to secure media support for the economic programs of the New Deal while the latter sections cover the overt efforts of the administration to overcome the isolationist sentiment in the country as world events pulled America ever closer to involvement in World War II.

Leonard deals only with the print media in his study, but Steele also covers radio and motion pictures.

The independent press of Leonard's study never completely succumbs to the charisma of FDR, and radio proved to be a medium more to his liking. He used it with skill, secure in the knowledge that what he said was what the public heard. Further, radio's sensitivity to regulation opened it to manipulation. Commentators like Johnson and Carter disappeared from the air while Winchell's interventionist reporting made him a darling of the administration.

Steele's account of the interventionist role of motion pictures is a significant contribution since movies receive little serious attention in most mass-media studies.

Taken together, these two books emphasize the independence and importance of the print media as seen later in the Nixon resignation. One wonders how FDR would have handled television's Sam Donaldson—certainly not like Boake Carter.

Both books belong in any serious library collection on communications and politics.

J. H. BINDLEY

Wittenberg University
Springfield
Ohio

LINK, ARTHUR S. et al., eds. *The Papers of Woodrow Wilson*. Vol. 53. Pp. xxxii, 751. Princeton, NJ: Princeton University Press, 1986. $52.50.

From one viewpoint, this volume is the high point of Wilson's career and collected papers. As he proclaimed to an assembled Congress that "the war thus comes to an end," adulation of him was all but worldwide, among the Allies. Supreme Court Justice Louis D. Brandeis was moved to quote Euripides in praise of Wilson's wisdom. King George V, "at this moment of universal gladness," congratulated Wilson and offered "deep thanks in my own name and that of the people of this empire." Colonel House, cabling constantly from Europe, the Armistice signed, wrote Wilson: "Autocracy is dead. . . . [Long live] democracy and its immortal leader. In this great hour my heart goes out to you in pride, admiration and love."

There was almost no one of high visibility among the leaders to affirm that a tragedy was being heaped on top of the tragedy of the war. Yet the Democrats had just been shocked by Republican triumphs in the November congressional elections. George Creel, Wilson's wartime director of information, somberly reported that dissent had been all but crushed by the 100-percenters, as superpatriots called themselves at the time. Indeed, progressives like Creel were soon to be themselves scorned not only by the patent reactionaries but by dissidents who would join the disillusioned of the 1920s.

Once news of the Armistice was released, Wilson issued a statement that read, "A supreme moment of history has come. The eyes of the people have been opened and they see. The hand of God is laid upon the nations." Yet even as he wrote, cables came that told him of the plans and strategems of his Allied associates. They would strip Germany of its substance as the sole instigator of war and raise specters of starvation from Austria to beleaguered Soviet Russia. Wilson addressed himself to the problem of hunger. He appointed Herbert Hoover to the critical position of director of relief operations, the tasks of which he would carry out with distinction. But Wilson's faith in the public will toward peace and democracy, at home and abroad, was not realistic. Although Samuel Gompers and others warned him of Bolshevik determination to survive on any

terms, and at whatever human cost, Wilson would not take their warnings seriously. "The real thing with which to stop Bolshevism is food," he advised his secretary of state, Robert Lansing.

This volume covers no more than three months of peace and preparations for a peace conference, from November 1918 to January 1919. Wilson, leading the American delegation in Europe, offers speeches in England, France, and Italy to national assemblies and admirers. Crystalized now is his unqualified faith in a league of nations that will outlaw aggressors and make national aggression impossible forever. The editors promise an estimate of seven forthcoming volumes that will present the Paris Peace Conference as Wilson and his coadjutors saw it and contributed to it. As always, the editors cull materials from other sources bearing on the American contribution. The present volume substantially concludes with a draft of the Covenant of a League of Nations, as drawn up by Wilson, in photograph and in type.

LOUIS FILLER

The Belfry
Ovid
Michigan

PLISCHKE, ELMER. *Diplomat in Chief: The President at the Summit.* Pp. x, 518. New York: Praeger, 1986. $42.95.

For reasons about which we can only speculate, the large literature on the presidency contains very little on the president's role in the making and implementing of American foreign policy. Even texts described as comprehensive typically give short shrift to the president's impact on the international environment. Elmer Plischke's latest book on the chief executive as diplomat in chief therefore fills an important gap. But it is also in its own right a distinguished and comprehensive examination of presidential politicking in foreign affairs since the beginning of the Republic.

The book focuses on those occasions on which diplomatic relations were conducted not by emissaries or bureaucrats but by the president himself. However, Plischke is not especially interested in the psychodynamics of the relationship between presidents and other national leaders. Instead he asks how summit meetings, which are by their very nature departures from the norm, alter relationships between states that generally communicate only through routine channels.

Plischke traces the beginnings of personal diplomacy at the presidential level all the way back to George Washington. However, since the technology of the twentieth century has made summit diplomacy far more viable than it was in the past, it is hardly surprising that well over half the book is devoted to the processes and outcomes of summit conferences that took place within the last fifty years.

At first glance the organization of the book is somewhat confusing. For example, a chapter titled "Summit Visits to the United States" does not contain the material on Brezhnev's visit to Washington in 1973, which is contained instead in a separate chapter on "East-West summit meetings since 1960." It also takes a while to understand certain distinctions Plischke makes, such as the one between a mere presidential trip or visit abroad and a full-fledged summit conference.

But the flaws are minor and the book contributes on at least two levels. First, it provides us with a lucid and thorough account of what actually happened whenever the American president conducted personal diplomacy. Second, it undertakes to estimate the costs and benefits of negotiating at the highest level of government. In a substantial concluding chapter Plischke contrasts summit and conventional diplomacy; explores the advantages, risks, and disadvantages of meetings at the top; and lists no fewer than 25 general postulates on presidential personal participation in foreign relations. Plischke is, in the end, an extremely cautious optimist. He is obviously alert to the problems and dangers of summits. At the same time he recognizes the value of having leaders become personally acquainted, and the potential efficacy of holding summit conferences when an impasse has been reached at the traditional diplomatic or ministerial level.

While only a few of our presidents have pursued active summit careers, there have been more than a few summit meetings with major consequences. But surely the best excuse for Plischke's timely book is that it finally draws attention to a diplomatic exercise with more potential than we generally realize.

BARBARA KELLERMAN
Fairleigh Dickinson University
Hackensack
New Jersey

SHIELDS, JOHANNA NICHOL. *The Line of Duty: Maverick Congressmen and the Development of American Political Culture, 1836-1860.* Pp. xix, 297. Westport, CT: Greenwood Press, 1985. $37.50.

In *The Line of Duty: Maverick Congressmen and the Development of American Political Culture, 1836-1860,* political scientist Johanna Nichol Shields joins historians Jean H. Baker, Ronald P. Formisano, Daniel Walker Howe, and Rush Welter in exploring the distinctive "political culture" of the antebellum era. The study takes as its starting point a quantitative analysis of roll-call votes in the House of Representatives between 1836 and 1860. Using data assembled by Thomas B. Alexander in his *Sectional Stress and Party Strength* (1967), Shields divides House members who served at least two terms into "mavericks" and "conformists." Eliminating members for whom no published source material was available at the Library of Congress, she then turns to those that remain in an effort to "integrate the concrete detail usually associated with classical historical studies" with "the functional abstractions about legislative behavior resulting from political science research."

Shields finds mavericks to be much more conversant than conformists with "nineteenth-century developments in the arts, philosophy, religion, literature, science, and technology." Yet they were also more likely to hold fast to increasingly anachronistic eighteenth-century republican notions of virtual representation and elite leadership. The tensions between these sets of ideas lay "at the center of the mavericks' attitudes towards their political situation." As she puts it, in a typical bit of lumbering prose, "[The mavericks'] capacity to perceive the predicament in this way was established by earlier influences which had produced within the matrix of their own attitudes a sort of microcosmic cultural conflict."

As a study of political culture, Shields's study is marred by its tendency to assume that the views of highly idiosyncratic individuals like Henry David Thoreau and Ralph Waldo Emerson were widely shared. For example, she claims that "the romantic protest against mechanism" was of "special importance" in the United States without adding Leo Marx's caveat that this was true for only a tiny elite. And as a study of behavioral politics, it is surprisingly vague about precisely how—besides giving long speeches—mavericks operated within the House. Shields is quite right to lament the shortage of scholarship on nineteenth-century congressional committees, yet she neglects both the published committee reports in the congressional serial set and the enormous body of manuscript records, including petitions and incoming letters, in the National Archives.

Shields declines to speculate on what role, if any, the mavericks played in the political developments leading up to the Civil War. She also declines to elaborate on the mavericks' "congressional significance," adding that to do so would entail passing judgment on "the moral nature of democratic politics," which is "surely beyond the necessary scope of the historian's work." She does, however, praise their defiant individualism, since it expresses the "constant hopes of Americans since their time that the material benefits produced by a society based on mass institutions will be accompanied by ample opportunity for individuals to achieve their different private aspirations." These are noble sentiments, to be sure, but hardly much help in making sense of the House of Representatives, past or present.

RICHARD R. JOHN, Jr.
Harvard University
Cambridge
Massachusetts

WINTERS, DONALD E., Jr. *The Soul of the Wobblies: The I. W. W., Religion, and America's Independent Progressives, 1905-1917.* Pp. xi, 159. Westport, CT: Greenwood Press, 1985. $27.95.

TOBIN, EUGENE M. *Organize or Perish: America's Independent Progressives, 1913-1933.* Pp. xiv, 279. Westport, CT: Greenwood Press, 1986. $37.50.

Even though Winters's Wobblies were far more radical than Tobin's Progressives, these two books still have at least some things in common. Winters's study is one of the most recent titles in Greenwood's ongoing Contributions in American Studies series, and Tobin's appears in that same press's series, Contributions in American History. The word "contributions"—too often bandied about by scholars—here takes on more than its ordinary meaning, for both these books are historiographically significant.

In marked contrast to the years before 1960, during the past two decades or so there has been a great deal written about the Industrial Workers of the World, and *The Soul of the Wobblies* is a welcome addition to this developing literature. Specifically, Winters has assigned himself the difficult task of analyzing the precise relationship between the Wobblies as a revolutionary labor movement on the one hand and American religion on the other. The greater portion of Winters's study is given over to a meticulous examination—and a clear explication—of the religious motif to be found in IWW songs, newspapers, and poetry. While Winters quarrels with those who have equated the IWW with a militant church, he himself nonetheless emphasizes the strongly religious quality of this system of symbols and beliefs that sought to create solidarity in the working class and to urge it on to an overthrow of the evil force of capitalism and to the creation of a new order of things. While a Protestant, Progressive America dreamed of class collaboration and while utopians imagined social harmony, "the I.W.W. raised an angry, prophetic voice of struggle and change, of building 'a new world in the shell of the old.' Like Christ, the members of the I. W. W. saw their mission 'not to send peace but a sword.'"

In their own special way, Tobin's later Progressives were still quite the zealots, too. Thus Tobin's greatest historiographical achievement is to help to show that progressivism was hardly so moribund in the conservative decade of the 1920s as many students and professors of American history and politics have previously imagined. To be sure, the research and writing that is the necessary foundation for such a reinterpretation as is here proposed have been in the making for a good many years now. Tobin's own bibliographic essay makes that abundantly clear. However, the vast documentation underpinning Tobin's work, much of it freshly culled from manuscript sources, clarifies in a heretofore unprecedented way the unending struggles of such liberal true believers as Amos R.E. Pinchot, George L. Record, Frederic C. Howe, and Mercer G. Johnston. If Tobin is correct, these later Progressives were not just vocal and active but were effective as well—though not, admittedly, in any actual political power they wielded in the 1920s as much as in their helping to keep the liberal vision alive for future use. As a group, Tobin concludes, these people hardly deserve to be dismissed, as they sometimes have been, as mere second-line Progressives.

To conclude with another comparison between these two authors, both deal with their subjects in highly intelligent, literate, critical, and yet very humane and sympathetic ways. Winters dedicates his book to the selfsame Wobblies he studies, and Tobin also admits to a somewhat grudging admiration of his subjects: "They annoy us with their persistence, embarrass us with their tirelessness, and occasionally affront us with their rudeness. But they will always be with us because they are organizers and survivors."

ROBERT P. HAY

Marquette University
Milwaukee
Wisconsin

SOCIOLOGY

AKERSTROM, MALIN. *Crooks and Squares: Lifestyles of Thieves and Addicts in Comparison to Conventional People*. Pp. 254. New Brunswick, NJ: Transaction Books, 1985. $24.95.

ELLIOTT, DELBERT S., DAVID HUIZINGA, and SUZANNE S. AGETON. *Explaining Delinquency and Drug Use*. Pp. 176. Beverly Hills, CA: Sage, 1985. $22.00.

In *Crooks and Squares: Lifestyles of Thieves and Addicts in Comparison to Conventional People*, Malin Akerstrom examines criminal life-styles based on three empirical studies involving the interviewing and surveying of incarcerated criminals. These data are compared to similar questions posed to a sample of noncriminal blue- and white-collar workers.

By asking inmates about their lives, hopes, fears, values, and plans, Akerstrom identifies the general, although not necessarily collective, experience of being a criminal. Her point is to describe a social world from the viewpoint of those who inhabit it and, through such description and appreciation, to understand why they choose to dwell there.

Akerstrom begins with the assumption that criminals are "competent social actors" who are capable of choice and action. She goes on to establish empirically that the inmates do indeed claim responsibility for their criminality, derive satisfaction and rewards from their illicit acts, and reject a more conventional livelihood. These criminals see themselves as responsible, entrepreneurial, independent men. They believe that their criminal life-style allows them much freedom, while affording them excitement and income. The rewards of this life are all the more attractive when contrasted with the lives of so-called squares. The inmates see the law-abiding as doomed to a dull, monotonous life entrapped by family, job, and mortgage. In a kind of sociological reversal, the criminals hold a there-but-for-the-grace-of-God-go-I view of the square johns. In this regard, their aspirations are revealing: to combine legitimate work with the freedom and fun of crime.

In assuming the viewpoint of the criminals, Akerstrom hopes to correct what she views as a predominant tendency by criminologists to depict criminals as cultural flotsam bobbing about in sociological currents. Unfortunately, her response is to overcorrect. To say that criminals can swim is not to say that there is no current. As theorists we must, critically and with as much value neutrality as possible, consider the extent to which the beliefs, values, and motives of criminals may be ideology or rationalization. We must consider not only their perception of the world and their place in it, but the world as it is objectively and empirically defined. Akerstrom has given us a penetrating and revealing look at the former.

Explaining Delinquency and Drug Use by Delbert S. Elliott, David Huizinga, and Suzanne S. Ageton begins by reviewing classic strain, control, and social-learning theories of delinquency. Based on this review of the literature and research, they propose an integrated theory in which delinquency is the result of differential bonding to conventional and delinquent groups. In addition to these

variables, suggested by the control and social-learning theories, they also test the direct effect of strain—perceived opportunity for achieving valued goals—on delinquency. The resulting integrated theory of delinquency consists of a sequential model with bonding to delinquent groups as the most proximate cause of delinquency.

Elliott, Huizinga, and Ageton test the empirical claims of this model using the National Youth Survey, a longitudinal study of delinquency and drug use among American youth. The total sample was interviewed for three consecutive years, 1977-79, regarding their involvement in delinquency during the previous year. Path analyses conducted on these data support the authors' hypothesis regarding the effect of bonding on delinquency.

The book concludes by considering the implications of these findings for the treatment of delinquency. In short, it warns against the unintended criminogenic consequences of using group interaction and bonding among delinquent youths as a control strategy.

PATRICIA EWICK

Wellesley College
Massachusetts

BLAU, JUDITH R. *Architects and Firms: A Sociological Perspective on Architectural Practice.* Pp. xv, 189. Cambridge, MA: MIT Press, 1984. $19.95.

This study of architecture as professional practice, as an occupation, and as a set of convictions is one of a very few serious analyses of architectural firms. Judith Blau provides architects, architectural educators, students, and social scientists with concepts from organizational theory for analyzing both the profession and individual firms.

Architecture is both an art and a business. Most architects are attracted to the profession because of its opportunities for creative design, but in practice these opportunities are limited. This is one of the basic contradictions in practice that puts the profession at risk—the very act of making decisions may solve one problem, but it creates others. Blau shows that these contradictions are an inherent part of practice.

The study is based on a 1974 survey and a 1979 survey of Manhattan architectural firms and architects. They enable Blau, fortuitously, to study the characteristics of firms that merely survived the recession of the late 1970s, those that died, and those that progressed. The latter two have essentially the same characteristics. She dispels a series of myths that architects have about the nature of firms and the quality of work they produce. The size of firms per se, for instance, is not a predictive variable. Rather, the type of firm and the nature of its internal features are what is important. Blau's statistical analysis goes well beyond simple correlations to reveal relationships between a firm's size, its convictions, the degree of voice that architects have in its decisions, and such characteristics as survival rate, level of gratification of designers, and the quality of work produced.

A by-product of the study is the demonstration of the use of a variety of research methods to obtain data that architects tend to think are unobtainable and to tease out explanations well beyond those revealed by simple correlational analysis. This does not mean that Blau's measures cannot be questioned. For instance, the use of awards as a measure of the quality of firms may be misleading, for many firms do seek awards.

Blau's findings will enable practitioners to assess the nature of their own firms in relationship to others, and educators and students to realize the discrepancies, perhaps necessary, between images created in architectural schools and the rigors of practice. They will provide architectural researchers with a base for further research—on the nature of schools, for instance—and will serve as an exemplar of the methods they might employ. Blau, however, wisely perhaps, leaves the normative principles of organizational design up to the reader to identify.

The book's potential is limited, particularly to the practicing architect, by the often obscure, turgid, and extremely dense writing. As a next step I hope Blau presents her findings in a form meaningful to architects. It will further the major contribution she has already made to the profession.

JON LANG

University of Pennsylvania
Philadelphia

BOULDING, KENNETH E. *The World as a Total System.* Pp. 183. Beverly Hills, CA: Sage, 1985. $25.00.

KAUFMAN, HERBERT. *Time, Chance, and Organizations: Natural Selection in a Perilous Environment.* Pp. xii, 179. Chatham, NJ: Chatham House, 1985. $20.00.

These two books are aptly chosen for joint review. Each deals with big questions, differing only marginally from the cosmic—total world system—to the slightly more contextually confined—the organization. Each of the authors is a distinguished scholar—Boulding, an economist; Kaufman, a political scientist—of theoretically creative bent who commands an international audience. Accordingly, the style of each is marked by vast learning that spans the conventional disciplines and sectarian literatures of science and humanism as well as the social sciences.

The more abstract and therefore more complex of these studies—Boulding's—produces a vision of the world as a total, or potentially total, system of components exhibiting order and pattern. Thus the world system is made up of interrelated and interacting subsystems ranging from the physical/biological to the human political/economic/communication/evaluation subsystems. The evolutionary pattern of most social subsystems has been a trend toward greater and greater similarity the world over. Relationships tend to be characterized by exchange (economic), threat (political), and/or integration (philosophical). An exploration of these dimensions involves observations, comparisons, and illustrations ranging from deoxyribonucleic acid (DNA) to deterrence, from cybernetics to bureaupathology. The style is of that digressive sort that nevertheless comes across as wisdom.

Herbert Kaufman's work is both more confined and more tightly organized and communicated. The basic question is, Why are organizations not immortal, or perpetually self-renewing? The basic answer is that their vital resources are dissipated as they are buffeted by a hostile environment, including, notably, other organizations. Yet the duration and life-cycle histories of organizations are variable. Thus the question becomes one of time—Why do some survive longer than others? A host of alternative hypotheses is entertained and found wanting. The available evidence suggests that superior management skill—rationality—is not the key. In spite of shrewd and heroic efforts of decision makers, bureaucratic dysfunction and failures of execution seem insurmountable. Nor does the functional quality of adaptability—flexibility in adjusting to environmental challenges—turn out to be very helpful. In the end, it seems to Kaufman, chance is the single most crucial determinant of organizational persistence. Even so, chance, over the long haul, is probably dictated by some developmental process comparable—not equatable!—to organismic evolution. Thus one dynamic of chemical, biological, and human organizational change is generally a thrust over time toward greater complexity. In organizations, increased specialization, technology, the manipulation of matter and energy are typical aspects of increasing complexity. One can only speculate about the ultimate state to which organizational evolution is leading. In addition to framing hypotheses and citing examples, Kaufman concludes this stimulating essay by enumerating many of the component variables and hypotheses that might be examined in ambitious empirical investigations of organizational life.

CHARLES E. JACOB

Rutgers University
New Brunswick
New Jersey

BURSTEIN, PAUL. *Discrimination, Jobs, and Politics: The Struggle for Equal Opportunity in the United States since the New Deal.* Pp. x, 247. Chicago: University of Chicago Press, 1985. $30.00 Paperbound, $12.95.

SNIDERMAN, PAUL M. with MICHAEL GRAY HAGEN. *Race and Inequality: A Study in American Values.* Pp. xv, 159. Chatham, NJ: Chatham House, 1986. $8.95.

The U.S. political system presents a major paradox: widespread support for egalitarian principles alongside pervasive inequalities among the population. This gap between ideology and outcomes is the focus of these two books. In a far-ranging and highly ambitious study, Burstein examines the utility of democratic politics for extending equal economic opportunities (EEO) to disadvantaged groups. Sniderman and Hagen intensively explore a narrower question: the ways in which white Americans account for continuing racial inequality.

Burstein uses a variety of both quantitative and qualitative data, from 1940 to 1978, to challenge the conventional explanation regarding passage of Title VII of the Civil Rights Act of 1964. Rather than being a contemporary product of an activist black civil rights movement, a crusading national media, and an engaged public opinion, Title VII is convincingly shown to be a classic incremental policy dating from the New Deal. Its passage came only after support for EEO—in principle and in policy terms— slowly gained a simple majority in all sections of the country and there existed ample state policy precedents for such action.

Burstein also provides a comprehensive and clear examination of the racial and gender earnings gap. He argues that EEO legislation has not been simply symbolic. Although white women, black women, and black men have differentially benefited, the gains of one disadvantaged group have not come at the expense of another. Burstein concludes with a speculative but intriguing discussion of the prospects for increased racial and gender equality.

Sniderman and Hagen, drawing upon national and San Francisco Bay Area polls taken in 1972, find four explanations for racial inequality: individualist, or personal responsibility; fundamentalist, or God's will; progressive, or economic exploitation; and historicist, or past discrimination. The bulk of their analysis is given over to further explicating these opinions in terms of associated personal characteristics, ideology, and psychological makeup.

Those interested in the structure of public opinion will be fascinated by some of the relationships uncovered here, such as, for example, the similar psychological profiles of progressives and fundamentalists. Those more concerned with egalitarian policy will not find much comfort here. The dominant U.S. orientation to racial inequality—individualist, held by close to 60 percent of the national sample—is deeply rooted in American culture and thus highly resistant to change. Further, individualists not only eschew collective action to attain racial equality, but also believe that equality of opportunity and condition already exist. This radical egalitarianism itself poses a significant barrier to equality.

Taken together, these studies underscore the ambiguous and tenuous nature of Americans' commitment to equality. And each is a model of the potentialities of quantitative social science research. Sniderman and Hagen's "deep analysis" is matched by Burstein's attempt to bridge interdisciplinary barriers and provide an integrated study of legal change. *Race and Inequality* is of greatest interest to the social scientist as teacher and *Discrimination, Jobs, and Politics* is of greatest interest to the social scientist as professional, but each deserves a wider audience.

JANET K. BOLES

Marquette University
Milwaukee
Wisconsin

EASTERLIN, RICHARD A. and EILEEN M. CRIMMINS. *The Fertility Revolution: A*

Supply-Demand Analysis. Pp. xix, 209. Chicago: University of Chicago Press, 1985. $24.95.

Richard Easterlin, professor of economics at the University of Southern California—formerly of the University of Pennsylvania, and a very well known and highly respected demographer—and Eileen Crimmins, assistant professor of gerontology also at the University of Southern California, are to be congratulated for presenting in this volume empirical tests of the supply-demand theory of fertility determination.

This book is well written, but it suffers from occasional lapses into repetitiveness. It is a very good book, however, and has rather important implications for public policy-makers—and their advisers—in the developing countries.

The reasons for persisting high fertility in the Third World and long-term fertility decline in other parts of the world are not fully understood by demographers and other social scientists. Recently a theory, known as the supply-demand theory of fertility determination, was put forth by an interdisciplinary National Academy of Sciences panel. According to Easterlin and Crimmins, "empirical research to test this theory has, however, been lacking," and their volume is an attempt to fill this gap. The work presented here grows out of research that Easterlin and Crimmins have been carrying out since the late seventies. Some of this research was in collaboration with other researchers. Some of it has been published in other places, for example, in *Economic Development and Cultural Change* (January 1984); *Population and Development Review* (June 1984); and volume 2 of R. A. Bulatao and R. D. Lee's *Determinants of Fertility in Developing Countries* (1983). Much new work is also to be found in this volume.

According to Easterlin and Crimmins, there

are two popular explanations for high fertility and low use of deliberate fertility control in today's developing countries. One is lack of accessibility to family planning services and techniques. . . . The other explanation is lack of motivation; that is, parents in these countries want so many children that there is no incentive to limit family size.

Easterlin and Crimmins argue that while both of these views have some merit, neither suffices, singly or conjointly, to explain crucial phenomena. Historically, the currently developed countries successfully accomplished deliberate control of fertility at a time when highly effective fertility-control techniques were not available and family planning programs were nonexistent. As for desired family-size explanation, they present data for Colombia, Sri Lanka, and India that show family-size preferences to be high in all three, yet fertility control tends to be the highest in Colombia, with the largest desired family size, and India, with the smallest desired family size, has the lowest use of fertility control. Easterlin and Crimins go on to state:

The theory of the present volume encompasses the explanations above but is not restricted to them. Family size desires correspond in the present theory to the "demand of children." Family planning accessibility is viewed as one element under the broader rubric, costs of fertility regulation. . . . In the present theory, however, "costs" also include subjective drawbacks of fertility control. . . . To these two factors—demand for children and regulation costs—the theory adds a third factor relating to the reproductive capacities of a couple, termed the "supply of children." The relevance of supply considerations, typically omitted from popular discussion and many scholarly theories, is illustrated by a modern couple that wants only two children but because of fecundity problems is unable to achieve its desires. For this couple, lack of fertility control stems, not from inordinately high family size desires or lack of access to fertility control techniques, but inadequate supply. In today's developing countries, an important limit on supply arises from high child mortality as well as fecundity limitations (p. 9).

In Easterlin and Crimmins's theory, then, "a couple's use of fertility control is hypothesized to vary directly with the excess of their supply of children over demand—their motivation for fertility control—and inversely with their perceived costs of regulating fertility, subjective as well as objective." Easter-

lin and Crimmins state that their theory, unlike a number of scholarly theories, does not assert the primacy of either motivation for fertility control or the fertility regulation costs. They leave the assessment of the relative importance of these two factors as an empirical issue.

The empirical testing of this theory—parts of it are not readily testable by virtue of the fact that subjective costs of fertility control and supply-of-children variables can at best be only approximated—is carried out in this volume by drawing upon data for households from Sri Lanka and Colombia, for geographic units in India, for rural and urban areas of the Indian state of Karnataka, and for Taiwan.

The main conclusions of the study are that both supply and demand for children contribute to the motivation for fertility control, and in the phase of the fertility transition, supply is as important as demand and possibly more important. As for the reasons for variations in the potential supply of children, Easterlin and Crimmins believe that "natural fertility and child survival are both contributing factors, but that neither one uniformly dominates." Regarding the importance of regulation costs, they find that it has the expected relation to use, but believe that the conclusion to which their "results uniformly point is the dominant importance of motivation . . . in the adoption and use of fertility control."

The implications of their analysis, they believe, are that "the optimum policy mix between socioeconomic development and family planning programs depends on the stage of modernization." In the early stages of modernization when motivation for fertility control may be low or even absent, socioeconomic development policies should take precedence. As development occurs, the supply of children increases, demand for children decreases, and motivation for fertility control increases. Development also lowers the costs of fertility regulation, and family planning programs' effectiveness should increase.

Easterlin and Crimmins close their volume rather optimistically:

Although some analysts see rapid rates of population growth as a serious obstacle to economic development, the fact is that since World War II living levels in the Third World have generally improved, often at rates higher than ever before. . . . [As development occurs] pressures for family size limitation are mounting as obstacles to use of fertility control diminish . . . [and] it appears that the more rapid the process of modernization, the more rapid the transition to lower fertility. Thus, this analysis of the causes of the fertility revolution leads to a view of the population explosion as a transient phenomenon (pp. 190-91).

SURINDER K. MEHTA
University of Massachusetts
Amherst

FAUSTO-STERLING, ANNE. *Myths of Gender: Biological Theories about Women and Men.* Pp. xi, 272. New York: Basic Books, 1985. $18.95.

The objective of this book is to assess the premises, evidence, and conclusions of scientific research on the biological and behavioral differences between males and females. Anne Fausto-Sterling provides interpretations of research projects directed to show the differences between males and females that challenge the methods employed, the data gathered, and the conclusions reached. Her viewpoint is original, openly expressed, and very persuasive. She demonstrates, at the very least, that beliefs such as that women are less intellectually gifted than men are not based on value-free, objective scientific studies and deserve much more thoughtful and careful testing and analysis. For those unfamiliar with fundamental biological concepts and laws, or who need a refresher course, she summarizes pertinent information and applies it to the broader questions of wide social interest, such as whether the physiological differences between men and women contribute to or detract from their behavior as citizens, professionals, or in any other ways.

Not all the research undertaken to explore the differences between male and female is scrutinized by Fausto-Sterling. She rests her case with the issues of mental ability emphasizing the ability to understand and do mathematics, the physiological changes associated with menstruation, menopause, and female behavior, and the role of aggression in the female and male psyches. She does not discuss women and depression, the mothering instinct, and the biological causes of homosexuality and transsexuality, which she believes would reveal the same lack of adequate experimental attention to the two-way interactions between mind and body and the complex forces affecting behavior, which affect the studies she does discuss, but which are not sufficiently taken into account by the researchers of the past.

Fausto-Sterling's main discovery is that present methods of biological research are not able to provide the parameters and tools needed to study either gender or humankind properly. She argues for a contextual research founded upon new analytical frameworks such as those suggested by Randi Koeske and others. Koeske, who theoretically analyzed research on menopause, concludes that both the biomedical and behavioral approaches to menopause ignore other important aspects of female existence. Employing a model-of-reality viewpoint that takes into consideration more physiological and psychological variables that have been ignored by researchers, the feminist-oriented biologist will, according to Koeske, create a

real alternative to biomedicine or a system of health research . . . which finds a way to reintegrate the whole person from the jigsaw of parts created by modern scientific medicine. The strength of the feminist perspective is the recognition that the parts biomedicine currently recognizes cannot be reassembled into a whole (p. 108).

One major result of these new methods and goals will not be more, but less, control of behavior.

Basically Fausto-Sterling underscores the increasingly tenable realization that good science needs the support of the social and political environment and, in this case, benefits from the insights raised by the feminist movement. Biological science as organized and pursued largely by male scientists has not cast its paradigm net widely enough, with the consequence that the most culturally esteemed qualities have been too often assumed and demonstrated inadequately to belong to males throughout the animal kingdom.

The subject of gender differences and inferiority are controversial and have long produced debate without satisfactory conclusions. Fausto-Sterling provides more satisfying commentary by employing a dual approach. She looks for the evidence in support of each claim about women and biology and then analyzes the data from a feminist viewpoint. Thus she sets up the basis for a feminist science that is not meant to be better or worse than normal science, but to be more complex and challenging. Fausto-Sterling's book about the biological nature of women will deservedly be cited along with Ruth Bleier's *Science and Gender* (1984) as a watershed volume.

AUDREY B. DAVIS

Smithsonian Institution
Washington, D.C.

GINZBURG, ELI, EDITH M. DAVIS, and MIRIAM OSTOW. *Local Health Policy in Action: The Municipal Health Services Program.* Pp. xiv, 136. Totowa, NJ: Rowman & Allanheld, 1985. $28.50.

Who would not want improved access to health care for the urban poor at no additional cost? This short book is a tale of five cities that painstakingly documents their attempt to create just that—better and more accessible medical services at a reduced cost.

The focus of the book is the Municipal Health Service Program (MHSP), a $15 million, five-year project, begun in 1978. MHSP was designed and funded by the Robert Wood Johnson Foundation and was supported by the U.S. Conference of Mayors

and the American Medical Association. The project was also supported by Medicare and Medicaid, which waived payment and copayment requirements for MHSP clinics. The five cities selected to participate in the program were Baltimore, Cincinnati, Milwaukee, St. Louis, and San Jose.

Local Health Policy in Action is actually a funded evaluation of MHSP that the Conservation of Human Resources at Columbia University was commissioned to do. The thrust of the evaluation was to identify the process by which political, community, professional, and organizational forces facilitated and retarded the goals of the project.

After providing details about the development of the project clinics in the first three chapters, Ginzburg, Davis, and Ostow go on in chapter 4 to describe major economic, political, and health industry influences on MHSP such as the conservative shift in Washington and the increase in the number of available physicians. In chapter 5, they identify factors in the local environment such as the jurisdictional structure of public health, and the roles of the mayor, medical school, voluntary hospitals, physician groups, and community groups that helped or hindered the goals of MHSP. In Chapter 6, Ginzburg and his coauthors attempt to evaluate the achievements of the program.

While the book is strong in sensitizing the reader to the myriad influences that affected the fledgling clinics in the five cities, the account fails in two important ways.

First, it fails to deliver data on the five city programs in a meaningful or usable way. Instead of providing the reader with information about the cities by preparing five separate case studies, Ginzburg, Davis, and Ostow absorb data about the five cities into such subthemes as staffing patterns, financial viability, utilization of clinics, and so forth. This method showers the reader with isolated facts, but provides no sense of the comparative urban experience.

The second failure of the book is its most disappointing aspect. It never cogently deals with the failure of MHSP. The "crux" of the project, the writers say, was developing "neighborhood health centers for the provision of ambulatory care to the inner city poor, in preference to the municipal and county hospital." But the project, no matter how worthwhile its other accomplishments, never succeeded in wooing patients away from the county or city hospital. Even though their descriptive evidence showed that the program failed in this regard, Ginzburg, Davis, and Ostow seem reluctant to acknowledge the failure and, in fact, at one point in their concluding chapter, they deny it.

ROBERTA ANN JOHNSON

University of San Francisco
California

NICHOLSON, LINDA J. *Gender and History: The Limits of Social Theory in the Age of the Family.* Pp. x, 238. New York: Columbia University Press, 1986. $27.50.

SOBLE, ALAN. *Pornography: Marxism, Feminism, and the Future of Sexuality.* Pp. x, 202. New Haven, CT: Yale University Press, 1986. $21.50.

What I like about Nicholson's *Gender and History* is its clear presentation of the nineteenth- and twentieth-century women's movements, including its sensitivity to the variety of contemporary feminist perspectives, and the generally excellent synopses of current research on gender and the family. Nicholson argues convincingly that research by feminist historians and anthropologists contributes to our understanding of evolving family, state, and economic interrelations.

Nicholson points to the feminist slogan "the personal is political" as a challenge to intellectual dualism. She goes on to show how feminist research illuminates differences in the meaning of family in women's lives across cultures and in different time periods. She then critiques Locke's theory of the individual-state separation and Marx's dialectical materialism for their blindness toward gender, acknowledging that their views were grounded in the social context of their times. As a socialist feminist, she is also critical of the search for a "universal cause" of women's oppression by some contemporary feminists, particularly Chodorow's assumption that mother-child relationships explain society or Mackinnon's view that sexuality is the linchpin for understanding social relations. Nicholson applauds feminists for claiming that "the personal is political," but cautions against ahistorical, single-cause explanations. She also criticizes a tendency to obscure racial and class diversity across cultures in explaining power relationships. *Gender and History* is a solid contribution to political theory and feminist studies.

There are a few common themes in *Gender and History* and *Pornography*. Each to some extent accepts Marxist analysis of society; each is critical of traditional theories; and each sees sexism as a factor in shaping society. Soble, however, touches a different context of personal and political in developing what he calls a Marxist defense of pornography.

It is a puzzling book, in part because some of what Soble argues seems reasonable. He argues that under an ideal communist state, where labor is neither coerced nor alienating, there is every reason to suppose that pornography would be pleasurable and not exploitive. Soble criticizes conservatives, liberals, Engels, Marcuse, Reich, Freud, those who would bring Marx and Freud together, and particularly the antipornography movement and radical feminists.

Unlike feminists who distinguish between pornography as woman degrading and erotica as mutually pleasing, Soble uses a sweeping definition: "any literature or film . . . that describes or depicts sexual organs, preludes to sexual activity, or sexual activity (or related organs and activities)." He argues that pornography arouses men "because it allows men to create women as men would like them to be," that it is not a reflection of men's power as some feminists claim, but rather a projection of men's sense of powerlessness. He does acknowledge that coercion, exploitation, and degradation of women are reflected in today's pornography, and that pornography serves men. He agrees that sexual expectations, like others, are formed in a social context and that current pornography reflects sexist assumptions and socialization.

If the social context were different—"given the collapse of the sexual division of labor..."" ...as long as pornography is not defined trivially as sexual material that degrades women"—pornography would be harmless and in fact could be of positive societal value. In his view, pornography or prostitution could become creative work, freely chosen. These are too many ifs and givens for me. The debate over causes, context, and consequences of pornography has been a lively, often bitter one. Soble's *Pornography* may fill one gap in Marxist theory, and certainly has some provocative moments, but overall it leaves too many difficult issues unresolved.

PAT HUCKLE

San Diego State University
California

REINER, ROBERT. *The Politics of Police.* Pp. xiii, 258. New York: St. Martin's Press, 1985. $29.95.

DALTON, THOMAS CARLYLE. *The State Politics of Judicial and Congressional Reform: Legitimizing Criminal Justice Policies.* Pp. xxi, 234. Westport, CT: Greenwood Press, 1985. $35.00.

The benign and dignified image of the English police has become badly tarnished in recent years. Labor unrest, race riots, and political demonstrations have thrust the police into the major controversies dividing English society. The left wing of the Labour Party condemns the police as oppressors of the people while the Thatcher government praises them as the basic guardians of Western civilization. As the police have come to be seen, both by themselves and by the general population, as allies of the Conservative Party, their legitimacy as a neutral peace-keeping force has been seriously undermined.

The Politics of Police is a fascinating study of the political dimensions of English policing and their implications for police management and administration. Author Robert Reiner, a lecturer in sociology of law at Bristol University, argues that the police are inescapably political but that "political analysis in general tends to underplay the significance of policing as both source and symbol of the quality of political civilization." But while acknowledging that policing is invariably political in terms of its uneven social impact, he argues that it need not be and should not be partisan in its intention. He believes that both ends of the political spectrum share responsibility for the recent politicizing of law enforcement, but that it is still possible to return to the type of consensus policing for which Britain was once famous.

The purpose of this book is to make use of the substantial body of research on law enforcement to analyze the positions of both sides in the increasingly polarized political debate over policing. While written in direct response to the current debate in Britain, Reiner is knowledgeable of American police practices and research and uses a great deal of comparative material in his analysis. A particularly fascinating chapter is "The Media Presentation of Policing." In it, Reiner identifies 12 types of law-enforcement narrative, ranging from the classic sleuth to Fort Apache, that have been popular in this century. Not only do media dramatizations of law enforcement influence how the public perceives the role of police in society, but they also influence how the police themselves perceive their role. Both fictional and factual reports of policing tend to overemphasize the law-enforcement functions of the police and downplay their peacekeeping and service activities.

Another chapter provides a provocative analysis of the different styles of policing that developed in the United States and England. While many sociologists have contended that the distinctive character of English policing was a product of that country's social homogeneity and tranquility, Reiner shows that the emphasis on service and the eschewal of force were deliberate strategies developed by early leaders to establish acceptance and support for the police in a time of political conflict and social upheaval. He argues that in the United States, by contrast, a more freewheeling and aggressive style of policing evolved, not as a consequence of social division, but because the political integration of American society had produced something approaching a property-owning democracy.

The current problem of reestablishing police legitimacy is not unlike the problem of establishing legitimacy faced by the founders of the English police in the 1830s. Reiner praises the conclusions reached by Lord Scarmon's report on the Brixton riots that explicitly draw upon instructions Sir Richard Mayne prepared for the New Metropolitan Police in 1829. These instructions emphasized preventive policing, minimal force, nonpartisanship, and recruitment from the working class. Reiner's conclusion is that the Scarmon reform iniatives are supported by past experience and research evidence and have the potential for reestablishing for the English police the public respect and support they enjoyed in the past. He warns that

the worst enemies of the current bid for police relegitimation are not their overt critics but their apparent benefactors—a "law and order" government which is unconcerned about destroying the social preconditions of consensus policing and the virtue of the British police tradition (p. 201).

Legitimacy is also the theme of *The State Politics of Judicial and Congressional Reform*. This study by Thomas Dalton, a former administrator in a state planning office responsible for the allocation of Law Enforcement Assistance Administration grants, analyzes state implementation of the *Mapp* and *Miranda* decisions and congressional policies regarding the privacy of criminal records. Like Reiner, Dalton believes that social turmoil and political unrest have led to an increasing politicization of law enforcement that in turn has produced a crisis of legitimacy in criminal justice. But while Reiner's concern is the effect this crisis of legitimacy has had on the police and their ability to carry out their basic peacekeeping and law-enforcement functions, Dalton's concern is the effect it has had on the commitment to protect defendant rights more fully.

Dalton provides an extensive review of the literature on policy implementation and judicial impact in an attempt to identify all the significant political constraints and supports that influence state implementation of national policies. From this literature, he develops an explanatory framework for policy implementation. The key variables identified by this framework are: (1) policy form—substantive, structural or procedural; (2) institutional structure and political culture; (3) the interests and priorities of elected officials; and (4) the expectations and beliefs of elites. Dalton uses this framework to analyze how the states of California, Colorado, Washington, and Massachusetts responded to federal mandates involving defendant rights and the privacy of records.

The study's conclusion is that federal mandates are exceedingly difficult to implement due to the "dispersal and fragmentation of the authority of national and state elected officials and the concentration of power and discretion in policy subsystems." Dalton believes that a serious gap exists between the promise and the reality of democratic politics and warns that it is in part due to the federal government's inability to bring about strict compliance with its mandates. The real danger to the American political system, he writes, "is institutional deadlock over achieving policy objectives which result in perpetuating the power and preferences of administrative and professional elites in policy subsystems."

The State Politics of Judicial and Congressional Reform will be of some interest to the student of judicial policy implementation, but its dissertation-style format and effort to relate its own relatively modest findings to the most fundamental research questions of political science make it a difficult work for the nonspecialist to follow. Even some specialists might have difficulty accepting Dalton's assumption that state reluctance to embrace controversial federal policies fully constitutes a crisis in legitimacy and poses a threat to basic democratic values. These aspects of the implementation system that give state and local officials influence over federal policies are seen by some as factors contributing to representative government and policy legitimation.

J. DAVID FAIRBANKS
University of Houston—Downtown
Texas

ROSE, MICHAEL. *Re-working the Work Ethic: Work and Society in the Eighties.* Pp. ix, 160. New York: Schocken Books, 1985. $17.50.

WOLFE, JOEL D. *Workers, Participation, and Democracy: Internal Politics in the British Union Movement.* Pp. xii, 258. Westport, CT: Greenwood Press, 1985. $45.00.

Chinese Communist leaders complain about the decline of service in Beijing. Margaret Thatcher complains about the loss of the Victorian work ethic among the British working class. Corporate leaders in Detroit complain about their work force's lack of interest in quality. Everywhere workers are being exhorted to revive the moral commitment to work of previous generations. But, as Michael Rose reminds us in the first part of this small but uneven book aimed primarily at students and industrial relations practitioners, there is no evidence that most employees have ever held anything but an instrumental attitude to work.

This is not to say that work values are not changing but, after reviewing the survey literature, Rose claims that employers and politicians have been exhorting the wrong group. It is among professional, managerial, and white-collar strata—the group where, in

the absence of close supervision, internalized values have probably played the most important role—that changes are taking place. Rose documents the growth of so-called post-bourgeoisie values—an increased hedonism, a lessened commitment to production at all costs, a generalized anti-authoritarianism, and growing demands for self-actualization—fostered, he argues, by the feminist stress on the reintegration of work and family; by the growth of the noncommercial state sector; by the rise of the service sector; and by the consumption orientation of modern economies. At present such values are restricted to a relatively small group, and Rose rejects the view that such values are necessarily inimical to capitalism in any revolutionary sense, but he does see their spread as posing a problem for traditional work-place organization with its reliance on more instrumental motivations. In a Durkheimian tone, Rose argues that employers, unions, and politicians need to take self-actualizing and participatory forms of work—including the controversial quality-of-work-life programs—more seriously if a performance ethic is to be maintained when instrumental controls lose some of their efficacy.

Wolfe has a more radical agenda. He is concerned to rescue the possibility of participatory democracy from the intellectual limbo in which Michels and the rational-choice theorists have left it. He does so, in a very interesting book, by examining the development of participatory democracy in the British labor movement during World War I. For participatory democracy to work, he argues, certain conditions have to be met: there has to be a moral base for communal action among the members, so that collective goals can supersede the individual self-interest on which the inevitability of oligarchy is postulated; and the members have to possess a commitment to equality as a substantive goal to which leaders can be held accountable.

The case-study material is interesting, and the theoretical model reinforces the growing recognition on the Left that socialism is a moral ideal that cannot be derived directly from the rational self-interest of the proletariat. But the question remains as to whether the preconditions Wolfe cites as necessary for participatory democracy were not the result of a structure of community and work place that suburbanization and the rationalization of work have now demolished. Wolfe is optimistic, however, and sees the post-bourgeoisie new social movements—feminism, environmentalism, the peace movement, and the like—as providing the basis for a resurgence of participatory democracy in the work place and elsewhere. As Wolfe himself notes, however, it was a commitment to equality rooted in a community of kind that provided the basis for the participatory democracy of the 1914-18 labor movement, and it remains to be seen whether this is to be found in the newer social movements with their largely middle-class base. In the sphere of work at least, Rose's cautious reformism probably provides a better guide to the best we can hope for in the near future.

Even more likely, employers will respond to any perceived absence of a performance ethic with a more traditional remedy: if workers will not work, they shall not eat.

PETER WHALLEY

Loyola University
Chicago
Illinois

VALENSTEIN, ELLIOT S. *Great and Desperate Cures: The Rise and Decline of Psychosurgery and Other Radical Treatments for Mental Illness*. Pp. xiv, 338. New York: Basic Books, 1986. $19.95.

Most people, inside and outside the medical profession, would see the lobotomy as an unfortunate aberration in the progress of modern psychiatry, now best forgotten. The prefrontal lobotomy and its many variants involved entering the skull and cutting through parts of the brain with the aim of altering the psychological state of the patient. The damage caused to thousands of people worldwide is incalculable. Valenstein's startling and fascinating book forcefully reminds us not only of the extensive practice of psychosurgery in the 1940s and 1950s, but also that the same factors that sustained the use of this mutilating operation are with us still. In the history of medicine, desperate need has often been the progenitor of desperate cures. Valenstein points to the contemporary concerns of cancer and acquired immune deficiency syndrome and the intense demand on the medical profession to find remedies—the miracle cure. The lure of fame and international renown for the miracle workers can lead to a selective perception of the facts, a disregard for troubling side-effects and conflicting evidence. Two ambitious men were most associated with the promotion of psychosurgery: Egas Moniz, a Portuguese neurologist and diplomat, and Walter Freeman, a neuropathologist from the United States. Valenstein describes, but cannot entirely account for, their unusual levels of drive and desire for success. Two separate and full biographies are needed to explain some of their extraordinary activities. Egas Moniz was awarded the Nobel Prize in 1949 for his work in pioneering prefrontal leucotomy, twenty years after he had first encouraged colleagues to seek it for him for an entirely different achievement. Freeman received many honors, but lived long enough to see psychosurgery superseded by tranquilizing drugs. In his heyday Freeman carried out lobotomies in his office without anesthetic by means of an ice pick. He was responsible for 3500 operations and indirectly responsible for thousands more through his tireless promotion of the technique.

It is not only the ambitious physician who is prey to self-deception; it is also the victims of disease and distress and indeed the media who like nothing better than to be harbingers of the latest medical breakthrough. The history of medicine is certainly replete with examples of treatments where judicious caution would have been a more appropriate response than rapturous enthusiasm. We have developed the knowledge and techniques to subject new treatments to proper assessment. What is missing all too often is the motivation to apply these critical techniques.

Valenstein's book is soundly and thoroughly researched. It is also as gripping as any detective story and as compelling as the best journalism. But read it for its importance.

SHEILA M. GREENE

Trinity College
Dublin
Ireland

ECONOMICS

JACOBY, SANFORD M. *Employing Bureaucracy: Managers, Unions, and the Transformation of Work in American Industry, 1900-1945.* Pp. ix, 377. New York: Columbia University Press, 1985. $35.00.

In this excellent study, Jacoby deals with the transformation of industrial labor from the nineteenth-century arbitrary pattern to the present system of good jobs, defined as jobs that pay well, offer stability and promotion opportunities, and protect against arbitrary discipline and dismissal. The vehicle through which this transformation took place was bureaucratization, which entailed the replacement of personal rule by foremen with professional personnel managers who were constrained to operate within a system of rules and structures. In his analysis Jacoby takes issue with both the Parsonian view that bureaucratization is an inevitable and automatic result of the technical imperatives imposed by large and complex organizations and the radical view, which sees bureaucratic devices as mechanisms of employer control over the work force. Although the changes were often brought about by management in the hope that the greater evil of unionization could be forestalled, the net result was less control by management over the decision-making pro-

cess. Indeed, the continuing irony in personnel management was that it best served the purpose of thwarting unionism by introducing the same reforms the unions sought. It was an illusion of freedom that management was able to preserve, not the real article.

Jacoby traces the emergence of personnel management from three earlier groups that focused on different aspects of work relations: the engineers who looked at job design and administrative practice, the welfare workers, who became concerned in the Progressive era with the factory environment and workers' edification, and the vocationalists, who emphasized employment policies and procedures. All of these strands of thought came together in the years before World War I to form a personnel movement that grew rapidly because of the members' involvement with the governmental effort to control the war labor market and finally became dominant after 1933.

The book has many virtues, not the least of which is that it puts major New Deal programs in perspective as part of a long-term drive for security, rather than as an entirely new departure. The belated governmental entry into the field served to set minimum standards of protection and to stimulate more interest in the subject. In the first four years after passage of the Social Security Act, for example, twice as many companies adopted pension plans as abandoned them. As industry advisers said, the act permitted a firm, "for a very small outlay," to earn its employees' gratitude by supplementing the inadequate pension provided by government.

Although Jacoby quite properly denies that the changes he details came automatically out of technological changes, he nevertheless gives technology its due by pointing out that the newer industries of the late 1800s, like electrical machinery and chemicals, were among the first to adopt personnel departments. In part, it was because these industries had little continuity with artisanal techniques, and it is important to note that the same technical innovations that destroyed artisans' traditions eroded the authority of the foreman. Technical innovations in manufacturing left the foreman with little authority and tended to transfer decision making to engineers and metallurgists.

I consider this to be an admirable book with no particular flaws worth mentioning. It is economic history in the best sense: based on an accurate reading of the historical record and informed in its interpretations by economic theory. Anyone interested in the social history of the twentieth century could read it with profit.

GEORGE H. DANIELS
University of South Alabama
Mobile

MARCHAND, ROLAND. *Advertising the American Dream: Making Way for Modernity, 1920-1940.* Pp. xxii, 448. Berkeley: University of California Press, 1985. $35.00.

There are many strengths in this book, not the least of which are its sources, introduction, content, and readability. Yet so vast is Marchand's mission in *Advertising the American Dream* that vulnerabilities are almost inevitable.

Marchand's sources, as manifested by his extensive bibliographical essay, are impressive. He has examined the secondary literature thoroughly and has scoured well the manuscripts of advertising agencies, corporations, and individuals related to the new advertising profession. He notes that many manuscript collections were worthless and that some were invaluable, such as the archives of the J. Walter Thompson Company, a leading advertising concern in the nation. I can imagine, as Marchand reports, that great manufacturing companies are usually "ahistorical, or even antihistorical" and are not especially interested in preserving and releasing material that might portray them as con artists. One caveat about Mar-

chand's sources: did he search enough for correspondence on his important subject? Were there no letters on the subject? None are reported in his over 1000 footnotes. Surely the Commerce Department files in the National Archives or in the Herbert Hoover and Franklin D. Roosevelt Libraries reveal something about advertising as a corporatist means of eliminating "waste" and "rationalizing the market."

Marchand's "Introduction" really whets the appetite with questions about the motivation, appeal, and downright distortion of advertising in the period. Distortion seemed everywhere in advertising—from emphasizing upper-class values to worshiping new products as American icons. In many respects advertising was bad social history, although Marchand notes correctly that it was no worse than much other documentary evidence. Moreover, advertising undoubtedly did reflect many of the people's needs and anxieties.

It is the basic content of this book, including fine illustrations, that make it so appealing. Portions of chapter titles hint at the appeal: "Apostles of Modernity," "The New Professionals," "[T]he Audience," "Abandoning the . . . Genteel Hope . . . [for plebian tastes]," "Art and Style," including the importance of color and modern design, "Advertisements as Eclectic Social Tableaux," "The Great Parables," "Fantasies and Icons," "Advertising in Overalls"—in order to adjust to the Great Depression—and "The Therapeutics of Advertising."

Marchand's last chapter, "The Therapeutics of Advertising," is appropriately the best. It addresses advertising's attempts at resolving the bifurcation of the increasing desire of consumers for personal interaction in an increasingly complex society. Advertising did so by denying the "seemingly chaotic complexity" of production—for example, by illustrating "the [tomato] soup can emerging directly and miraculously from the ripe tomato of the fields." If consumers' choices were too proliferated, advertisements decided for the consumer. If the products were too technical for consumers, advertisements rejected any attempt at explanation and proclaimed useless phrases as literal descriptions—like "Knee-Action" for General Motors car engines. And if modernity depersonalized life, advertisers concocted a Betty Crocker who asked consumers to write to her—and tens of thousands did. In short, the new professionals blended the hard work of "economic transaction . . . and the soft . . . world of home . . . [and] family." The last chapter, like the whole book, addresses its important subject almost definitely. Yet, presumably because "the 1920s and 1930s [do importantly] provide the optimum era for . . . historical interpretation" of advertisements as "reflections of American culture," I wish Marchand had concluded the book with a more thorough summing up and a clearer statement of his own interpretation of the meaning of advertising in the period. One expects, following 400 pages of such fine manuscript material, *finis coronat opus*.

> MARTIN L. FAUSOLD
State University of New York
Geneseo

ROTHSTEIN, LAWRENCE E. *Plant Closings, Power, Politics and Workers*. Pp. xv, 201. Dover, MA: Auburn House, 1986. $27.95.

It appears that in some ways the captains of industry have learned the lesson of modern warfare better than the captains of armies. That lesson concerns the primacy of mobility. Those who must defend centers of population and their social and political networks are at a disadvantage in a war movement. The advantage goes to those who can abandon the towns and cities and who can isolate their opponents from the support of the general population. This is exactly what business is doing.

According to Rothstein this is the inevitable conclusion of his situational analysis of Youngstown steel plant closings and a similar labor defeat in Longwy, Lorraine, France. The two plant closings and layoffs resulted in different worker responses, but in both instances certain "myths" enabled management to dominate the processes preceding final plant closings.

Rothstein sees power in its institutional frame as the measure by which any individual or group can achieve a goal reflecting its original purposes. Latently, "people and issues are left out of public decision making."

Decisions on where to relocate plants in exchange for lower labor costs and tax incentives and development loans are secretly arrived at in corporate and bank board rooms. Experiences of workers in both the Longwy and Youngstown plants indicated employers' "power to suppress" and limit the influence of aggrieved groups.

Three "myths" have their bases in the "power to suppress." They are the "myth of big labor," the "myth of the business climate"—including the "myth of foreign competition"—and the "myth of legality."

For Rothstein, big labor does not exist in contemporary America. It may have been influential in the early organizing days of John L. Lewis and the Reuthers, encouraged by the sympathetic New Deal dedicated to balancing the power of management and labor.

The business-climate myth symbolizes the idea that union or government activities aimed at strengthening the labor movement inherently threaten economic growth and investment interests in the community. Hence, jobs will be lost, and the entire community and its economy will be affected negatively. One prevailing argument used in Youngstown claimed that the closing of the U.S. Steel plant would be a good thing because big labor would be broken, and the town would become "economically diversified"; new investment capital would be attracted when labor costs became more "flexible." Rothstein claims this position invalid, considering the mobility of capital measured by the extent to which American investments end up in rural areas or more significantly in Third World countries where cheap labor is plentiful.

The myth of legality assumes the legal

system as "neutral" and "fair." This notion accepted by union and management buttresses management rights to close plants regardless of the effects on communities and workers. The long processes in grievance procedures, arbitration clauses, and layoff procedures in collective bargaining agreements attest to the inherent power of the myth of legality. The instrument in and of itself, "negotiated in good faith" by both parties, is, according to the accepted myth of legality, protective of both parties.

Rothstein notes that proposed local state policies to protect workers against plant closings and relocation have been defeated at the legislative level in state capitals. There have been instances in which national and state union headquarters have opposed local union efforts to resist plant closings.

How can a revived trade union movement resist plant closings or at least gain compensatory treatment through the enactment of legislation? A long list of recommendations is approved by Rothstein; these have been supported by a select group of labor leaders.

The losses by labor in Youngstown, in Rhode Island where Rothstein was a close participant, and in Longwy are considered to be "political defeats."

The book is a challenging presentation of a serious situation facing urban America and should be considered by students as well as political and union leaders.

GEORGE H. HUGANIR
Temple University
Philadelphia
Pennsylvania

STEUERLE, C. EUGENE. *Taxes, Loans, and Inflation: How the Nation's Wealth Becomes Misallocated.* Pp. xii, 205. Washington, DC: Brookings Institution, 1985. $26.95. Paperbound, $9.95.

This book provides an excellent coverage of the major tax and financial factors that lead to a serious misallocation of capital resources in the American economy. While it has long been recognized, especially among economists, that efficiency distortions arise from the manner in which the federal income tax treats capital income, there has not been written—to the best of my knowledge—any one work that has assembled this analysis into a complete, yet concise and meaningful, picture—that is, not until this brilliant effort by C. Eugene Steuerle.

Not only does the book convey to the reader the logical basis of economic decisions that distort capital allocation, as prompted by the interaction of the federal personal and corporation income tax laws, loan markets, and inflation; it also provides insight into various other economic phenomena that have been influenced by these distortions such as the failure of many saving and investment incentives as well as the performance of supply-side economic policies. Clearly portrayed is the central role played in capital misallocation by tax arbitrage, which, in essence, is a situation in which taxpayers borrow money using deductible interest payments in order to acquire tax-preferred assets. The reader thus obtains an understanding of the normally elusive message of just why and how a highly differentiated income tax structure distorts economic decisions pertaining to the use of capital, whether they be made by individuals, businesses, or governments.

Following an introductory chapter, the six chapters of part 1 explain, in detail, the intricacies of the nonuniform treatment of capital income under the federal income tax laws, both as to the sources of capital and as to its differential treatment with respect to wage income, and the resulting misallocation of capital. Next, the four chapters of part 2 apply this analysis to selected important issues such as macroeconomic policies, business organizational structure and mergers, and tax burden equity. In part 3, the final three chapters expertly consider tax and nontax alternatives for making the treatment of capital more uniform, leading to an improvement in allocational efficiency. The final chapter of this sequence offers a seven-part agenda for reform in which a federal income tax with a more comprehensive base and lower rates plays a major role. It is interesting that Congress has moved toward this general pattern of income tax reform as the present review is being written.

BERNARD P. HERBER
University of Arizona
Tucson

WEAVER, R. KENT. *The Politics of Industrial Change*. Pp. xi, 291. Washington, DC: Brookings Institution, 1985. $31.95. Paperbound, $11.95.

Industrial policy debate is usually cloaked in arguments of competitiveness in world markets. R. Kent Weaver, in his book *The Politics of Industrial Change*, helps clarify this debate by arguing that the barriers to effective industrial policy result from domestic political forces rather than international factors. The book presents a good history and analysis of Canadian and U.S. public policy toward railroads that would be a useful case study for students of regulation and industrial policy. Emphasis on public enterprise in the railroad industry provides an anatomy of a policy failure, but it also makes the book narrow in scope. The suggestion that the analysis is generally applicable across industries, countries, and policies is heroic.

Weaver begins with an assumption of the desirability of accelerationist policy over market-oriented and protectionist policies. Accelerationist policies speed up industrial transitions when a market failure prevents rapid industrial adjustment. However, too little attention is paid to making the case that widespread market failures require an accelerationist policy.

The stated thesis of the book is that "national variations in political constraints give countries differing comparative advantages in pursuing particular governmental activities, just as variations in economic resources create comparative advantages in specific industries." The book really focuses on the political economy of accelerationist industrial adjustment policy, concentrating on public enterprise. The book is a comparative case study of public policy toward rail transportation in Canada and the United States. The analysis is organized around three questions: (1) how capable are these governments in implementing accelerationist policies? (2) what factors influence government choice of policy instruments? and (3) how does the political system affect the implementation of industry policies? These are not completely independent questions. Consequently, addressing the questions separately makes the book repetitive in parts.

To address each question, a theoretical chapter is presented followed by chapters discussing the evolution of rail policy in each country. Weaver does a good job of synthesizing and presenting details of the politics of rail policies in each country. The theoretical chapters, however, lack rigor. Weaver loosely formulates a theory that is consistent with the facts presented in the chapters that follow. He discusses the political costs and benefits of the choice of public policy and specific policy instruments, yet he fails to discuss more rigorous theories of regulation that are consistent with the facts he presents in the case of rail policy. Weaver works toward developing a theory of public enterprise behavior by suggesting hierarchical objectives of security, autonomy, and public service. However, the theory is too general and vague, limiting its usefulness.

Finally, the concept of comparative advantage in industrial policy choice is distracting from the main thrust of the book. Specialization and comparative advantage have little relevance for nontraded goods and services. What Weaver actually suggests is that governments have different least-cost—economic and political—policy instruments, given different political and economic situations. The comparative-advantage issue is confusing since the political costs are the result of different factional demands rather than supply-side constraints, which traditionally determine comparative advantages. Despite the stated thesis, the comparative-advantage concept is discussed only in the introductory and concluding chapters and is not essential.

KELLY EAKIN

University of Oregon
Eugene

YORK, NEIL LONGLEY. *Mechanical Metamorphosis: Technological Change in Revolutionary America*. Pp. xviii, 240. Westport, CT: Greenwood Press, 1985. $35.00.

Writing on a topic that has had comparatively little systematic analysis, Neil York sets out to record "the shifting technological outlook of the Americans during the Revolutionary Era." An explicitly social context frames the study; thus the topics selected are those that, in York's view, "accurately depict the social nature of technology and technological change and the American pairing of political and technological goals." Those topics span a range from the late colonial through the early national period: home manufactures and "the isolated inventor" of prewar years; then wartime technological capability and experimentation—the munitions industry, "visionary" instruments of war like David Bushnell's submarine, military engineering efforts to erect barriers in the Delaware River approaches to Philadelphia, and the technical limitations of the Pennsylvania rifle as opposed to the conventional musket. Finally York analyzes the postwar industrial and inventive activity as a period during which the "American appreciation for and identification with technology took shape . . . the intellectual equivalent to Walt Rostow's pre-condition to takeoff."

Careful—often fascinating—in detail and wide in scope, York's book envisions technological change in forms far broader than the usual narratives of developments in industrial processes. That perception leads York to the provocative thesis that technological and inventive activity was inextricably linked with sociopolitical circumstance; he writes, for example, "As far as many Americans were concerned, there was a direct connection between national prosperity and the rate of technological change. They treated the political republic and the technological republic as obverse sides of the same coin." In providing evidence for that thesis, York points to "technological visionaries," "technological agitators," and "manufacturing enthusiasts," all of whom alledgedly reacted to political concerns. Readers may, however, be nagged by the thought that economic opportunity could have dominated political commitment. York himself notes that prospect: "As one would expect, market pressures often dictated the rate of technological change." Those market pressures receive little attention in the book—a distinct surprise given the encompassing nature of the discussion. In light of the book's objectives, then, the social nature of technological change is better demonstrated than is the "pairing of political and technological goals."

Yet if the work does not succeed in all that it attempts, it clearly succeeds in presenting technological change in its broader context, a "landscape perspective," in David Jeremy's words. That perspective is particularly valuable because it evokes a spirit of technological enterprise—the beginnings of one of the major themes in American history.

H. A. GEMERY

Colby College
Waterville
Maine

OTHER BOOKS

ACKLAND, LEN and STEVEN McGUIRE, eds. *Assessing the Nuclear Age.* Pp. xvii, 382. Chicago: University of Chicago Press, 1986. $29.95. Paperbound, $12.95.

ALEXANDER, JEFFREY C., ed. *Neofunctionalism.* Pp. 240. Beverly Hills, CA: Sage, 1985. Paperbound, no price.

ANDERSON, ALFRED F. *Liberating the Early American Dream: A Way to Transcend the Capitalist/Communist Dilemma Nonviolently.* Pp. viii, 272. Ukiah, CA: Tom Paine Institute, 1985. $24.50. Paperbound, $12.50.

ARRIGHI, GIOVANNI, ed. *Semiperipheral Development: The Politics of Southern Europe in the Twentieth Century.* Pp. 279. Beverly Hills, CA: Sage, 1985. No price.

BEKERMAN, GERARD. *Marx and Engels: A Conceptual Concordance.* Translated by Terrell Carver. Pp. xxxi, 205. New York: Basil Blackwell, 1986. Paperbound, $12.95.

BERGSTEN, C. FRED and WILLIAM R. CLINE. *The United States-Japan Economic Problem.* Washington, DC: Institute for International Economics, 1985. Paperbound, $10.00.

BERKE, JOEL S., MARGARET E. GOERTZ, and RICHARD J. COLEY. *Politicians, Judges, and City Schools: Reforming School Finance in New York.* Pp. xxii, 279. New York: Russell Sage Foundation, 1984. No price.

BICKEL, ALEXANDER M. *The Least Dangerous Branch: The Supreme Court at the Bar of Politics.* 2nd ed. Pp. 303. New Haven, CT: Yale University Press, 1986. Paperbound, $12.95.

BINNENDIJK, HANS, ed. *Strategic Defense in the 21st Century.* Pp. xii, 151. Washington, DC: Center for the Study of Foreign Affairs, 1986. Paperbound, $5.50.

BLECHMAN, BARRY M. and VICTOR A. UTGOFF. *Fiscal and Economic Implication of Strategic Defenses.* Pp. xiii, 152. Boulder, CO: Westview Press; Washington, DC: Johns Hopkins Foreign Policy Institute, 1986. Paperbound, $22.50.

BRODY, ANDREW. *Slowdown: Global Economic Maladies.* Pp. 151. Beverly Hills: Sage, 1985. No price.

CAMPBELL, COLIN D. and WILLIAM R. DOUGAN, eds. *Alternative Monetary Regimes.* Pp. xi, 251. Baltimore, MD: Johns Hopkins University Press, 1986. $29.50. Paperbound, $12.95.

CARAMAZZA, I. F. and U. LEONE. *Phenomenology of Kidnappings in Sardenia: Towards an International Perspective of a Local Crime Problem.* Pp. 211. Rome: United Nations Social Defence Research Institute, 1984. Paperbound, no price.

CHELIUS, JAMES, ed. *Current Issues in Workers' Compensation.* Pp. vi, 372. Kalamazoo, MI: W.E. Upjohn Institute for Employment Research, 1986. $19.95. Paperbound, $14.95.

COLLINS, H. M. *Changing Order: Replication and Induction in Scientific Practice.* Pp. vii, 187. Beverly Hills, CA: Sage, 1985. Paperbound, no price.

COLLINS, PATRICK. *Currency Convertibility: The Return to Sound Money.* Pp. xvi, 249. New York: St. Martin's Press, 1985. $29.95.

COLLINS, RANDALL. *Max Weber: A Skeleton Key.* Pp. 151. Beverly Hills, CA: Sage, 1986. Paperbound, no price.

COQUERY-VIDROVITCH, CATHERINE and PAUL E. LOVEJOY, eds. *The Workers of African Trade.* Pp. 304. Beverly Hills, CA: Sage, 1985. No price.

CORSON, WALTER, ALAN HERSHEY, and STUART KERACHSKY. *Nonmonetary Eligibility in State Unemployment Insurance Programs: Law and Practice.* Pp. xvii, 138. Kalamazoo, MI: W.E. Upjohn Institute for Employment Research, 1986. Paperbound, no price.

COWEN, REGINA H.E. *Defense Procurement in the Federal Republic of Germany: Politics and Organization.* Pp. xvii, 334. Boulder, CO: Westview Press, 1986. Paperbound, $29.50.

DANIELS, ROBERT V. *Russia: The Roots of Confrontation.* Pp. xxiii, 411. Cambridge, MA: Harvard University Press, 1985. $25.00. Paperbound, $8.95.

DEVINE, C. MAURY, CLAUDIA M. DISSEL, and KIM D. PARRISH, eds. *The Harvard Guide to Influential Books.* Pp. xxix, 303. New York: Harper & Row, 1986. Paperbound, $7.95.

DOERINGER, PETER B. and MICHAEL J. PIORE. *Internal Labor Markets and Manpower Analysis.* Pp. xxxv, 212. Armonk, NY: M.E. Sharpe, 1985. $30.00. Paperbound, $13.95.

DOUGLAS, MARY. *Risk Acceptability According to the Social Sciences.* Pp. 115. New York: Russell Sage Foundation, 1986. Distributed by Basic Books, New York. Paperbound, $6.95.

DRAPER, HAL. *The Marx-Engels Glossary: Glossary to the "Chronicle" and "Register" and Index to the "Glossary."* Pp. xx, 249. New York: Schocken Books, 1986. $28.50.

DUNLOP, JOHN B. *The Faces of Contemporary Russian Nationalism.* Pp. xii, 363. Princeton, NJ: Princeton University Press, 1983. Paperbound, $13.50.

DYSON, KENNETH, ed. *European Detente: Case Studies of the Politics of East-West Relations.* Pp. xi, 279. New York: St. Martin's Press, 1986. $32.50.

ELWORTHY, FREDERICK THOMAS. *The Evil Eye: An Account of This Ancient and Widespread Superstition.* Pp. xi, 471. New York: Harmony Books, 1986. Paperbound, $7.95.

EVANS, PETER, DIETRICH RUESCHE-MEYER, and EVELYNE HUBER STEVENS, eds. *States versus Markets in the World-System.* Pp. 295. Beverly Hills, CA: Sage, 1985. Paperbound, no price.

FATHY, HASSAN. *Natural Energy and Vernacular Architecture: Principles and Examples with Reference to Hot Arid Climates.* Pp. xxiii, 172. Chicago: University of Chicago Press, 1986. $25.00. Paperbound, $10.95.

FEIGENBAUM, HARVEY B. *The Politics of Public Enterprise: Oil and the French State.* Pp. xvii, 194. Princeton, NJ: Princeton University Press, 1985 $25.00. Paperbound, $8.95.

FRANSMAN, MARTIN. *Technology and Economic Development.* Pp. xi, 161. Boulder, CO: Westview Press, 1986. $35.50.

FURLONG, WILLIAM L. and MARGARET E. SCRANTON. *The Dynamics of Foreign Policymaking: The President, the Congress, and the Panama Canal Treaties.* Pp. xx, 263. Boulder, CO: Westview Press, 1985. Paperbound, $19.00.

GHOSH, ARABINDA. *Competition and Diversification in the United States Petroleum Industry.* Pp. xiv, 124. Westport, CT: Greenwood Press, Quorum Books, 1985. $35.00.

GIDDENS, ANTHONY. *The Constitution of Society: Outline of the Theory of Structuration.* Pp. xxxvii, 402. Berkeley: University of California Press, 1986. Paperbound, $12.95.

GLENNON, JOHN P., ed. *The Near and Middle East.* Vol. 9, *Foreign Relations of the United States: 1952-1954.* Pt. 2. Pp. xxxvi, 908. Washington, DC: Government Printing Office, 1986. No price.

GOLDSTEIN, MORRIS. *The Global Effects of Fund-Supported Adjustment Programs.* Pp. vii, 49. Washington, DC: International Monetary Fund, 1986. Paperbound, $7.50.

HAAS, EDWARD F. *DeLesseps S. Morrison and the Image of Reform: New Orleans Politics, 1946-1961.* Pp. xii, 368. Baton Rouge: Louisiana State University Press, 1986. Paperbound, $9.95.

HAGEMAN, MARY JEANETTE. *Police-Community Relations.* Pp. 159. Beverly Hills, CA: Sage, 1985. Paperbound, no price.

HALL, RICHARD H. *Dimensions of Work.* Pp. 351. Beverly Hills, CA: Sage, 1986. No price.

HAMOUDA, O. F., ed. *Controversies in Political Economy: Selected Essays by G. C. Harcourt.* Pp. 293. New York: New York University Press, 1986. Distributed by Columbia University Press, New York. $40.00.

HARASYMIW, BOHDAN. *Political Elite Recruitment in the Soviet Union.* Pp. xviii, 277. New York: St. Martin's Press, 1984. $27.95.

HARRINGTON, CHRISTINE B. *Shadow Justice: The Ideology and Institutionalization of Alternatives to Court.* Pp. x, 216. Westport, CT: Greenwood Press, 1985. $29.95.

HAWORTH, LAWRENCE. *Autonomy: An Essay in Philosophical Psychology and Ethics.* Pp. vii, 248. New Haven, CT: Yale University Press, 1986. $18.95.

HIGGINS, PAUL C. *The Rehabilitation Detectives: Doing Human Service Work.* Pp. 240. Beverly Hills, CA: Sage, 1985. Paperbound, no price.

HOWE, IRVING. *The American Newness: Culture and Politics in the Age of Emerson.* Pp. 99. Cambridge, MA: Harvard University Press, 1986. $12.50.

HUNT, MORTON. *Profiles of Social Research: The Scientific Study of Human Interactions.* Pp. xxiii, 337. New York: Russell Sage Foundation, 1986. Distributed by Basic Books, New York. $17.50. Paperbound, $8.95.

The Inauguration of George Rupp. Pp. viii, 54. Houston, TX: William Marsh Rice University, 1986. No price.

JACOBS, JAMES B. *Socio-Legal Foundations of Civil-Military Relations.* Pp. ix, 190. New Brunswick, NJ: Transaction Books, 1986. $19.95.

JEFFREYS, SHEILA. *The Spinster and Her Enemies: Feminism and Sexuality, 1880-1930.* Pp. vii, 232. London: Routledge & Kegan Paul, Pandora Press, 1985. Paperbound, $9.95.

JEWSIEWICKI, BOGUMIL and DAVID NEWBURY, eds. *African Historiographies: What History for Which Africa?* Pp. 320. Beverly Hills, CA: Sage, 1986. No price.

JONES, ROBERT ALUN. *Emile Durkheim: An Introduction to Four Major Works.* Pp. 167. Beverly Hills, CA: Sage, 1986. Paperbound, no price.

KEOHANE, ROBERT O., ed. *Neorealism and Its Critics.* Pp. x, 378. New York: Columbia University Press, 1986. $45.00. Paperbound, $13.00.

KERNELL, SAMUEL and SAMUEL L. POPKIN. *Chief of Staff: Twenty-Five Years of Managing the Presidency.* Pp. xx, 244. Berkeley: University of California Press, 1986. $15.96.

LAIRD, ROBBIN F. and ERIK P. HOFFMANN, eds. *Soviet Foreign Policy in a Changing World.* Pp. xxiv, 969. New York: Walter de Gruyter, Aldine, 1986. $57.95. Paperbound, $27.95.

LARWOOD, LAURIE, ANN H. STROMBERG, and BARBARA A. GUTEK, eds. *Women and Work: An Annual Review.* Vol. 1. Pp. 312. Beverly Hills, CA: Sage, 1985. No price.

LEE, DWIGHT R., ed. *Taxation and the Deficit Economy: Fiscal Policy and Capital Formation in the United States.* Pp. xxvii, 554. San Francisco: Pacific Research Institute for Public Policy, 1986. $34.95. Paperbound, $14.95.

LESSARD, DONALD R. and JOHN WILLIAMSON. *Financial Intermediation beyond the Debt Crisis.* Pp. xii, 118. Washington, DC: Institute for International Economics, 1985. Paperbound, $12.00.

LONG, SAMUEL, ed. *Political Behavior Annual.* Vol. 1. Pp. xii, 191. Boulder, CO: Westview Press, 1986. $35.00.

MALDONADO, LIONEL and JOAN MOORE. *Urban Ethnicity in the United States: New Immigrants and Old Minorities.* Pp. 304. Beverly Hills, CA: Sage, 1985. Paperbound, no price.

MARRIS, STEPHEN. *Deficits and the Dollar: The World Economy at Risk.* Pp. xxxviii, 343. Washington, DC: Institute for International Economics, 1985. Paperbound, $15.00.

MARSHALL, VICTOR W. *Later Life: The Social Psychology of Aging.* Pp. 352. Beverly Hills, CA: Sage, 1986. Paperbound, no price.

McADOO, HARRIETTE PIPES and JOHN LEWIS McADOO, eds. *Black Children:*

Social, Educational, and Parental Environments. Pp. 279. Beverly Hills, CA: Sage, 1985. Paperbound, no price.

MILLS, EDWIN S. *The Burden of Government.* Pp. x, 188. Stanford, CA: Hoover Institution, 1986. $23.95.

MUSKIE, EDMUND, KENNETH RUSH, and KENNETH W. THOMPSON. *The President, the Congress, and Foreign Policy.* Pp. xv, 311. Lanham, MD: University Press of America, 1986. $24.75. Paperbound, $14.25.

NEWMAN, W. RUSSELL. *The Paradox of Mass Politics: Knowledge and Opinion in the American Electorate.* Pp. 241. Cambridge, MA: Harvard University Press, 1986. $29.95. Paperbound, $12.50.

OKA, YOSHITAKE. *Five Political Leaders of Modern Japan.* Translated by Andrew Fraser and Patricia Murray. Pp. viii, 232. Tokyo: University of Tokyo Press, 1986. Distributed by Columbia University Press, New York. $24.50.

O'SULLIVAN, NOEL. *Terrorism, Ideology, and Revolution: The Origins of Modern Political Violence.* Pp. xv, 232. Boulder, CO: Westview Press, 1986. $28.00.

PAIGE, R. MICHAEL, ed. *Cross-Cultural Orientation: New Conceptualizations and Applications.* Pp. viii, 346. Lanham, MD: University Press of America, 1986. $28.75. Paperbound, $16.50.

PIERRE, ANDREW J., ed. *A Widening Atlantic? Domestic Change and Foreign Policy.* Pp. xii, 107. New York: New York University Press, 1986. $19.50.

PIOTT, STEVEN L. *The Anti-Monopoly Persuasion: Popular Resistance to the Rise of Big Business in the Midwest.* Pp. x, 194. Westport, CT: Greenwood Press, 1985. $35.00.

PREEG, ERNEST H. and DIANE B. BEN-DAHMANE, eds. *New Dimensions in Foreign Economic Policy.* Pp. xiii, 117. Washington, DC: Center for the Study of Foreign Affairs, 1986. Paperbound, $3.75.

PRESTON, PAUL. *The Spanish Civil War: An Illustrated Chronicle, 1936-1939.* Pp. viii, 184. New York: Grove Press, 1986.

Distributed by Random House, New York. $20.00.

PUNCH, MAURICE. *Conduct Unbecoming: The Social Construction of Police Deviance and Control.* Pp. xi, 249. New York: Tavistock in association with Methuen, 1985. Paperbound, $13.00.

ROACH, JAMES R., ed. *India 2000: The Next Fifteen Years.* Pp. xxi, 228. Riverdale, MD: Riverdale, 1986. No price.

ROGERS, HELEN P. *Social Security: An Idea Whose Time Has Passed.* Pp. xii, 93. Carmel, CA: Wellington, 1985. Paperbound, $9.95.

RONEN, DOV, ed. *Democracy and Pluralism in Africa.* Pp. xi, 220. Boulder, CO: Lynne Rienner, 1986. $26.50.

RYAN, ALAN. *Property and Political Theory.* Pp. viii, 198. New York: Basil Blackwell, 1984. $34.95.

SAPIRO, VIRGINIA, ed. *Women, Biology, and Public Policy.* Pp. 272. Beverly Hills: Sage, 1985. Paperbound, no price.

SCOTT, W. RICHARD and BRUCE L. BLACK, eds. *The Organization of Mental Health Services: Societal and Community Systems.* Pp. 311. Beverly Hills, CA: Sage, 1986. Paperbound, no price.

SHAFFER, BUTLER D. *Calculated Chaos: Institutional Threats to Peace and Human Survival.* Pp. 338. San Francisco: Alchemy Press, 1985. Paperbound, $10.95.

SHAPIRO, MARTIN. *Courts: A Comparative and Political Analysis.* Pp. ix, 245. Chicago: University of Illinois Press, 1986. Paperbound, $9.95.

SHEFFER, GABRIEL, ed. *Modern Diasporas in International Politics.* Pp. 349. New York: St. Martin's Press, 1986. $32.50.

SINGER, BENJAMIN D. *Advertising and Society.* Pp. 240. Reading, MA: Addison-Wesley, 1986. Paperbound, no price.

SINGH, INDERJIT, LYN SQIUIRE, and JOHN STRAUSS, eds. *Agricultural Household Models: Extensions, Applications, and Policy.* Pp. xi, 335. Baltimore, MD: Johns Hopkins University Press, 1986. $34.50.

SKINNER, ELLIOTT P., ed. *Beyond Constructive Engagement: United States Foreign Policy toward Africa.* Pp. xx, 282. New York: Paragon House, 1986. $21.95.

SLANEY, WILLIAM Z. et al., eds. *Western European Security and Integration.* Vol. 4, *Foreign Relations of the United States, 1955-1957.* Pp. xxiii, 659. Washington, DC: Government Printing Office, 1986. No price.

STEIN, ARTHUR. *Seeds of the Seventies.* Pp. v, 184. Hanover, NH: University Press of New England, 1985. $18.00. Paperbound, $8.95

STOCKMAN-SHOMRON, ISRAEL, ed. *Israel, the Middle East, and the Great Powers.* Pp. xvi, 389. Jerusalem: Shikmona, 1984. No price.

SULLIVAN, JOHN L., MICHAL SHAMIR, PATRICK WALSH, and NIGEL ROBERTS. *Political Tolerance in Context: Support for Unpopular Minorities in Israel, New Zealand, and the United States.* Pp. xv, 264. Boulder, CO: Westview Press, 1985. Paperbound, $20.00.

TEEVAN, JAMES J., ed. *Introduction to Sociology: A Canadian Focus.* 2nd ed. Pp. viii, 552. Scarborough, Ontario: Prentice-Hall Canada, 1986. Paperbound, no price.

Universal Child Immunization by 1990. Pp. xxvi, 473. Geneva: United Nations Children's Fund, 1985. Paperbound, no price.

URBANSKA, WANDA. *The Singular Generation: Young Americans in the 1980's: Who We Are, What We Want, What We See Ahead.* Pp. xiv, 245. New York: Doubleday, 1986. $16.95.

VITO, GENNARO F. and DEBORAH G. WILSON. *The American Juvenile Justice System.* Pp. 133. Beverly Hills, CA: Sage, 1985. Paperbound, no price.

WHITE, STEPHEN and DANIEL NELSON, eds. *Communist Politics: A Reader.* Pp. xii, 416. New York: New York University Press, 1986. Distributed by Columbia University Press, New York. Paperbound, $16.50.

WHITNAH, DONALD R. and EDGAR L. ERICKSON. *The American Occupation of Austria: Planning and the Early Years.* Pp. xiv, 352. Westport, CT: Greenwood Press, 1985. $39.95.

WILLIAMS, HOWARD. *Kant's Political Philosophy.* Pp. xii, 292. New York: St. Martin's Press, 1986. Paperbound, $12.95.

WILSON, ROBERT N. *Experiencing Creativity: On the Social Psychology of Art.* Pp. vii, 171. New Brunswick, NJ: Transaction Books, 1986. $24.95.

YOUNG, ALMA H. and DION E. PHILLIPS, eds. *Militarization in the Non-Hispanic Caribbean.* Pp. ix, 178. Boulder, CO: Lynne Rienner, 1986. $20.00.

YOUNG, ROBERT. *Personal Autonomy and Positive Liberty.* Pp. ix, 123. New York: St. Martin's Press, 1986. $22.50.

INDEX